Praise for *Chanel's Riviera*

"A history of the Côte d'Azur, from the frivolity and decadence of its post–Jazz Age heyday to the terror and desperation of World War II." —*The Wall Street Journal*

"Intoxicating descriptions . . . of Chanel's life, specifically her fashion innovations and love affairs, are woven throughout the book. . . . But glamour on the Riviera would soon give way to a fight for survival." —*The New York Times Book Review*

"De Courcy's book is entertaining . . . a peek, at once envious and satisfyingly censorious, at the lifestyles of the rich and famous." —*The Washington Post*

"De Courcy deploys gleaming, well-chosen details to make *Chanel's Riviera* as vivid and entertaining as a novel. Her careful research, coupled with her polished narrative style, illuminates an era of opulence and starvation, of heroes and collaborators, in a world that soared high and swiftly plummeted." —*Shelf Awareness*

"Dishy and well-researched . . . this fluidly written history succeeds in capturing the era's intoxicating mix of glitz and grit." —*Publishers Weekly*

"De Courcy is adept at describing displays of opulence, and proves equally capable when portraying the deprivations and reversals of fortune occasioned by the onset of WWII . . . this will be popular with royal-watchers, fashionistas, and readers who relish the international social scene." —*Booklist*

"A gleaming social history of the French Riviera in the 1930s . . . [a] lovingly researched portrait of paradise." —*Kirkus Reviews*

"[A] sparkling, anecdote-rich narrative." —*The Times* (UK)

Praise for *The Husband Hunters*

Editors' Choice, *The New York Times*

"[A] diverting new study . . . [the American heiresses] were just what was needed to shake the cocktail and bring some pizazz to the party. De Courcy conjures it all with skill."
—*The New York Times Book Review*

"Anglophiles fascinated by the intricate tribal codes of the British upper classes will find plenty to feed their interest . . . if we're looking to history to better understand our own time, *The Husband Hunters* has something to say about how we got here."
—*The Boston Globe*

"A true account of the women who inspired *Downton Abbey* . . . [de Courcy] gets in their heads and in their homes, exploring what life was like for them after their moves and the clash of cultures that ensued."
—*Vanity Fair*

"Amusing [and] breezily readable."   —*The Washington Times*

"Vanderbilts, Astors, Churchills, Marlboroughs; diamonds, tiaras, yachts, mansions; all are documented in glorious detail and should satisfy those readers with insatiable thirst for all things peerage."
—*Booklist*

"Fascinating . . . enough glitz and glamour to enthrall those who couldn't get enough of the recent royal nuptials."
—*Publishers Weekly*

"*Downton Abbey* fans will swoon over this trip through the privileged turn-of-the-century world of cash, class, and coronets. . . . A highly readable social history that contains all of the juicy drama of a prime-time soap opera."
—*Kirkus Reviews*

"Witty and well-researched, Anne de Courcy brings to colorful, dramatic life these dollar princesses whose vast fortunes propelled them to glittering transatlantic marriages that captivated international society."

—Daisy Goodwin, *New York Times* bestselling
author of *The Fortune Hunter*

ALSO BY ANNE DE COURCY

The English in Love

A Guide to Modern Manners

1939: The Last Season

Society's Queen

The Viceroy's Daughters

Diana Mosley

Debs at War

Snowdon: The Biography

The Fishing Fleet

Margot at War: Love and Betrayal in Downing Street

The Husband Hunters:
American Heiresses Who Married into the British Aristocracy

CHANEL'S RIVIERA

GLAMOUR, DECADENCE, AND SURVIVAL
IN PEACE AND WAR, 1930–1944

Anne de Courcy

ST. MARTIN'S GRIFFIN
NEW YORK

Published in the United States by St. Martin's Griffin, an imprint of St. Martin's Publishing Group

www.stmartins.com

The Library of Congress has cataloged the hardcover edition as follows:

Names: De Courcy, Anne, author.
Title: Chanel's Riviera : glamour, decadence, and survival in peace and war, 1930–1944 / Anne de Courcy.
Other titles: Glamour, decadence, and survival in peace and war, 1930–1944
Description: First U.S. edition. | New York : St. Martin's Press, 2020. | Includes bibliographical references and index.
Identifiers: LCCN 2019043188 | ISBN 9781250177070 (hardcover) | ISBN 9781250177094 (ebook)
Subjects: LCSH: Riviera (France)—History—20th century. | World War, 1939–1945—France—Riviera—History. | Chanel, Coco, 1883–1971—Homes and haunts—France—Riviera. | Riviera (France)—Social life and customs—20th century. | Socialites—France—Riviera—History—20th century. | Celebrities—France—Riviera—History—20th century.
Classification: LCC DC608.8 .D33 2020 | DDC 944.9/40815—dc23
LC record available at https://lccn.loc.gov/2019043188

ISBN 978-1-250-17708-7 (trade paperback)

Our books may be purchased in bulk for promotional, educational, or business use. Please contact your local bookseller or the Macmillan Corporate and Premium Sales Department at 1-800-221-7945, extension 5442, or by email at MacmillanSpecialMarkets@macmillan.com.

Originally published in Great Britain by Weidenfeld & Nicolson, an imprint of The Orion Publishing Group Ltd, an Hachette UK company

First St. Martin's Griffin Edition: 2021

10 9 8 7 6 5 4 3 2 1

CONTENTS

ILLUSTRATIONS

>-+-+>-·-O-·-<+-+-<

SECTION ONE

Women wearing beach pyjamas, 1934 *(Getty Images/Hulton Archive/Stringer)*

Coco Chanel with Boy Capel, 1917 *(Getty Images/Hulton Archive)*

Chanel with the Duke of Westminster *(Getty Images/Hulton Archive/Stringer)*

Chanel in the garden at La Pausa *(Shutterstock/Grange)*

The colonnade inside La Pausa *(Berard Christian,* Vogue © *Conde Nast)*

A dinner party at La Pausa *(Jaques Wochiler)*

La Pausa *(Alamy/age fotostock)*

Misia and Jose Maria Sert, Chanel and Igor Stravinsky, c.1921 *(Getty Images/Fine Art Images/Heritage Images)*

Roussy Sert *(Getty Images/Bettman)*

Jean Cocteau *(Getty Images/Albin Guillot/Roger Viollet)*

Chanel with Serge Lifar *(Brigitte Moral SAIF Paris)*

Chateau de la Croë *(Getty Images/Pool BENAINOUS/DUCLOS/Gamma-Rapho)*

The Duke and Duchess of Windsor *(Alamy/Everett Collection Inc)*

Villa E.1027 *(Photograph by Gaelle le Boulicaut/Figarophoto, Camera Press)*

Le Corbusier *(© FLC/DACS, photographer Lucien Hervé*

Doris Delevigne and Lord Castlerosse *(Getty Images/Bettmann)*

Lord and Lady Furness *(Getty Images/Corbis)*

INTRODUCTION

❧

This book is neither a biography of Chanel nor a history of the Riviera – both have been written many times before – but the story of the years during which Chanel spent her summers in that part of France.

The French Riviera is probably the most famous piece of coastline in the world, while Coco Chanel has a good claim to be the most famous dress designer ever. In 1930 they so to speak joined forces, with Chanel building a glamorous villa there, known as La Pausa. All through the decade that followed she came down to spend the summer in it, often with a lover, almost always with friends. It was, in many senses, her only real home: she had had apartments in Paris, but from 1934 onwards lived in the (Paris) Ritz, whereas La Pausa, built to her specifications, furnished and run exactly as she wanted, was hers and hers alone.

The 1930s were probably the heyday of the Riviera in its modern sense – that is, as a place to visit for its long, glorious summer rather than, as Queen Victoria did, for winter warmth. Not yet smothered in concrete, newly opened up by the Murphys, Fitzgeralds, Hemingways and their friends, it was at first known as a place to live simply and cheaply, with the rich and fashionable swarming to Antibes, Nice and Cannes, driving out at night along the coast to eat at one of the little fishermen's restaurants or into the hinterland for something a bit grander.

Few of those who had settled there, as many English had, thought much about what was going on in the rest of Europe. It was another life, warm, golden, easy, with reassuring visits by British naval ships, far removed from politics or conflict.

Then came the war years. At first, no one took much notice and life went on as before, with the French and the resident British placing their trust in the Maginot Line, believed impregnable. With the Franco-German armistice in June 1940 first came Vichy France, and a tide of Jewish refugees escaping from the Nazis, and then invasion by the Italians, followed by the Germans.

Through it all, Chanel spent summers at La Pausa, in the later years with her German lover until, with the liberation of the coast in 1944, her business still closed and her lover gone, she left for the peaceful neutrality of Switzerland. Although she visited La Pausa several times afterwards, it was no longer her home; and its sale in 1953 snapped her final link with the coast.

PROLOGUE

➤━◆➤━○━◆◄━◆◄

In the summer of 1938, the burning question on the Riviera was not what Germany was going to do next but whether or not to curtsey to the Duchess of Windsor.

It was less than two years since the Duke had abdicated the throne of England to marry, as he famously put it, 'the woman I love', but – largely because she, Wallis Simpson, had already been divorced twice and no one knew whether she would stop at that – she had been denied the HRH title that would have brought with it this automatic obeisance.

Would courtesy – the Duke was insistent that respect be shown to his wife – win over correctness and the feeling of some that neither of them deserved it?

It was fitting that they had come to the Riviera, the glamorous, golden, sun-filled coastline famous for uninhibited enjoyment and where nobody enquired too deeply into your past. Here, every year, the rich, the famous, the beautiful and the eccentric gathered to swim, gamble and soak up the sun in a hedonistic lifestyle that then seemed never-ending. As for any threat from Germany – well, France had the impregnable Maginot Line, did she not?

That summer, it felt as though this state of things would go on for ever. By the thirties, France had become full of self-confidence. She was at the forefront of the arts, her ocean liners were the fastest and the most luxurious, her writers, her sportsmen and women, like the great tennis players Jean Borotra and Suzanne Lenglen, were known worldwide; no other nation could compete with her food, her culture and her couture. France's prestige was epitomised by the greatest and most original designer of them all,

3

Gabrielle Bonheur Chanel, more usually known as 'Coco' Chanel. The Windsors were but the latest arrivals on that famous littoral. In early May they had leased the Château de la Croë from the press magnate Sir Pomeroy Burton.

It was not surprising that this celebrity couple had decided to settle here for much of the year. The coastline, its charming fishing villages not yet submerged under the later tide of building, was exquisitely beautiful, with sparkling blue seas, little bays, pines, groves of ancient olive trees, balmy air scented with rosemary and thyme, small houses covered with brilliant bougainvillea, pots of tumbling geraniums and colourful markets where the fish and vegetables of the coast could be bought fresh every day. No wonder it drew an increasing number of visitors.

Writers too had flocked to the Côte d'Azur, many because of danger in their own country, or scandal. One of the wealthiest and most successful in the English-speaking world was W. Somerset Maugham, who had left England in 1926 following the arrest for gross indecency and enforced deportation of his American companion Gerald Haxton.

On Maugham's gatepost at his house, the Villa Mauresque, was his personal talisman, the mystical Moorish sign that appeared on all his books – the hand of Fatima warding off the evil eye. He was rich, generous and hospitable, his household with its thirteen servants running seemingly on oiled wheels and known for delicious food and entertaining conversation. 'Everyone on the Riviera accepts an invitation from Maugham at any time that they are lucky enough to get one,' said another very successful writer, E. Phillips Oppenheim. That August of 1938, the Windsors did so.

Harold Nicolson, staying with Maugham, described the party in a letter to his wife Vita: 'Willy Maugham had prepared us carefully. He said that the Duke gets cross if the Duchess is not treated with respect.' When the Duke and Duchess arrived, Maugham and his daughter went into the hall to greet them while the rest of the guests waited in the drawing room. Nicolson described their entrance. 'She, I must say, looks very well for her age [Wallis

4

was then forty-two]. She has done her hair in a different way. It is smoothed off her brow and falls down the back of her neck in ringlets. It gives her a placid and less strained look. Her voice has also changed. It now mingles the accents of Virginia with that of a Duchess in one of Pinero's plays.

'He entered with his swinging naval gait, plucking at his bow tie. He had on a *tussore* dinner jacket. He was in very high spirits. Cocktails were brought and we stood around the fireplace. There was a pause. "I am sorry we were a little late," said the Duke, "but Her Royal Highness couldn't drag herself away."

'He had said it. The three words fell into the circle like three stones into a pool. Her (gasp) Royal (shudder) Highness (and not one eye dared meet another).'

No matter that the threat from Germany was profound – that spring it had occupied Austria, with a ruthless and barbarous persecution of minorities, and was casting covetous eyes towards the Sudetenland, its troops massing on the Czech border, while in England gas masks were being issued in preparation for war – on the Riviera the question of the day had been settled. HRH and a curtsey it would have to be. Now life in the playground of Europe could go on as normal.

For, as Nicolson wrote from the Villa Mauresque: '[This] really is the perfect holiday. I mean, the heat is intense, the garden lovely, the chair long and cool, the lime juice at hand, a bathing pool there if one wishes to splash, scenery, books, gramophones, pretty people – and above all, the sense that it is not going on too long.'

Nor did it . . .

CHAPTER I

><>–○–<><

1930, the Beginning: La Pausa

By 1930 the long love affair between Coco* Chanel, the world's best-known dress designer, and the Duke of Westminster, the richest man in England, was coming to what seemed its inevitable end. Bendor, as the Duke was known, longed for an heir and at forty-seven Chanel† was unlikely to provide him with one. Nor could she bear the repeated infidelities that his enormous wealth made all too easy for him.

They had met seven years earlier, in Monaco's Hôtel de Paris, where Chanel was dining with Vera Bate, an old friend of the forty-four-year-old Bendor.

Although there was ambiguity about Vera's birth, it was generally acknowledged that she was a connection of the royal family – it is believed that she was an illegitimate daughter of the first Marquess of Cambridge, a younger brother of Queen Mary – and as such she was at the heart of English upper-class society. She was then married to her first husband, an American officer named Fred Bate but, beautiful and popular as she was, she was perennially hard up. Chanel, whose lightning grasp of opportunity was one of the reasons for her success, had employed her, largely as a kind of walking advertisement: she wore clothes so beautifully that every other woman longed to possess what Vera had on her back at that moment. These were, naturally, given to

---

* Her nickname Coco originated in her brief early career as a singer, when the chorus of one of the songs she sang began 'Co-co-co-co . . .'.

† She was born on 19 August 1883.

her by Chanel, and the two had already become close friends.

When the Duke spotted Vera across the room he had been planning to visit the Casino, but he went over to talk to her and to his delight the pair asked him to join their table. They talked, they laughed, they danced; Bendor forgot about the Casino and asked them both to dine with him the next night on his yacht, the four-masted schooner *Flying Cloud*, hiring a gypsy band to serenade them and then taking them to a nightclub to dance.

Bendor was immediately fascinated by Chanel. She was beautiful, elegant, witty and fiercely independent; from a poverty-stricken girlhood she had climbed, step by step and man by man, to the pinnacle of success on which she now stood. She had surmounted her past as a kept woman – something that usually remained a lifelong social barrier – and many of her wealthy clients were now her friends, entertaining her and being entertained by her.

She had revolutionised fashion, designing simple, supple, pared-down clothes for women in materials hitherto thought unfashionable, like jersey, that allowed the body to move freely. 'The purpose of fashion', she had declared (in French *Vogue*), 'is to make women look young. Then their outlook on life changes. They feel brighter, and more cheerful.'

Already a fashion force two years before she met Bendor – she had been noted by *Harper's Bazaar* as early as 1915 – she had launched what became the most famous scent in the world: Chanel No.5. It was an overwhelming success, making her rich for the rest of her life. As she explained on numerous occasions to Bendor, while refusing his advances, what did he have that she could possibly want? For although she claimed to live for love, what she really valued was her independence – and work. She did, however, leave the door open a chink, agreeing to meet him the following year. Meanwhile, he wooed her with everything from flowers and jewels to salmon sent by air from his Scottish estate.

Finally she relented. In the late spring of 1924, she went aboard the black-hulled, piratical-looking *Flying Cloud* to sail with Bendor on a Mediterranean cruise and to enter a world of unimaginable luxury. As well as the crew of forty, the four-poster beds, the silk curtains, he had brought along a small orchestra so that the two of them could dance every night. If he entertained on the yacht, as he often did, the rigging was illuminated.

Bendor, tall, blond and good-looking, had houses scattered everywhere. As he seldom stayed longer than three or four days in one place and often arrived without notice, all were ready for immediate use – cars fuelled, silver polished, servants in Grosvenor livery, food in the larder. He showered Chanel with presents, from jewellery and works of art to a town house in London.

When they visited the Westminster estate in Cheshire, she acted as his hostess at his country house, Eaton Hall. Here she rode, played tennis and sailed; when they visited his Scottish estates, she learnt to fish, acquitting herself well. She became a friend of Winston Churchill, to whom Bendor was close, so that often they were at the same house party or aboard *Flying Cloud* at the same time. 'Coco is here in place of Violet,' Churchill wrote to his wife Clementine. 'She is vy agreeable – really a gt & strong being fit to rule a man or an Empire. Bennie vy well & I think extremely happy to be mated with an equal – her ability balancing his power.'

When Bendor bought a house in the Highlands she decorated it, painting the drawing rooms beige and installing the first bidet in Scotland; during the season she hunted three days a week. She charmed all his friends and got on well with his children and his first wife. But none of this affected her dedication to her work; and, although she had come to love Bendor ('My real life began with Westminster,' she told a friend, 'I'd finally found a shoulder I could lean on, a tree against which I could prop myself'), she was still determined to preserve her independence. One way of doing so was to have a house that was completely her own, where she could live 'without a footman at every door'.

It had to be in France, it had to be within reasonable reach of Paris and it had to be in the sun, which she loved – it was when she came back from one cruise with Bendor 'brown as a cabin boy' that sunbronzed skin became a fashionable accessory. There was only one answer: the Côte d'Azur, past which she had sailed so many times in her lover's yacht.

For Chanel, it would be the first time in her life that she could live entirely by her own rules and according to her own wishes. The site she first saw from the Duke's yacht in December 1927 was at the top of a small village called Roquebrune, 180 metres above the sea, with wonderful views over Menton and the Italian border on one side and Monaco and its bay on the other. Behind the villa, the foothills of the Alps can be seen in the distance. In all, by buying several adjacent parcels of land, she managed to acquire twelve acres that included an olive grove. The name of the property, La Pausa, came from the story that it was here that Mary Magdalene had paused to rest when she had fled the Holy Land in a rudderless boat after the crucifixion and resurrection of Christ.

There were three existing buildings, which would be transformed into the main house, with two smaller cottages for guests; she gave one of these, 'La Colline', to Vera Bate, now Lombardi. Vera, who had divorced her husband two years before, had earlier that year married an Italian officer named Alberto Lombardi, a brilliant horseman highly thought of by Mussolini. With Vera in situ, inviting the Duke's friends over would be an easy matter – she knew them all.

The transformation of the dilapidated buildings into a beautifully designed home was effected by a young local architect, Robert Streitz. One of Chanel's friends, Count Jean de Segonzac, had had his own nearby villa so well restored by Streitz that the Count recommended him to Chanel. Soon after signing the deed of sale in February 1929, Chanel invited Streitz to a drinks party on board *Flying Cloud*, then moored off Cannes. Three days later he brought drawings of the proposed villa that featured three wings wrapped around an open courtyard bordered with columns. For the twenty-eight-year-old Streitz this would be a wonderful commission.

Chanel liked his plan so much that she accepted it straight away, with the proviso that before starting work he went to look at the convent of Aubazine, where she had spent much of her childhood and adolescence, so that he could incorporate its atmosphere and some of its main features into the proposed villa. (While there, he met the Mother Superior and asked if she remembered Gabrielle Chanel. Yes, she answered, she remembered her well, that unfortunate waif, 'an illegitimate child born in the poorhouse'.)

With this brief, Streitz designed the great central staircase, almost exactly like the one at the convent up and down which she must have trodden hundreds of times. Chanel's well-known secrecy over her early years did not extend to these architectural 'reminiscences' as the house, long and low, with three sides facing inwards over a shady courtyard, held more echoes of Aubazine in its cloistered colonnades, vaulted ceilings and heavy doors.

On the ground floor it was dominated by a large hall with a beautifully carved front door, an antique wrought-iron chandelier and five windows above the entrance – five was Chanel's lucky number (her zodiac sign was Leo, the fifth sign). She ordered more than 20,000 hand-made, curved tiles for the roof, as she wanted it to look old. For the same reason, the wooden shutters were distressed and even the olive trees, transplanted from Antibes, were 100 years old.

Outside, purple irises, lavender and lawns made gardens original for their time. She was the first to cultivate 'poorer' plants, like lavender and olive trees, discarding the more conventional ones such as lilies, although climbing roses were allowed. At the top of the garden, tucked away behind yew hedges, was a superb tennis court – Chanel was a great believer in exercise.

The making of the house, bought and paid for by Chanel, was a project in which she was deeply involved. Once or twice a month she would come down from Paris to check progress. 'She was always in the best of moods when she visited Roquebrune,' remembered the builder, Edgar Maggiore. 'On the site one day she slipped into a pool of mud. Instead of lamenting the loss of a dress, she laughed until the workers pulled her out. If her work kept her in Paris, we made the trip to see her if we had a delicate problem on which we wished to consult her. I remember sending the stucco worker to see her so she could choose the colour of the plaster to be used on the façade.'

Once, Streitz's car broke down and, having had to take the bus to Roquebrune, he arrived late, fearing a scolding from the imperious Mademoiselle. Instead, she was sympathetic and, finding out what sort of car he had, said she had a similar one in her garage – and presented it to him as a gift. 'We never had a contract or any kind of correspondence,' recalled Streitz later, from his retirement at Valbonne in the Alpes-Maritimes. 'For me, Mademoiselle's word was as good as gold. Nine months after the completion of La Pausa, every last bill had been paid on the nail.'

Much of the house was made of white marble; there were large fireplaces in each room, eighteenth-century English-oak floors and panelling, and Tudor and Jacobean furniture* from Bendor's attics – in his bedroom, separated from Chanel's quarters by a bathroom, was a massive Elizabethan oak bed. The main colours were white and beige; even the piano was beige. 'It is only possible to relax if one is not diverted by colourful backgrounds,' said Chanel. In the living room there were three large beige leather and chamois sofas, pieces of Provençal and Spanish furniture (then completely out of fashion), with bowls of white lilac on the oak tables. Her own bedroom was done up in beige taffeta with a blue rug on the floor; her bathroom next door was in white opaline.

Her feeling for luxurious simplicity carried through to her style of entertaining. In the mornings the house was silent; Chanel slept late and so did many of her guests, although anyone who wanted to swim or shop would find small cars with drivers ready to run them down the two kilometres of twisting mountain road to Menton or the beach.

The real beginning of the day was lunch: more like a sparkling party, it was filled with conversation, chat and plans. The food, from cold roast beef to various pastas, was kept hot with antique silver warmers from England and served buffet-style from a table covered with dishes at one end of the dining room. Sometimes

---

* Today in the Dallas Museum of Art.

these lunches took place on the terrace, the guests sitting on grass covered by tarpaulins of coarse linen.

Heavy beige silk curtains hung at the huge windows which formed almost two sides of the main room, with their view of Monte Carlo seen through a grove of orange trees. Dark-green blinds kept off the extreme heat of summer. In the dining room, with its enormously long table, white taffeta curtains matched the white walls. Each bedroom had an en suite bathroom and each bathroom also had another, separate entrance, so that a servant, summoned by electric bell, could slip in and out unnoticed to run a bath or pick up clothes to wash. In the bedrooms there were antique Italian beds with gold mosquito curtains and heavy rugs on the oak floors.

As well as being a home, La Pausa was a deliciously seductive setting for lovers whose lives, like Chanel's and Bendor's, were deeply entwined. How near they came to marriage is a moot point, as neither ever made a definitive statement on this, although Chanel said later that if she had become pregnant she would have married him – and pregnant was what she longed to become. She may have thought that the romantic atmosphere of La Pausa would help to bring this about; pragmatically, she took advice from others. 'She tried everything,' said Madame Patricia Marinovich, whose mother and grandmother had worked at La Pausa and were privy to the gossip of the household. 'She would even lie on her back with her legs in the air for ages after making love to try and achieve it.'* Or, as she herself described it in her later years, she went in for 'humiliating acrobatics'.

Although the Duke still had his bedroom at La Pausa, he had, in fact, already met and begun courting the woman he would later marry. This was Loelia Ponsonby, the daughter of Sir Frederick ('Fritz') Ponsonby, then Keeper of the Privy Purse to King George V, and twenty-seven to his fifty. They had met the previous November in the Embassy, the favourite London nightclub of the Prince of Wales and his circle, to which Loelia,

---

* A popular theory of the time was that this enabled sperm to travel up the vagina more successfully.

hastily pulling on a purple chiffon dress, had dashed in response to a friend's last-minute invitation. Three weeks later Bendor proposed to her – only two days after Chanel, who went to stay with him in mid-December, had left Eaton Hall. The engagement was announced on 2 January 1930, as they cruised down the Dalmatian coast.

'Ten years of my life have been spent with Westminster,'* Chanel said later. 'The greatest pleasure he gave to me was to watch him live. For ten years, I did everything he wanted. But fishing for salmon is not life.'

Chanel was not the only person who had decided to put down roots on the Riviera. It had become highly fashionable, indeed the playground of the rich,† with development along the coast and Hispano-Suizas, Bugattis and Rollses parked everywhere. Nor were they 'ordinary' cars: many of them expressed the personalities or quirks of their owners, with custom-made upholstery of any shade, fittings of marquetry, ivory, mother-of-pearl or gold, sides emblazoned with family crests, monograms or basketwork. Out of them stepped titled men and women, rich businessmen and film stars, for whom Chanel had opened another salon in Monte Carlo, to stay at the villas now steadily crowding the coast, or at one of the grand hotels.

Except in the smaller villages, cheap suppers of bouillabaisse and local wine were becoming a thing of the past; the restaurants were beginning to charge top prices and some of the bistros had become nightclubs. But the swifts still wheeled round the oleander trees, market stalls were piled high with lemons, aubergines and tomatoes, the air was pine-scented and flower sellers sold armfuls of carnations. On spring nights there were still fireflies and the croaking of colonies of small, jade-green tree frogs, followed by nightingales, while all summer long the cicadas thrummed in the background.

The barefoot fishermen still went out in their *pointes* (as the

---

* She always said ten – he went on seeing her after he married.
† Holidays with pay did not come in until 1936 in France and 1938 in England.

fishing boats were called), their catch served that night in restaurants where it might be cooked by their wives, wearing the
capacious coarse black aprons used by all local women to save
their often threadbare clothes. On rocky parts of the coast men
would hunt for octopuses with a long pole, at the end of which
was a hook hidden in a bunch of red rags. They would jiggle the
rags over cavities in the rocks, and if an octopus was hiding in
one of these it would often make a dart at the rags and impale
itself on the hook.

Towards Marseilles, a simpler life was still possible. Near
St-Tropez Colette, already famous for her masterpiece *Chéri*,
and her lover, later husband, Maurice Goudeket* had four years
earlier bought a four-room peasant *mas* in two and a half acres
of land planted with vines and fig trees. It had no electricity,
which they later installed; water came from a deep well, in which
Colette would also cool white wine. It had a charming terrace
which faced north, shaded by an old wisteria, and a little path led
directly from the house to a nearby hidden beach. Because there
was an ancient muscat vine circling the well, Colette decided to
call her house 'La Treille Muscate'.

Here she spent every summer. One person described her as
'a short [she was five foot four inches], heavy-bodied woman
with a crop of wood-coloured hair, with long grey luminous
eyes and a deep alto voice'. Her eyes were always made up with
kohl, which she believed would help preserve her faulty sight.
She began to garden energetically immediately after breakfast
– hard work that included digging an irrigation ditch for her
tangerine trees and mulching them with seaweed carried up from
the beach. Later in the morning there would be a swim followed
by a lunch of Provençal dishes: green melons, bouillabaisse with
aïoli, *rascasse farci*.

She wrote constantly and prolifically, settling down to work
after a short siesta. She had built herself a workroom, a cube
with thick walls that kept it cool. Here were her large work table
and a wide divan with a mosquito net; books filled a large Breton

* They married in 1935.

cupboard, green pottery stood against the creamy walls, and on a shelf was a sheaf of the blue paper on which she always wrote. In the summer she often bathed at night on the little beach, so deserted that it was almost her private property, and would sleep on her verandah after dragging her mattress on to it. Sometimes she and Maurice would dine out with the artist friends who lived in and around St-Tropez; at one restaurant, recorded Maurice, if they wanted to eat game out of season, 'we had to give warning forty-eight hours in advance, so that the poachers would have time'.

Also living there, in a castellated villa on a ledge between the road and the rocks of the seashore, was one of Chanel's earlier rivals and almost as great an innovator, the couturier Paul Poiret, now suffering from Parkinson's disease, his hands that had once created beautiful clothes shaking uncontrollably. As stylish as ever, he owned a pale-grey Hispano-Suiza and wore coral-pink scarves and a beret to match.

The Riviera was a magnet for writers, like D.H. Lawrence who in 1930 was still hoping for an English publisher for his controversial novel *Lady Chatterley's Lover*.* When P.G. Wodehouse, at first scathing about Cannes ('the most loathly hole in the known world'), rented a villa near Grasse he was an almost nightly visitor to Cannes Casino, where he gambled by walking from table to table and putting *mille-franc* notes on his preferred colour or number.

The novelist Edith Wharton lived in Hyères, in a house in the grounds of a ruined seventeenth-century convent, where she created a wonderful hillside garden – although there was nothing of the simple life about her ménage. It was not where she had expected to settle, but she had fallen in love with the village of Hyères at first sight. She was then fifty-seven, she had been divorced from her husband of thirty years, Teddy Wharton, for six years and she was getting over a three-year love affair with the brilliant dandy and womaniser Morton Fullerton; and when she

---

* It had been published privately in Italy in 1928 and in France and Australia in 1929.

bought her house she had exclaimed, 'I feel as if I were going to get married – to the right man at last!'

Not far off, in the little village of Sanary-sur-mer, Aldous Huxley and his Belgian wife Maria lived in the cube-shaped villa they had bought in 1930, with their red Bugatti driven by Maria (Aldous was near-blind). Huxley's health was delicate; his lungs needed a warm climate. Their house was known as Villa Huley because the mason, thinking to welcome them with a surprise, had painted this misspelling of Huxley's name on the gateposts in bright-green letters. It was halfway between two villages and was fortunate to have mains water and electricity. An even greater luxury was a telephone, from which calls could be made between 7.30 a.m. and 9.00 p.m.

The interior was filled with the Huxleys' eclectic collection of objects – Mexican rugs, piles of straw hats, an enormous sofa by Raoul Dufy. They installed central heating, a water filter for their tea and an electric refrigerator. They always had Earl Grey tea and thinly sliced brown bread (rare in France) and butter for tea. 'Here all is exquisitely lovely,' wrote Huxley to his sister-in-law. 'Sun, roses, fruit, warmth. We bathe and bask.'

Huxley's reputation – he had already published four successful satirical novels and was one of the most famous writers of the twenties – drew others, among them the newly married Cyril Connolly. After honeymooning in Majorca, Cyril and his wife Joan took a lease on Les Lauriers Roses, a two-bedroom house just east of Sanary at Six-Fours. It had a garden, which allowed them to add ring-tailed lemurs to the ferrets they already kept. The lemurs chattered in the moonlight, responded to the different intonations of the human voice, and swung gracefully through the trees.

Later in the year Connolly wrote of that time, when he would bicycle down to the port to fetch their dinner, 'past the harbour with its bobbing launches and the cafés with their signs banging. At the local restaurants there would be one or two "plats à emporter", to which I would add some wine, sausage and Gruyère cheese, a couple of "diplomats" to smoke and a new "Detective" or "Chasseur Français"; then I would bowl back heavy laden with the mistral behind me, a lemur buttoned up inside my jacket with his head sticking out. Up the steep drive it was easy to be blown off into the rosemary, then dinner would be spoilt. We ate it with our fingers beside the fire ... at last we would go to bed, bolting the doors while the lemurs cried in the moonlight, house-ghosts bounding from the mulberries to the palms, from the palms to the tall pines whose cones the dormice nibble, from the pines to the roof and so to our bedroom window ...'

Connolly was a passionate admirer of Huxley, and when the red Bugatti appeared in the drive of Les Lauriers Roses he was thrilled, hoping that it would herald the start of a close and satisfying friendship. But it turned out to be a mere courtesy call: Huxley was under immense deadline pressure for his next two novels and whenever the Connollys turned up at the Huxley house they were intercepted by Maria, who told them her husband was working and must not be disturbed. It was true, but another reason was that Maria found the Connolly ménage distasteful. 'Eating your dinner with your fingers reading before the fire meant leaving grape skins and the skeletons of sardines between the pages,' she commented. 'The ferrets stank; the lemur hopped upon the table and curled his exquisite little black hand around your brandy glass.'

The result was that Connolly's initial hero-worship for the Huxleys curdled into bitterness* when the close friendship he had envisaged did not materialise. He felt rejected and, when he contrasted his own lethargy with Huxley's feverish activity, humiliated. Later he said about his rejection by the Huxleys: 'The cut was deep and added ten years to my life.' He had come to the Riviera to write, but although he filled notebooks with ideas, nothing constructive emerged. 'Writing is an accident arising out of certain unhappinesses,' he claimed defensively. He had no financial need to write, but without this spur could not force himself into the self-discipline of his wealthy neighbour up the coast, Somerset Maugham.

---

* In his only novel, *The Rock Pool* (1936), Connolly refers to the 'competent intellectual vulgarity of Aldous Huxley'.

Maugham, who could seldom speak without stuttering, had just published *Cakes and Ale*, which had created a huge sensation – hitherto he had been thought of as a playwright and short-story writer. His dedication to his work did not prevent his entertaining a constant flow of guests. Among them were Evelyn Waugh, that year on his first visit to the Riviera, and his brother Alec, then much the better known of the two. Both dined with Maugham, who asked Evelyn what a certain person was like. As Evelyn recorded, 'I said: "A pansy with a stammer." All the Picassos on the walls blenched.'

The Waugh brothers were staying at the Hôtel Welcome in Villefranche (to the east of Antibes). This, facing the harbour, with the Old Town behind it, was for much of the time a creative powerhouse: here, in a second-floor room, lived Jean Cocteau, polymath intellectual at the heart of Paris's avant-garde musical, artistic, film-making and design world. He was a painter, novelist, poet, script-writer, playwright, essayist and critic who had become a national celebrity in the early twenties. He was openly homosexual* and, from time to time, flung himself into the taking of opium and other drugs.

'One day I went through the Welcome lobby while Cocteau was on the telephone [there were none in the bedrooms]', wrote a young American also staying there. 'He was speaking in a pleading voice, almost in tears. Later it was explained to me that he had been begging Mlle Coco Chanel to allow him to go on smoking opium longer than had been agreed.' Chanel, who knew that he was overdue for a cure, and who was constantly paying for them, said firmly: '*No!*'

Cocteau spent much of the day in his room, usually with a friend, smoking heavily, the unmistakable fumes filling all the corridors. 'It was pleasant to buy it from the Chinese in a sordid street hung with washing,' he wrote, 'pleasant to return home quickly and try it out in one's hotel ... to unroll it, stretch out on it, open the window onto the port, and take off.' Somehow,

---

* Homosexuality had not been illegal in France since the Penal Code of 1791.

he never got into trouble with the authorities. 'Addiction ruins the liver, affects the nervous cells, causes constipation, makes the temples like parchment and contracts the iris of the eye,' he wrote. After one cure he tried to describe opium's allure. 'It is hard to find oneself dismissed by opium . . . it is hard to know that this magic carpet exists and that one will no longer fly on it.'

It was here, at the Hôtel Welcome, that Cocteau wrote the novel for which he is best remembered, *Les Enfants terribles* (1929). Several of his friends, attracted by his presence and the atmosphere of Villefranche, followed him and stayed nearby, among them the composer Stravinsky and the ballet maestro Serge Diaghilev. But Villefranche was also a base for the American and Russian navies, and when the fleets were in the hotel changed character. 'I live in a brothel for American sailors,' wrote Cocteau to one friend, ' . . . the sailors dance and fight day and night. You hear nothing but loud jazz, each machine playing a different tune.'

There was no doubt, however, that the epicentre of the mélange of high life and low morals that characterised so many of the summer crowd was Antibes. Here, for instance, Sir Oswald ('Tom') Mosley and his wife Lady Cynthia* took a villa or stayed at the Hôtel du Cap or Eden Roc (the hotel's seaside pavilion) every year. Tom Mosley, for whom philandering was as natural, and almost as frequent, as breathing, was always in pursuit of his latest flame, to the often obvious misery of his good-looking wife. Staying with them in 1930 were the Castlerosses.

Valentine Castlerosse was a man so hugely fat that he was often known as Lord Elephant and Castlerosse. His salient quality was boundless extravagance. 'There is nothing more boring than money in the bank, especially if it belongs to someone else,' he once said, and it was a philosophy he lived by, depending on his charm and wit to keep him out of trouble. Once, returning in the small hours after a fancy-dress ball, his vast bulk clad in nothing but skins, an early-rising female guest met him in the

---

* One of the three daughters of Lord Curzon, she was always known as Cimmie.

hotel corridor. 'My God!' she exclaimed in horror. 'Yes, Madame,' replied Castlerosse smoothly, 'but tonight strictly incognito,' and passed in dignified fashion to his room.

Castlerosse had for years been obsessed by Doris Delevingne, a dazzling blonde who lived a life only one step away from that of a top courtesan. Her lifestyle was just as lavish as that of Castlerosse and it, too, was subsidised by others – in her case, her numerous lovers. Lord Beaverbrook, for whom Castlerosse wrote his immensely successful *Sunday Express* gossip column *Londoner's Log* and who picked up most of Castlerosse's enormous bills – and who certainly did not want to find himself responsible for Doris's equally vast outlay – had done his best to prevent their marriage. When he learnt in late December 1927 that a notice of marriage had been put in Hammersmith register office, he hastily invited Castlerosse to join him on a visit to Cannes on the day scheduled for their nuptials, taking the *Golden Arrow* – which he knew left before the register office opened.

He was a little surprised when Castlerosse readily accepted. But when the bill for their stay at the hotel was brought to him, he realised why. On it was not only a room that he had not ordered, but a daily bottle of champagne delivered every afternoon to that same room. Soon he discovered that shortly after he and Castlerosse had arrived at the hotel, so had Doris, and every afternoon Castlerosse visited her for love and champagne – on Beaverbrook.

Beaverbrook's efforts at preventing the match were in vain; the two were married shortly afterwards, in May 1928. Within months Doris, whose way of life remained unaltered, had a fling with Tom Mitford; and the unhappy Castlerosse moved into the International Sporting Club but was soon driven from it, he said, 'by the depressing sound of young men's muscles flexing and old men's arteries collapsing', and the Castlerosses were briefly reunited.

In August 1930 the Mosleys and their children went as usual to Antibes, staying at the Hôtel Eden Roc, where Cimmie's sister Lady Ravensdale joined them. Also staying nearby were the youngest Curzon sister, Lady Alexandra (Baba) Metcalfe, and her husband Fruity Metcalfe. (One Sunday, Castlerosse's weekly column had reported: 'Played golf with Fruity Metcalfe. He went round the course in 20,000 words.') Drink flowed freely both there and at the various villas they visited where friends lived or were staying.

There were always ructions when the extended Mosley family was together: the first was caused when Irene Ravensdale over-heard her brother-in-law Tom Mosley's whispered speculations as to which of the three sisters would succeed in attracting the (married) silent-movie star John Gilbert, also staying at the hotel. Would it be, Mosley wondered, 'the heavyweight, the lightweight or the middle weight', i.e. Irene, Baba or Cimmie. For everyone wanted a crack at John Gilbert, from the notorious man-eater Daisy Fellowes,* who hoped to be asked to their moonlight party on the top balcony of the Eden Roc, to Baba, who successfully pounced on the seat next to him at dinner. The evening ended in altercations, with Tom Mosley accusing his wife of being drunk.

The next day was equally alcohol-fuelled: 'Fruity was well over the odds with Baba very annoyed,' wrote Irene in her diary that night. 'He disappeared and made up like John Gilbert and came in with Gilbert and Cim and proceeded to circle all the ladies as the great lover and was very funny. The fun was entirely ruined at 10 p.m. by Maurice and Miss Stephenson both dead drunk . . .'

Cimmie's birthday, on 23 August, was similarly social. After a family lunch at the hotel the sisters, Tom and the children joined Wolf (Babe) Barnato's party at the next table. Babe Barnato, the son of the Rand diamond millionaire Barney Barnato, was a rich man who lived for speed; he was one of a set known as the Bentley Boys. He was a scratch golfer, a county cricketer, bred racehorses and was a superb skier as well as being an expert driver – he had won for the past three years at Le Mans.

The parties at his large and luxurious Surrey house started at around 10.00 p.m. and went on well into the next day. At one of them, the waiters were dressed as motor-racing drivers,

---

* See page 101.

with linen helmets and goggles, and Brooklands-style racing pits were constructed along the quarter-mile gravel drive. Guests in powerful cars, with beautiful girls aboard, tore into the 'pits' for champagne (Barnato himself could drink two bottles with no visible effect) and sped on to the house.

His most recent exploit was to race, for a bet, his Bentley Speed Six coupé against the famous Blue Train (the Calais-Mediterranée Express, to give it its proper name), so-called because of its dark-blue sleeping cars* with room for eighty first-class passengers in connecting luxury compartments, panelled with wood and equipped with everything from heavy folding metal washbasins to hooks on which to hang keys. It was so well known that in 1924 Cocteau had designed a ballet, *Le Train Bleu*, around it featuring swimmers, tennis players and weightlifters. Chanel had designed the clothes for it and Picasso had painted the curtain – two giantesses leaping across a beach, against a bright-blue sky.

The Blue Train was fast and luxurious: there were only ten berths to each sleeping car and plenty of attendants. The china in the dining car was white instead of the customary blue, with a gold-leaf motif, there were fresh flowers on every table, the menu was handwritten. Even the corridor was thickly carpeted, so that those who dined late did not disturb those who had turned in early (the waiters slept in hammocks slung from hooks in the dining car when this had finally emptied).

Naturally, it was the preferred train of wealthy and famous passengers. When Cole Porter and his wife went south they booked a complete car, with a bedroom for each of them and two more for a valet and maid, a drawing room in which to take their meals and another for work or entertaining. Gamblers going to Monte Carlo used it, playing bridge for high stakes en route; high-grade courtesans – *poules de luxe* – travelling down to the Riviera to try their luck might allow the winners a night of joy on the way. English passengers joined it at Calais; along the coast it stopped at St-Raphael, Cannes, Juan-les-Pins, Antibes, Nice, Monte Carlo and Menton.

---

* All other French trains were brown.

That March, Barnato had been at a dinner party on board a yacht near Cannes when the subject of racing the Blue Train came up and Barnato bet £200 that he could beat it on its journey from Cannes to Calais with ease. The next day, as the Blue Train departed from Cannes railway station at 5.45, Barnato left the Carlton Bar in Cannes and with a companion set off in the Speed Six.

Their progress was slowed by heavy rain, they lost time searching for their prearranged fuelling rendezvous, met dense fog near Paris and had a puncture. Despite this, their average speed on the 570-mile journey was 43.43 mph. They reached Calais so far ahead of the train that Barnato decided to extend his side of the bet to London. They scrambled aboard a ferry to Dover and set off again. At 3.20 p.m. Barnato parked the Speed Six outside the Conservative Club in St James's Street, four minutes before the Blue Train arrived at Calais. The French got their own back for this snub to national pride by fining him £160 for racing on public roads and barring Bentley Motors (of which Barnato was Chairman) from that year's Paris Salon.

Babe Barnato figured again during the evening of Cimmie's birthday, when she gave a floodlit birthday dinner on the rocks below the hotel, and Barnato, Gilbert and other men had diving races after dinner. Again it was an evening of scenes and quarrels. Irene, who sat next to Gilbert at dinner, listened to his confidences that 'things were screw-eyed between him and Ina [Gilbert's wife]'. Nevertheless, after Mosley, never averse to making mischief, had taken Ina some distance away to talk to Fruity and left her with him, the furiously jealous Gilbert, finding her missing, 'went mad', in Irene's words. He 'dragged her savagely into the street where Cim and Dudley witnessed a fearful scene . . . Baba and Cim had hour after hour battling and appeasing Ina and him'. Irene was driven home at 5.00 a.m., 'exhausted with waiting on other people's rows', and when the party rose in the morning it was discovered that John Gilbert had left for Paris at dawn in a taxi, saying to the driver: 'Don't have an accident – my face is my fortune.'

*

For the golden couples who had first invented summertime holidaying on the Riviera, all was not going well. This dark side was perhaps best summed up in the disintegrating lives of Zelda and Scott Fitzgerald (often guests of Gerald and Sara Murphy, the original settlers on that coastline and on whom Fitzgerald's novel *Temder is the Night* is based). That summer of 1930 the thirty-year-old Zelda entered the first of the clinics in which she would stay intermittently for the rest of her life, as their relationship slowly and tortuously unravelled and her mental state became ever more fragile.

In a long letter that summer Scott described Zelda's 'almost megalomaniacal selfishness and my insane indulgence in drink . . . we ruined ourselves – I have never honestly thought that we ruined each other.' Money, once plentiful, was now harder to earn: although Scott was only thirty-four, his alcoholism had caught up with him and he was finding writing more of a struggle. Zelda began sending him miserable, accusing letters from hospital to which he replied: 'the rotten letters you write me I simply put away under Z in my file'. What had stung him most was the accusation of homosexuality flung at him once by Zelda. It was a sad dwindling of what had seemed charmed lives.

Financially, too, the Riviera was beginning to suffer. The Wall Street stock market crash of October 1929 was rippling through to the Riviera as the world economic depression began. Properties were for sale, the shares of the casinos dropped, the number of visitors plummeted, hotels and shops cut their prices in an attempt to attract more visitors. At Nice's Hôtel Splendide, revenues almost halved from 1929 to 1930. But none of this stopped the men and women in search of what this magic coastline could offer: glamorous, sun-drenched hedonism.

One of those was a German diplomat called Baron Hans Günther von Dincklage, who had settled in Sanary with his beautiful half-Jewish wife named Maximiliana but known as Catsy, an heiress whom he had married in 1927 and whose half-sister was the writer Sybille Bedford. Von Dincklage was tall and athletic, with open-faced, blond good looks, had graceful, urbane manners and was fluent in English and French. His mother was English and his father came from an old Westphalian noble family, so he fitted easily into the minor diplomatic post he held with the German Embassy. Later, he would figure largely in Chanel's life.

CHAPTER 2

>-+-<>-O-<>-+-<

Misia Sert and Her Circle

All through the thirties one of the most constant and frequent visitors to La Pausa was Misia Sert. She and Chanel were each other's most intimate friend, a bond that was lifelong despite an underlying rivalry* and several fallings-out. When an invitation came, Misia and Chanel went together, Misia always in clothes by Chanel; at La Pausa, Misia's rooms were next to Chanel's. They had met at a dinner party in 1917, when Chanel was beginning her rise to fame. From the very start, Misia was fascinated by Chanel, then a rather silent but supremely elegant young woman, realising at once that she had encountered someone extraordinary. The next day she called on her, and they talked for hours.

Of Polish-Russian extraction, Misia was intensely musical and artistic and, when married to her first husband, her cousin Thadée Natanson, quickly became the centre of a circle that included Debussy, Renoir, Monet and Gide, among others. All were enthralled by her youth and charm, painted her often, dedicated musical compositions to her, and she became muse and patron to many of them. After being hotly pursued by one of the richest men in Paris, Alfred Edwards, she divorced Natanson and in 1905 married him, but only a year later Edwards fell in love with the courtesan he would eventually marry and the couple parted.

---

* It is noteworthy that Chanel's name is never once mentioned in Misia's memoirs, despite the months they would spend together and the depth of their intimacy.

In 1908 Misia began an affair with the Spanish painter José-Maria Sert, a man who was nothing much to look at – heavy-set, dark, bearded – but vibrantly alive and with perfect confidence in his star. As for Misia: 'I now had the absolute certitude that Sert was the man I had always waited for, that the others had not existed, and that no one else would ever exist,' she wrote after they had travelled through Italy together. 'For the first time, I knew the dazzling, calm and frightening feeling of something final.'

By now Misia was famous throughout Paris for her influence on the cultural scene – and Paris, in the twenties, was considered the cultural capital of the world (not least in its own eyes). Many of the traits Proust assigned to his hostess Madame Verdurin were Misia's. The writer Paul Morand described her as a 'collector of geniuses, all of them in love with her'. You had to be gifted, it was said, before Misia wanted to know you.

Unsurprisingly, from the moment Misia and Sert became a couple, Sert's career prospered. Soon commissions poured in and on the walls of the houses and castles of the rich appeared his fantasy creations – elephants, dwarfs, acrobats, nude gods and goddesses under palm trees, billowing curtains. Ballrooms, pavilions, music rooms and staircases were the canvases for his huge frescoes and soon he was asked to decorate public buildings: the town hall in Barcelona, the Palace of the League of Nations in Geneva, the Rockefeller Center in New York. Being rich suited them both, so much so that, later, Sert would put his art and what it brought in before anything else.

It was Misia, once the model for painters like Toulouse-Lautrec, Vuillard and Renoir, and the close friend of the ballet impresario Serge Diaghilev, who introduced Chanel to the seething artistic life of Paris, then a ferment of ideas. With Misia and Sert, Chanel learnt about music, painting and the arts, and a certain stylish way of living; it was through Misia that Chanel met artistes like the brilliant dancer and choreographer Serge Lifar and France's polymathic intellectual Jean Cocteau.

At the same time, there was a latent rivalry: Misia regarded Chanel as her protégée and anything that undermined that feeling caused jealousy. When Chanel, who had been introduced to the ballet by Misia, paid the impresario Serge Diaghilev's debts she said to him: 'Misia must never know, never!', telling one biographer:* 'I'd learnt enough by then to know that Misia would be jealous of me because she couldn't do what I could do for Diaghilev.'

It was also Misia who had rescued Chanel from a despair to which she had almost succumbed – and in doing so, had in a sense also saved Chanel's career. This career had originally been launched through the great love of Chanel's life, Arthur 'Boy' Capel. Capel, green-eyed, dark-haired and good-looking, was an Englishman who spoke fluent French and, unlike most of his friends, enjoyed work as much as pleasure. It was an attitude that resonated with Chanel, as did his belief in the ability of women, whom he thought were wrongly held back from worldly success. 'The door to the future city is still closed to women,' he wrote. 'The time has come to liberate them . . . the inferiority of women was only an illusion of the other sex.'

Chanel would certainly prove him right.

Her beginnings were not auspicious. Gabrielle Bonheur Chanel was born on 19 August 1883, to unmarried parents. Her absent-ee father was an itinerant peddler, her mother died when she was eleven, upon which her father took his three daughters to an orphanage for girls run by the nuns of the Cistercian abbey. Here he left them, and vanished for ever from their lives. Their young-er brothers, Alphonse and Lucien, aged nine and five respectively, were treated even more harshly, placed with peasant families to be regarded, as was customary, virtually as slave labour. Not until they were about thirteen were they removed from the small farms on which they had worked, to become market traders like their father.

The orphanage was strict, secluded, monastic and mono-chrome. The girls wore black skirts and white blouses and were closely chaperoned on days when they emerged into public view.

---

* Marcel Haedrich.

Here, in this bleak, lonely place, with lessons six days a week, Chanel remained for six years, with everything from more interesting clothes to novel-reading forbidden. It was literally an incarceration, and at times it must have seemed to the teenage Chanel that she would never escape it. But here she learnt to sew, and when she was eighteen – the age at which girls left the orphanage – she was despatched as a charity pupil to a convent school in Moulins, a town around which several regiments were stationed. Here, with her aunt Adrienne, a beautiful girl only a year older than herself, she found work as a seamstress.

By now a lovely young woman of singular and striking looks, Chanel sang in a cabaret-concert to earn extra money. It was at this time she met Étienne Balsan, a former French cavalry officer, now gentleman rider and textile heir and, at twenty-three, became his mistress – or rather, his second-string mistress. For Balsan was keeping a well-known cocotte at his château, Royallieu, near Compiègne, famous for the hunting in its forests. Chanel, pragmatic from her earliest days, accepted this state of affairs as an escape from her earlier life, became an expert horsewoman, watched how his aristocratic friends behaved – and fell in love with one of them. This was Boy Capel, for whom she left Balsan after three years to live in Capel's chic Paris apartment.

Here she ran a small millinery business. Her hats were strikingly simple and elegant, as different as possible from the creations piled with flowers, feathers and sometimes jewels that were then in vogue; and soon she began to be known. When she needed to expand, Capel subsidised her; before long, the simplicity and elegance of her creations received publicity. It was a happy time: she was deeply in love ('he was my father, my brother, my entire family', she said) and she was establishing herself as independent, one of the most powerful elements of her character.

Both of them were hugely energetic, and while Capel was often absent, playing polo at the various grounds that had sprung up around France, Chanel had her work and had also taken up the new idea that exercise as a routine helped shape a slim and beautiful body, in her case with dance classes. This was something she would practise all her life. With her growing success and Capel's frequent absences on business, Chanel was becoming increasingly self-reliant. She was soon going to need every ounce of strength: in the spring of 1918 Capel told her that he was going to marry the young widow Diana Wyndham, an aristocrat who would consolidate his social position.

Chanel was devastated. It seemed that she was only a mistress, after all. She left their apartment and took one that Misia found for her. When Diana and Capel married in August 1918, Chanel, afflicted by what was in effect a nervous collapse, fled Paris. Capel, too, suffered deeply at the loss of Chanel; only a few months later he was drawn back to her again and their liaison continued. His wife Diana was no obstacle as she was spending more time in England, where she had resumed an affair with Duff Cooper ('She doesn't care at all for me and I not really very much for her but it amuses us,' wrote Cooper in his diary).

By now Chanel was registered as a *couturière* (rather than a milliner) and had established her *maison de couture* at 21 rue Cambon, Paris, conveniently near the Ritz.

Then, several days before Christmas 1919, driving to the South of France, Capel was killed in a car accident when one of his tyres burst, the car turned upside down and exploded into flames. A friend, Comte Léon Laborde, went round to Chanel's house in the early hours to break the news. He was greeted by the butler but insisted that he must speak to Madame. Chanel, her black hair tousled with sleep, came down the stairs in her white satin pyjamas. When the Count had told her the terrible news, she said nothing but stared at him with stricken eyes, 'crying with dry eyes', as Laborde put it later. She knew immediately what she must do. She dressed, packed an overnight bag and insisted that Laborde drive them south at once.

They reached Cannes late the following evening. Laborde went from hotel to hotel to find Capel's sister, whom he knew was there. Finally, at three in the morning, he tracked her down and took Chanel up to her suite. Here she learnt that she could not even look at Capel's face for the last time, as he was so badly burnt the coffin had been sealed up at once. She would not go to the funeral next day but asked the chauffeur to take her to the place of the accident. There she walked round the debris of the car, touching it, and finally sat on a milestone beside the road and at last began to weep. Many years later she said: 'I lost everything when I lost Capel. He left a void in me that the years have not filled.' She mourned like a widow, ordering the furniture in her bedroom suite to be covered in black, black curtains for the window and black sheets for the bed.

Added to the terrible sense of loss was one of humiliation and betrayal: Chanel discovered that she had not been Boy Capel's only lover. It was revealed in *The Times* that in his will he had left a bequest equal to the one she received to an Italian countess. It was the final humiliation and she sank into what seemed a bottomless gulf of misery, hopelessness and apathy.

It was only when the Serts, who had just married in a religious ceremony, took her with them to Venice on their honeymoon that her recovery began. Despite being still almost mad with grief, she flung herself into work again, investing the £40,000 that Capel had left her in her business and taking larger premises at 31 rue Cambon.* She also began what would become a lifetime habit: love affairs that were either simultaneous or overlapping, and the ability to keep most of her lovers as lifelong friends.

In 1921 her lover was one of the Sert circle, the composer Igor Stravinsky. His financial position was precarious and he was unable to find an affordable apartment in Paris for his family. Chanel had handed over her Paris house to his wife and four children, herself taking a suite at the Ritz. Here Stravinsky took to visiting her, often escorting her to clubs and parties. Soon, she was making him a regular allowance. The restaging of his ballet *The Rite of Spring*, largely financed by Chanel, was a huge success, and brought her into ever closer contact with the artistic circle around Diaghilev. 'I liked him [Stravinsky],' she said, 'because he was very kind.' She was also drawn both by his Slavic temperament and his talent, learning much about music from him.

---

* By 1927 she owned five properties in the rue Cambon, the odd numbers from 23–31 inclusive.

Soon they were launched into an affair. In that world, nothing was ever a secret for long – even from the betrayed spouse. When Chanel, who had come to his rescue as a family man, reminded Stravinsky that he was married and asked him what his wife would say, he merely answered: 'She knows that I love you. To whom, if not her, would I confide a thing as great as this?'

Being Stravinsky, the relationship was a tortured affair, its drama heightened by the Serts, to whom the highs and lows of others' relationships were meat and drink. As for Chanel, although fascinated by the interior landscape of the Russian soul, she did not feel the same passion for Stravinsky that he felt for her. When the Ballets Russes left for a tour of Spain and Stravinsky asked her to come with them, she told him merely that she would follow.

A month or two later she gave a lift home one night to a young man she had earlier met briefly. The thirty-year-old Grand Duke* Dmitri Pavlovich, the grandson and favourite of Tsar Alexander II, was one of the aristocratic Russian émigrés who had escaped to Paris and were now supporting themselves as waiters, taxi drivers and by any other means they could think of. His childhood, though privileged, had been spent almost as an orphan: his mother had died at his birth and when he was eleven his father was exiled for contracting a morganatic marriage disapproved of by the Tsar. With his sister, he heard the guns and bombs of the 1905 Revolution as they sheltered in the Kremlin.

Then, in 1916, Dmitri had been involved in the plot to murder Rasputin – he had been one of the conspirators in the house where Rasputin was first poisoned and then shot – and had therefore been exiled by his first cousin, the ill-fated Tsar Nicholas II. This had saved his life when the Revolution came; his father, brother and aunt were all murdered by the Bolsheviks. He was tall, exceptionally good-looking – and eight years younger than Chanel. Of the night she drove him home to his apartment, where she stayed until 4.00 a.m., he wrote: 'we suddenly found ourselves on an amazingly friendly footing'.

---

* Grand Dukes were the sons and grandsons of the Tsars.

Their liaison was not without its complications. When Misia
Sert discovered that Chanel, whom she thought of as *her* protégée, had been sleeping with the handsome Dmitri without her
knowledge, she sent a telegram to Diaghilev and Stravinsky that
was guaranteed to cause trouble. 'Coco is a little shop girl who
prefers Grand Dukes to artists,' it read. Diaghilev sent it straight
to Chanel, adding that in no circumstances should she now come
to Spain as Stravinsky wanted to kill her. As far as Chanel was
concerned, it was the end of the affair with Stravinsky (although
she continued to support him financially) – and almost the end of
her friendship with Misia, to whom she did not speak for weeks.

Meanwhile Chanel saw Dmitri every day. Soon she took him
down to the Riviera, a jaunt for which she bought a new car.
This was a pale-blue convertible, a Rolls-Royce Silver Cloud: she
was, after all, a rich woman now – and about to get richer. They
stayed at Menton, where they were joined by Chanel's maid and
Dmitri's valet Piotr, a giant of a man who had followed him into
exile. Dmitri played golf in the mornings while Chanel stayed
in bed late; they met for lunch then drove to see villages and
churches in the surrounding countryside, they ate out, they gambled at the Casino.

In his diary Dmitri wrote of Chanel's 'rare goodness' and 'surprising sweetness'. Although he had no money and was largely
supported by her, he gave her marvellous family pearls, which he
had managed to save when he fled the Revolution. She had them
copied and launched the fashion for long strings of real or fake
pearls. Their liaison, though brief (Dmitri also wrote that he was
not in love with Chanel), became an enduring friendship and
also proved to be the greatest source of Chanel's wealth. It was
Dmitri who introduced her to the Russian-French *parfumeur*
Ernest Beaux.

The scents then worn by smart women were pure flower essences – gardenia, rose, heliotrope, jasmine – light and innocent,
that quickly wore off. The deeper, more sexual aromas based on
musk and civet, which were also much longer-lasting, were left to
the demi-mondaines. Chanel, however, believed that women – by
which she meant her society clients – were now more liberated

and ready to embrace perfumes that were sophisticated and sensual, which would serve as a counterpoint to the almost spartan chic of her clothes. Underlining perfume's erotic appeal, she added: 'Spray it on wherever you expect to be kissed.'

She herself had always loved scent, wearing it every day and leaving a trail of perfume in her wake. Often she would quote Paul Valéry's aphorism: 'A woman who doesn't use perfume has no future.' Already well aware of the value of publicity, especially by word of mouth, she saw the new scent as becoming so much part of the Chanel 'image' that the influence of the entire brand would reach a whole new market.

Beaux, a master *parfumeur*, had created blends of natural essences and synthetics (which stabilised these essences), so that a scent became an abstract, long-lasting perfume instead of a short-lived and identifiable flower fragrance. He offered Chanel several of his creations to choose from and she selected the fifth. When he asked what they should call it, she determined to stay with what she regarded as her lucky number, and replied: 'I'm presenting my dress collection on the 5th of May, fifth month of the year; let's leave the name No. 5.' Even its bottle had the same economical elegance as her clothes: unlike the usual curvy, elaborate flagons it was a simple, square-cut phial of clear glass with her double C insignia.

She gave samples of it to her favourite clients, who loved it. But selling perfume was quite a different business from the sale of couture clothes to individual clients. Through a friend, Théophile Bader, the owner of Galeries Lafayette, she was introduced to the Wertheimer brothers, the owners of Les Parfumeries Bourjois, France's largest cosmetics and fragrance company. With them she signed a deal to produce, market and distribute Chanel No. 5, the Wertheimers taking 70 per cent of the profits, 20 per cent going to Bader as commission and Chanel receiving a mere 10 per cent, a deal she would furiously regret for most of her life. Success was immediate, the impact on the American market was huge, and soon Chanel No. 5 was the world's best-known scent and Chanel herself, with her 10 per cent of the profits, a multi-millionaire.

At the same time she began another affair, with Picasso's friend the married poet Pierre Reverdy, whose work inspired many of the Surrealists. Unlike her two previous liaisons, it lasted for five years (from 1921 to 1926). They had met for the first time in Misia Sert's fifth-floor apartment with its blue butterflies, baroque statues and Venetian glass. Reverdy was small, with thick black hair, swarthy olive skin and a warm, harsh voice. Given to sudden silences, he was also moody, difficult and mystical. Misia, who had known him for some time, described him as seeming 'fundamentally shattered by life. He was a curious mixture of deeply Christian humility and violent revolt, one was almost physically aware of the permanent torture of his soul.'

His nature was full of contradictions: he loved the good life, with its fullness of sensual enjoyment, but was equally drawn to an existence of asceticism and contemplation. Love of Chanel, coupled with remorse at his infidelity, meant that he would suddenly disappear from the social glamour and luxury of life with Chanel to his small attic in Montmartre.

This temperament, uncomfortable to say the least in a lover, coupled with his reclusiveness, drove him to take refuge near the monastery of Solesmes, accompanied by his wife. Here he lived for several years. This meant that when Chanel wanted a holiday on the Riviera, it was Dmitri she took with her.

After Chanel's affair with Bendor ended in 1930, Reverdy came back into her life ('I cannot resist the joy of seeing you . . .') and spent much of the summer of 1931 at La Pausa. Here, he wrote for her a series of aphorisms that she could later pass off as her own when magazines approached her. ('One can be driven to deceit by an excess of tact in love.')

Her wealth both intrigued and appalled this man of tortured sensibilities, so when she wished to help him financially she had to do it secretly, largely by buying his manuscripts through his publisher. Although he left her at the end of 1931, consumed with guilt over his unfaithfulness to his wife, their relationship remained one of the deepest of both their lives.

By this time Chanel had become the most famous *couturière* in the world, clients booked fittings with her months in advance, and the Riviera the top summer destination – from the late 1920s, its grand hotels had decided to stay open for the summer months. To them came kings (of Norway, Sweden and Denmark), princes, maharajas, millionaires, film stars, peers and the rich and social without number. Some rented, or bought, villas along the coast, an influx that pushed up prices to the disgruntlement of those English who had settled here earlier in search of a life quieter, cheaper and warmer than in their homeland.

No one was better known than Chanel. Her alluring looks, sensual, androgynous and chic, her short hair, her slender figure, which showed off the pared-down elegance of her clothes to their best advantage, and her high-profile lovers ('My love life got very disorganised,' she said) that everyone gossiped about had created a powerful public image. Well aware of this, she never shirked the limelight or turned away from a photographer; on the Riviera, she was seen at all the smartest evenings. She and her style ('To my mind, simplicity is the keynote of all true elegance') had, in fact, become a brand, of which she was the living expression.

Ideas poured forth. Already, she had invented what perhaps is her most famous creation: the little black dress. 'That won't last,' she had said one evening at the theatre, looking around at all the women in their over-elaborate clothes. 'I'm going to dress them all simply, and in black.' It is difficult nowadays to understand what a revolutionary concept this was: hitherto, black had been worn solely, and strictly, for mourning, so she was inaugurating not only a new idea but breaking a social taboo. In 1926 *Vogue* published a photograph of a Chanel black dress, calling it Chanel's Ford (Henry Ford's Model T, affordable for everyone, came only in black). She brought in tweed jackets for women, costume jewellery piled on simple sweaters, striped Breton tops.

Her output was prodigious. In an average year Chanel made around 400 garments for the two collections she showed every year. The first step was to choose the fabric from hundreds of samples, fingering it to feel the texture and crumpling it to check for creasing. She couldn't draw so there were no sketches; instead, she would describe what she wanted, which assistants would interpret. Once a toile had been cut out, sewn and put onto a house model, Chanel would go to work.

With pins and scissors, she would cut or rip out sleeves, adjust shoulders, pin waistlines. The garment would then be made up in the fabric of her choice and the whole process would start again until she felt she could do no more. This occupied her entire working day, roughly eight hours from noon onwards. It could have been called a treadmill – except for the long months that from 1930 onwards she spent at La Pausa.

The Depression that began at the end of 1929 meant even more wealth for Chanel. In 1932 she was approached by De Beers, the diamond-industry giants, as their business was suffering both because of the global downturn and the enormous success of costume jewellery, as popularised by Chanel herself. Hitherto most jewellery, as worn by Chanel's well-heeled clients, had been real; even so, few could afford more than one or two, probably smallish, pieces for daytime wear. 'It's disgusting to walk around with millions of dollars around the neck because one happens to be rich,' she said, adding, 'I only like fake jewellery . . . because it's provocative.' What it provoked was the fashion for mixing real and fake jewellery together in copious amounts, the strings of pearls, the ivory or white enamelled cuffs set with Maltese crosses and the necklaces of mingled precious stones and glass beads, dramatic against the minimalist simplicity of her clothes.

Her inspiration for these had come from the wonderful family jewels that her former lover Dmitri had been able to smuggle out of Russia and from her own collection, much of it given to her by Bendor. She owned ropes of pearls in every length and size of pearl, eight yards of mixed diamonds, rubies, pearls and emeralds, chokers, bracelets, rings and earrings of emeralds surrounded by diamonds, diamond, ruby and emerald bracelets, enamelled cuffs set with jewels, a fifteen-strand necklace of small rubies twisted into a rope as well as many loose and uncut stones. With these – sapphires, topazes, rubies, diamonds – together with pieces of coloured glass, she would work out the semi-precious necklaces for which she became known.

For the De Beers collection Chanel turned for help to her latest lover, Paul Iribe (born Iribarnegaray). He was a brilliantly talented illustrator and designer in the fields of textiles, advertising, graphics and stage design, and a celebrated caricaturist. He and Chanel, both forty-nine, had begun to work together in the late twenties.

Iribe, a Basque, was a controversial character, anti-democracy, anti-fascist, anti-German and, like Chanel herself, antisemitic. He was ferociously patriotic: the rallying cry for *Le Témoin*, the magazine he had started many years earlier, now relaunched because subsidised by Chanel, was '*Le Témoin* speaks French!' Chanel figured in it identifiably as Marianne, the iconic figure of French liberty.

Theirs was a stormy, passionate relationship. Given to outbreaks of temper, shouting matches and even fist fights, Iribe was one of an intellectual bohemian circle rife with emotional entanglements and fuelled by drugs and alcohol. The writer Colette believed him to be a demon. ('He coos like a dove,' she wrote to a friend, '. . . you will find in old texts that demons assume the voice and form of the bird of Venus'.)

Chanel admired and respected his talent, as he did hers. Together they created a collection for De Beers that had the elegant simplicity of the best of Art Deco, as well as an intriguing practicality – four slender diamond bracelets that would interlock to form a glittering cuff, necklaces that could become a tiara.

The exhibition was shown for two weeks during November 1932 at Chanel's suitably sumptuous Paris apartment, on the ground floor of 29 rue du Faubourg St-Honoré, to visitors who included Paris's grandest. Her rooms, decorated in her favourite colours of cream, beige, black and gold, provided a fitting background, with their mirrors, sculptures and a huge Regency sofa covered in orange velvet making a dramatic splash of colour. (Her bedroom, by contrast, was muted, with cream silk curtains, and an entire wall covered with mirror glass.)

Also in the apartment were most of Chanel's wonderful Coromandel screens. These screens had become part of Chanel's life, perhaps in part because it was with Boy Capel that she had discovered them. 'I've loved Chinese screens since I was eighteen years old . . . I nearly fainted with joy when, entering a Chinese shop, I saw a Coromandel for the first time . . . Screens were the first thing I bought', she affirmed. She used these black-lacquered folding screens, some decorated with exquisite images of birds or flowers, some inlaid with ivory, tortoiseshell or mother-of-pearl, as wall coverings, to create a more intimate corner in a larger room or to hide doors.

Screens or no, Chanel's diamond designs were so successful that De Beers shares rose twenty points on the London Stock Exchange two days after the opening of the exhibition.

On the Riviera, the economic downturn had a parlous effect, with hotels cutting their prices as the number of visitors dropped and tradespeople fought for survival. But despite the Depression one class of people, the rich, kept on coming. An attraction to many Americans was the release from Prohibition which reigned at home, where even a simple glass of wine with dinner was illegal; on the Côte d'Azur they could openly drink what they pleased without fear of running foul of the law.

Most people still arrived by the Blue Train. Although air travel had begun,* many of the flights to France were extremely uncomfortable, so cold that the airline provided fur-lined boots for the feet, and so noisy that passengers were advised to put cotton wool in their ears and sometimes cabin crew had to use small megaphones to speak to them. On Evelyn Waugh's flight passengers sat in wicker armchairs on either side of an aisle.

Air pockets meant that planes randomly dropped several hundred feet, which often made the brown-paper bags or sickness bowls under the seat a necessity. Some Americans travelled by liner, especially the superb new Italian ones, the *Conte di Savoia* and the *Rex*, coming from New York to Cannes or Villefranche en route for Genoa.

Edith Wharton, while complaining that Hyères was a 'social desert' in a February 1931 letter to a friend, nevertheless in March

---

* Only about 6,000 people travelled by aeroplane in 1930, but by 1938 the figure was 1.2 million.

had the Kenneth Clarks, the Rex Nicholsons, Lady Desborough, Lord Stanmore and Louis Mallet to stay.

Maxine Elliott entertained as usual. 'Cim, Viv, Nic and I went to Maxine Elliott's at 11,' wrote Irene Ravensdale in her diary on 12 August 1931. 'Bit by bit, hordes swarmed in to bathe. Beatrice Guinness, two daughters, Syrie Maugham, David Margesson,* Peter Watson, Whitney Straight ... every combination was adopted down the chute, it was the greatest fun. After lunch we all lay on cushions and slept or read.'

Maxine Elliott was perhaps the best-known hostess on that strip of coast. A former actress and legendary beauty, she had so successfully transformed herself into a facsimile of an Edwardian great lady that she had become a member of society's inner circle when she lived in England. Many of this set now came out to stay with her at the Château de l'Horizon. With her theatrical presence she could still give an impression of glamour, often dressing in white that set off her well-coiffed white hair, and flashing with diamonds, although on leaving the stage she had given in gladly to her love of good food and wine and now weighed almost seventeen stone. Conversation, except when Winston Churchill was staying, was nothing but frivolous, fashionable gossip.

Just along the coast from Maxine Elliott was someone else with whom Churchill stayed, and who was also politically aware, the press baron Lord Rothermere, a man both rich and generous: he was said to give away £30,000 a year to nephews and nieces. His villa at Cap Martin, La Dragonnière, was so called from a legend that once a terrifying dragon had been slain there. It stood in two acres of orange groves, 200 metres from the sea overlooking Monte Carlo. Rothermere, owner of much of the popular press, including the *Daily Mail*, spent much time there after the failure of his marriage, often entertaining one of his string of mistresses, equally recipients of his largesse (he once told his nephew Cecil King that old mistresses were much more expensive than Old Masters).

---

* Promoted from Assistant Government Whip to Chief Whip of the Conservative Party a few months later, in the November 1931 election.

*

At about this time, Chanel's only serious rival was emerging, although Chanel was not to realise it for some years. Elsa Schiaparelli, in 1932 forty-two to Chanel's forty-nine, could hardly have been more different. She was an eccentric Italian who had fled the life in which she had been brought up, considering it cloistered and restricting. Although, like Chanel, she was hugely energetic and loved exercise – especially swimming and skiing – she could not sew and regarded herself as an artist rather than a dressmaker. Her first, and instantly successful, design had been a sweater with a *trompe l'oeil* design of a bow at the neck with sleeves seemingly ending in cuffs.

Other differences were more profound. Where Chanel had burst like a dragonfly from a poor, peasant background, Schiap – as her friends called her – came from a well-connected and cultivated ambience: her mother was a Neapolitan aristocrat, her father an accomplished scholar, and she had been born in a palazzo. By the early thirties she was employing a workforce of 2,000 and the seventy new pieces she showed twice a year were simple and wearable – wrap dresses, black suits – and fitted the lives of wealthy, conservative clients. Already, though, she was displaying the originality for which she became famous, from zips that were visible rather than concealed to evening dresses with jackets (these had never yet been seen). Soon her hallmark flamboyance would contrast vividly with Chanel's discreet elegance.

Chanel's style and fame brought her another stroke of luck. One evening in Monte Carlo, Dmitri, already indirectly responsible for the creation of Chanel No. 5, introduced her to Samuel Goldwyn. In 1931, the Depression was reducing the size of American cinema audiences and Goldwyn, who believed that 'women went to movies to see how other women dressed',* felt that to clothe his stars in the creations of the world's most famous *couturière* would be a huge draw. He offered Chanel a million dollars to dress his stars both on and off screen. With couture

---

* According to A. Scott Berg, Goldwyn's biographer.

clothes – even her own – affected by the economic downturn, it was too good a deal for Chanel to refuse.

Goldwyn treated her like a princess, laying on an express-train car to Los Angeles with an all-white interior and buckets of champagne, a reception in Hollywood attended by Marlene Dietrich, Greta Garbo, Fredric March and Erich von Stroheim and a special costume department with 100 workers to use as she chose.

In the event, Chanel's visit was shorter, with fewer films dressed by her than either she or Goldwyn had anticipated: she clothed the stars of only three films, *Palmy Days*, *The Greeks Had a Word for It* and *Tonight or Never*, starring Gloria Swanson – who was pregnant but did not wish this known. 'Coco Chanel, tiny and fierce, approaching fifty, wearing a hat, as she always did at work, glared furiously at me when I had trouble squeezing into one of the gowns she had measured me for six weeks earlier,' wrote Swanson. 'It was black satin, cut on the bias, a great work in the eyes of both of us.' The problem was eventually solved with a special rubber corset that effectively concealed the pregnancy.

But though Chanel's dresses won acclaim, the films in which they appeared did not and, unperturbed, she left Hollywood a million dollars richer – and, at the very least, one up on her new rival Schiaparelli. Later she would say: 'Hollywood is the capital of bad taste.'

What she returned with was a vital piece of knowledge, gleaned from touring the American department stores, where she saw plenty of rip-offs of her own designs. Piracy, she realised, was impossible to stop: far better to regard it as valuable publicity and perhaps later to cash in on the desire for cheaper versions of Chanel dresses.

Chanel had taken Misia with her on her Hollywood visit, largely so that her friend could leave her tangled private life behind. Six years earlier, in 1925, a beautiful nineteen-year-old Russian princess called Roussadana Mdivani, known as Roussy, had entered the lives of Misia and Sert. By then the Serts were living in an apartment at the Hôtel Meurice, an Ali Baba cave full of the treasures Sert had found – gilt-encrusted black-lacquer armoires, malachite tables, heavy, glittering chandeliers, huge pieces of rock crystal placed in front of fireplaces to send sudden glimmers of coloured light to unexpected corners as the flickering firelight was refracted through them.

Both Misia and José-Maria, aged fifty-three and fifty-one respectively, had fallen in love with Roussy. Tall, slim, with ash-blonde hair streaked with gold and large grey eyes, and gifted with great charm, she had rung the bell of Sert's large new studio, ostensibly to ask advice about where to find a studio (she was a sculptor). 'How can one man need so much space?' she asked with one of her enchanting smiles. Sert, intrigued, offered her a corner of his. With such daily contact, it was not long before he had fallen under the spell of this alluring young woman and she had fallen into his bed.

Misia had either given tacit permission or turned a blind eye, as she herself quickly became infatuated with Roussy, seeing her as the daughter she had never had. Roussy returned this affection; the two Serts took her with them everywhere and talked of her constantly. To all three of them, it seemed natural that Roussy should come and live with the Serts at the Hôtel Meurice, where she shared Sert's bed. Soon the three were inextricably entangled, Misia managing to convince herself that she was behaving generously and nobly to the man she loved in allowing him this sexual freedom. 'The poor girl was not responsible for the feeling she had for you,' she wrote to Sert. 'I found it very natural that she should adore you.'

Chanel did not see it like that. She constantly told Misia that she was an idiot to play such a dangerous game, spending hours on the telephone trying to convince her of this. She was right. It was only when Misia found a letter to Roussy in her husband's pocket that she realised this was not merely an infatuation. The letter said that he planned to leave Misia and marry Roussy. 'Never in my whole life had I believed that a few written words could hurt so much,' wrote Misia, 'but I refused to take it as inevitable . . . a few written words – could they obliterate twenty years of love?' Her reaction was to seize a pencil and scrawl across the pages that this was impossible, that she knew he still loved her. 'We belong together. Whatever happens, I am yours.' Then she stuffed the letter back in his suit pocket. But Sert never spoke of either the letter or her message.

By the following summer the strain was such that both Misia and Roussy were taking drugs – Sert had always used cocaine and drugs were common among the artistic circles in which Chanel moved. Eventually, Roussy cut the Gordian knot, telling Misia that she, Misia, was the only obstacle to her marriage to Sert. Still the triangle continued: when the Serts went to Italy, Roussy went too. In Florence came the incident that finished the marriage, recorded by Misia years later in a letter to Sert. 'My God! How vividly I remember that bedroom, with the shutters closed against the early afternoon heat, where for the last time I was yours . . . Suddenly a faint creaking revealed her presence; she had crawled in on all fours to make less noise! You were not even angry.'*

At the end of 1927, Sert divorced Misia. Devastated by the loss of the two people she adored, Misia fell ill and Chanel took her to stay with her. Sert, who was now extremely rich, began to resent Misia's intrusive love and her expectation of always being included – her presence was still everywhere: she took Roussy to Chanel for her trousseau, she even helped Sert choose the magnificent ruby necklace that was his wedding present to Roussy. Cocteau, an interested onlooker, described her as 'like someone waiting for a table in a crowded restaurant, whose presence prevents the diners from enjoying their food'.

But nothing stilled her unhappiness. For Misia, the only refuge from it was Chanel and her practical good sense and, as the years passed and her misery remained unabated, especially La Pausa, where she would spend months at a time. Here the atmosphere was of calm and freedom, with plenty of time for solitude if wished. For Chanel, it was a complete contrast to the life she had led with the Duke of Westminster when she stayed in his houses. She had had another reminder of this when she visited him after

* Quoted in *Misia* by Arthur Gold and Robert Fizdale.

her return from Hollywood, when the Duke told her: 'I've lost you. I cannot get used to the idea of living without you.'

It was with her, said Chanel, that he could not have everything. They would always be close but his life was not for her. 'Everyone forever doing needlepoint, looking at rose gardens, changing their clothes, boiling in front of a fire and freezing away from it,' she would say. At La Pausa, everyone could be themselves.

CHAPTER 3

> ❧ ❧ ❦ ❧ ❧ ❦ ❧ ❧

Fun, Games and the Beginning of Terror

As well as being the world's most fabled holiday resort the Riviera was, for many, an intense stimulus to creativity. Around Christmas 1931 the writer Georges Simenon had rented the villa Les Roches Grises in Antibes. To get about, he imported a Chrysler Imperial from the US and settled down to write three of the Maigret novels for which he would become famous. He was not the only one to have found sudden, spectacular fame on the Riviera.

In Sanary, Aldous Huxley wrote his seminal novel *Brave New World* (published in 1932) in four months between May and August. Set in London in the year AD 2540 (632 AF – 'After Ford' – in the book), it anticipated developments in reproductive technology, attitudes to sex, addiction, sleep-learning, psychological manipulation and conditioning. The mechanistic society it produced, governed at a distance by the Resident World Controller of Western Europe, gives a horrific vision of what Huxley himself called 'a negative utopia'. The Connollys, who had given up trying to form an intimate friendship with Huxley, returned to London.

Three years earlier, in 1928, Kurt Weill and Bertolt Brecht, both regarded as *enfants terribles* in the Berlin of the Weimar Republic, were working on an adaptation of Gay's *The Beggar's Opera*. Brecht had already written a first draft, to be called *The Threepenny Opera*. With rehearsals planned for August, the pair fled with their wives in mid-May to the Riviera, where they could work hard and uninterruptedly. They settled in Le Lavandou, where Weill's wife, the well-known actress Lotte Lenya, described the intensive collaboration of the two men. '[They] wrote and rewrote furiously, night and day, with only hurried swims in between.'

The peace and sunshine of the Riviera worked their magic. Their revolutionary 'play with music', like nothing that had been seen before, was shown in Berlin on 31 August. When it ended, the applause was deafening. The smart set loved it. 'One simply has to have been there,' said the Anglo-German aesthete Count Harry Kessler. Perhaps predictably, the National Socialist press, frothing at the mouth, could barely find words vitriolic enough to condemn it. 'Some especially noxious cesspool they find in a corner of any big city is barely good enough for the celluloid romance of this two-bit culture,' was one comment.

Others simply sought pleasure on the coast. In 1932 the Mosleys returned to the Riviera as usual, arriving on 2 August, this time to a rented villa. The financial blizzard was looming: halfway through August an Austrian bank went bankrupt, foreign depositors called in their money from London, there was a run on the pound and gold reserves were depleted. Harold Nicolson, left in charge at Mosley's New Party headquarters, wrote to him: 'I recognise that people may say that at the gravest crisis in present political history you prefer to remain upon the Mediterranean. On the other hand, I do not see what you would do were you here at the moment.'

Life in Antibes went on in its usual way. For the Mosleys, this meant dinner with Michael Arlen, the celebrated author of *The Green Hat*, visits to the bar at the Eden Roc in a chattering group of the ultra-social – Sylvia Ashley, Cecil Beaton, Doris Castlerosse, as always in the brief shorts that made the most of her superb legs, while other women wore the beach pyjamas and ropes of pearls made so fashionable by Chanel. And inevitably, Tom Mosley pursuing yet another woman.

One evening Mosley's pursuit of this inamorata was so

blatant that Cimmie, as her sister Irene recorded, 'ran out of a dinner party and down the street in a blind rage'. But next day the round of lunch parties, dinners, nightclubs, cocktail chatter and drunkenness began again.

In Germany, the effects of the Depression had been immediate and catastrophic. America called in all its foreign loans and the Weimar Republic was destroyed. The government cut wages, workers were laid off everywhere and there were six million unemployed. In this time of extreme poverty and political turmoil, of anger and bitterness, some turned to communism, others to the rising Nazi Party, which seemed to offer a way forward. Where in 1928 the Nazis had only had twelve seats in the Reichstag, by July 1932 they held 230 of the 608 seats – and were the largest party.

The government was in chaos, only able to pass laws by using Article 48 (this allowed the President, under certain circumstances, to take emergency measures without the prior consent of the Reichstag). In January 1933 Hindenburg and the then Chancellor, von Papen, came up with a plan to get the Nazis on their side by offering to make Hitler Vice-Chancellor. He refused, demanding instead to be made Chancellor. Thinking they could control him, they agreed. Hitler immediately urged the dissolution of the Reichstag and the calling of new elections. Simultaneously, the Nazis unleashed a campaign of violence and terror, first against communists, trade unions and anyone suspected of being left-wing, then the centre and Social Democrats.

When, in late February, the Reichstag was set on fire by a Dutch communist, the Nazis had the excuse they wanted to imprison communists. The elections that took place in March 1933 were closely 'monitored' by Hitler's Brownshirts; unsurprisingly, there was a large increase in the Nazi vote. Two weeks later Hitler was able to pass an 'Enabling Act', which gave him dictatorial powers, and within months all other parties were banned and their supporters dismissed from all government offices. The Nazi takeover was complete.

*

Although what happened that spring in Germany seemed far removed from the serenity of life on the Riviera, one ripple effect was quickly felt: the arrival of some of Germany's best-known writers.

On 10 May 1933 German students burned more than 25,000 'un-German' books. Nationalist students marched in torch-lit parades against the 'un-German' spirit; in Berlin, some 40,000 people gathered to hear Joseph Goebbels declaim: 'No to decadence and moral corruption! Yes to decency and morality in family and state! The era of extreme Jewish intellectualism is now at an end.'

'The Burning of the Books', as it became known, heralded an era when only Nazi-approved books could legally be published or sold. On the banned list were any authors critical of Nazi Germany, anything communist, liberal or democratic in tone or which supported the Weimar Republic, writings on sexuality that suggested sex could be a pleasurable activity rather than one to be encouraged purely for reproductive purposes, and anything by Jewish writers.

These sweeping categories included respected foreign writers like Victor Hugo, André Gide, Ernest Hemingway, H.G. Wells, Upton Sinclair, James Joyce, Leo Tolstoy, Joseph Conrad and D.H. Lawrence as well as most of the best-known names in German-language literature, science and philosophy, from Sigmund Freud and Albert Einstein to Erich Maria Remarque, Stefan Zweig, Thomas Mann and Weill and Brecht (whose play had now been translated into eighteen languages and performed more than 10,000 times on European stages).

As public libraries immediately removed all banned works from their shelves, private libraries – referred to by the Nazis as 'literary brothels' – were attacked. That of the eminent doctor Magnus Hirschfeld's Institute for Sexual Science was a prime target on several counts – one was that Hirschfeld had campaigned to decriminalise consensual sex between adult males – and it was destroyed by a hundred-odd students who arrived in trucks accompanied by a brass band. Hirschfeld, fortunately, was abroad on a lecture tour, and after briefly staying in Paris moved to Nice, where he hoped to reopen his Institute (he died just over a year later, before he could do so).

Although few of them could speak the language, France was a natural destination for these German-Jewish intellectuals. Over the past decade the country had gladly absorbed many refugees; with a low birth rate and the loss of so many men in the First World War, it needed more manpower, so entry permits were comparatively easy to obtain. That year, 1933, France accepted 25,000 refugees* – 40 per cent of all those who fled the Reich – of whom the majority were Jews.

As well as the welcoming – for the moment – arms of France, there was another consideration. For anyone who had to escape illegally, the long border between France and Germany was easier to cross than the shorter ones between Switzerland and Austria (although the fact that German was spoken in the latter countries was a draw). As for where to go in France, while Paris was the natural magnet for writers and artists, most had little money so were drawn to the cheap living in the south.

It was also natural for them to congregate together and Sanary, popular with writers, was already known to them. The German-born Sybille Bedford began her writing career there, and Colette lived at nearby St-Tropez. On arrival, many stayed at the Hôtel de la Tour before finding a place to rent. The most famous was Thomas Mann, the greatest name in contemporary German literature, whose family found a house for him in June. He had agonised long and hard about leaving Germany – his wife was Jewish – and had done his best not to antagonise the Nazis; his departure meant that he lost his house in Munich, and the half of his Nobel Prize money† that he had had transferred to Germany. With Thomas Mann was his elder brother, the novelist Heinrich Mann (on one of whose books the film *The Blue Angel* was based). Mann rented the Villa La Tranquille, up a hill with a view across the bay.

Others who arrived were the pacifist writer Wilhelm Herzog,

---

* PRO FO 371/16757,C8140.
† Thomas Mann won the Nobel Prize in Literature in 1929 for his novel *Buddenbrooks*.

who had predicted the rise of Nazidom, and the novelist and playwright Lion Feuchtwanger, author of *Jud Süss*, whose opposition to Hitler was so violent that his German citizenship had been removed. The secluded Villa Lazare, just outside Sanary, which Feuchtwanger rented in June, soon became a literary centre, with his elegant wife Marta hosting tea parties for up to sixty; the villa, as well as having its own private beach, had a beautiful garden, with fig, cherry and olive trees. What it did not have was heating or cooking facilities, so the Feuchtwangers regularly drove into Sanary in the small battered Renault that Lion had bought for fifty francs for the café life that the immigrants had imported.

At first they were welcomed respectfully. The local people, mainly of Italian-Provençal extraction, saw in them a source of income and the French had always admired men of letters. But the ancient enmity between France and Germany quickly rose to the surface (although the French painters living there, fiercely anti-Nazi, were welcoming) and soon, as Sybille Bedford pointed out, it took only a minor incident or disagreement to evoke the muttered words: 'Un Boche, c'est toujours un Boche'.

In complete contrast, another former Sanary dweller, Hans von Dincklage, who had lost his lucrative job with a textile firm after the Depression, moved to Paris and began working for the new German government in their embassy. Once Hitler's power was firmly established, von Dincklage left his wife Catsy, saying it was because she was Jewish. Catsy returned to Sanary. Despite their break, von Dincklage came often to Sanary, and when he did the couple continued to live together as if nothing had happened. In the autumn, as the Manns left for Switzerland, Bertolt Brecht and Arnold Zweig visited Sanary, where the leather-jacketed Brecht played the guitar and sang his anti-Reich songs to fellow exiles.

By now there was such a complete colony at Sanary that it became known as Weimar-on-Sea. The exiled writers and artists congregated together, sipping coffee in the little cafés on the quay, arguing in the bars, strolling under the pines, slapping at the mosquitoes in the evening. As the years passed they, more than anyone, realised how the shadow of war was drawing closer.

They gave anti-Nazi talks, they wrote for anti-Nazi publications. But they were an enclave and no one outside Sanary listened. As one of them remarked mournfully: 'We live in paradise, against our will.'

At the other end of the Riviera from Sanary was one of the coast's greatest allurements and biggest industries – gambling. It was glamorous, sophisticated, exciting and impossible to ignore (the politician Leslie Hore-Belisha went on gambling at the Cannes Casino right up to the time of the Munich Crisis, when he was Secretary of State for War). Even those with no intention of betting so much as a sou would go and dine in one of the casinos, partly because the food there was so good and there was often an excellent cabaret, and partly for the sheer fun of watching the gamblers themselves.

For most of the previous century, gaming in public had been illegal in France. However, Monaco was not part of France and the first casino there was opened in the 1850s. Its success was such that in 1907 the French government allowed baccarat and chemin-de-fer to be played in public. Casinos sprang up all over France, the best known and most successful at Deauville, Biarritz, Nice and Cannes. But none really touched that of Monte Carlo, its wealth described by Evelyn Waugh as deriving 'wholly and directly from man's refusal to accept the conclusion of mathematical proof'.

It was here that 'everyone', from Charlie Chaplin, Gloria Swanson, the Aga Khan, Maurice Chevalier, Schiaparelli and Gertrude Lawrence to statesmen and politicians like Clemenceau, Churchill, Lloyd George and Hore-Belisha as well as millionaires, maharajas, grand dukes, cocottes and kings, came to gamble. Here Chanel would be seen, usually in a white evening dress slung with pearls that set off her dark looks and tanned skin, on the arm of whichever man was then in favour.

It was here, too, that the Dolly sisters gambled so heavily that they almost cleaned Gordon Selfridge out; it was here that the Queen of Sweden arrived at the roulette tables followed by her six ladies-in-waiting. It was here, too, that Somerset Maugham saw, in one of the Casino's spectacular cabarets on the stage overlooking the sea, a turn so dangerous that it formed the basis of his short story 'Gigolo and Gigolette', in which a girl dives thirty metres into two and a half metres of water.

The Casino was run like the business it was, with a strict but almost invisible eye kept on those who came to gamble. A man standing inconspicuously in a corner would sometimes jot down words or symbols in the small notebook he carried everywhere. A red line signified a cocotte, a triangle meant a suspicious character, a little red dot was an officer of the Légion d'honneur, *acajou** stood for a redhead. No domestic servant could enter the Casino without the express permission of his employer.

So frequent were the attempts to swindle the Casino or its regular gamblers that there was said to be a list of over 100,000 'undesirables' in a strongroom near the entrance. Some had been in prison, others had been detected trying to cheat the system, women might be banned for constantly importuning the big players for money or men for writing menacing letters to the Casino authorities. The biggest categories were those gamblers reported as undesirables by other casinos, those who cheated and those who did not repay the passage home given them by the Casino after they had been cleaned out.

This sad finale happened all too often. One of the most successful of the Belle Époque courtesans, the Spanish actress and dancer La Belle Otero, had had jewels, houses and fortunes showered on her, only to gamble them all away when she finally retired to the Riviera. The great dancer Anton Dolin saw her when he visited the gaming tables in Monte Carlo late one evening. 'Sitting at a table was La Belle Otero ... looking very elegant and regal in a black velvet dress, long black gloves and a rope of pearls. She was playing chemin de fer, the only game I ever liked playing ... When La Belle Otero rose to leave the table all the men stood up. The double doors at the entrance of the Juan-les-Pins Casino were normally manned by an attendant but when La Belle Otero left the building both of those portals were

---

* Literally, 'mahogany'.

opened by a pair of smartly uniformed commissionaires and she made a majestic exit . . .'

Gradually she lost everything, pledging her assets to pay her debts – the Pacific island given to her by the Emperor of Japan, the villa in St Moritz, the fabulous jewels. The Tsar (she complained that he stank), the Kaiser and Edward VII had all been her generous lovers; William K. Vanderbilt had given her the Empress Eugénie's famous pearls and the black velvet jacket she often wore was sewn back and front with diamonds.

Her effect on men had been nothing short of mesmeric, or, as she herself put it: 'The declarations I have received! The men I have seen weeping, sighing, imploring! Every one of them approached me with a face transfigured by longing; you could read it in every wrinkle on their brows, in the nervous smiles on their mouths. Rough or tender seducers; ironic satyrs that look upon you hungrily; ingenuous adorers, full of timid attentions; hard, complacent rich men who can pay for their pleasure and will take no refusal; greedy old men seized with a last access of ardour, and possessed by the longing to recapture once more the thrills of their first youth . . .'

Yet in 1941 she had to move into a small hotel in the students' quarter of Nice, sandwiched between a plumber's shop and a hairdresser. Even here, she had to move from a large suite to a smaller one, then finally into just one room, no. 11, in a corner on the second floor with a tiny balcony from which she hung her underwear to dry. On one side was a gas ring, in the corner were a bidet, a lavatory and a washbasin in a curtained recess. In this room she spent the last years of her life, financed only by a small municipal pension from Nice, and one from the casinos of Monte Carlo and Cannes into which she had poured the whole of her enormous fortune.

At the nearby Hôtel de Paris, the watchword was opulence and glamour, much of it provided by the clientele. When Prince Peter of Montenegro died in 1932, the hotel allowed his widow, Princess Violet, to live there free for the rest of her life – a princess could only add to its upmarket ambience. Even the road to the roulette tables was made as easy as possible: an underground tunnel had been built between the hotel and the nearby Casino, so that any diner who wanted a flutter could slip over almost between courses. In the lobby stood a bronze statue of Louis XIV on horseback, its nose, right knee and fetlock gleaming brightly where countless gamblers had touched them for luck before an evening's gaming.

Nothing was spared to make Monte Carlo and its Casino *the* place to visit, from a fifty-metre swimming pool and terraced tennis courts to pigeon-shooting, practised on a terrace at the far side of the Casino. The unfortunate birds, which had had wing and tail feathers plucked so that they could only flutter, not fly, were released, to be blown to bits by the waiting guns. If one poor wretched bird escaped, to descend erratically to the beach below, it was instantly seized by one of the waiting small boys, who wrung its neck and took it home to the family stewpot.

Monte Carlo was not the only place on the coast where one could gamble: the casinos in Nice and Cannes were also famous. Here Florence Gould, the wife of a wealthy property entrepreneur, regularly dropped huge sums, often in one of her husband's casinos. She had persuaded Chanel, of whom she was a friend and client, to design her special beach pyjamas, with extra-large pockets for gambling chips; for the evening, these were made of sequinned velvet or satin.

Florence, née La Caze, had been born to French parents in San Francisco, who had for safety sent her and her sister to boarding school in Paris after the 1906 earthquake. A siren with an eye to the main chance and limitless social ambitions, she had returned to Paris after a brief first marriage hoping to become an opera singer and instead had met the millionaire Frank Jay Gould, son of the nineteenth-century 'robber baron' Jay Gould. When the twice-divorced Frank spotted Florence, then working in the Folies Bergère, he fell for her straight away; she became his mistress and married him in 1923. He was forty-five to her twenty-seven; and although the two had what would now be called an 'open' marriage, Frank enjoyed Florence's beauty, admired her sharp intelligence and business brain – and was also conscious of what a third divorce would cost him.

Frank had realised that Prohibition would increase the number of rich Americans coming to the South of France, and built accordingly. His creation, the $5 million Art Deco Palais de la Méditerranée in Nice, had a casino, theatre, restaurant and cocktail bar; earlier he had put Juan-les-Pins on the map by revamping its shabby wooden Casino and adding a cabaret. He then bought up the 200-room Hôtel Provençal, which would soon become a glamorous modern landmark, with a jetty for yachts, gourmet restaurants, beaches of white sand and a private bathroom (and a new piece of soap) for every guest. Although Juan-les-Pins had earlier been beyond the social orbit, with the alluring Florence's gift for publicity it soon attracted a glittering clientele, from stars like Rudoph Valentino and Harpo Marx to writers such as Ernest Hemingway and Scott and Zelda Fitzgerald and the tennis champion Suzanne Lenglen.

A green-eyed, chestnut-haired beauty, Florence was also athletic – she introduced water-skiing to the Riviera – and a noted hostess, entertaining lavishly at El Patio, the Gould villa near Cannes, surrounded by her Impressionist paintings, eighteenth-century French clocks and furniture, English silver and Renaissance objects. Here artists, writers and actors, from Cocteau and Matisse to Maurice Chevalier and Colette, ate off her marvellous Chinese flower-decorated porcelain, simply kept in the pantry in piles rather than on display. Stacked in the silver cupboard were a dozen superb silver plates made in 1770 for Catherine the Great to give to one of her favourites. Florence also loved the nightlife of Paris, where Frank had bought her an apartment on the boulevard Suchet, by the Bois de Boulogne – Frank, older and a recovering alcoholic, seldom followed her there.

Florence was even more famous for her jewels. Her pearls were huge, lustrous and evenly matched, she had an enormous sixty-five-carat sapphire ring, emerald and diamond, sapphire and diamond, ruby and diamond bracelets, an enamelled Art Deco card case set with precious stones, rings, pill boxes, brooches and watches, an emerald fish cigarette lighter, cigarette cases and powder compacts in gold and diamonds.

Usually seen drinking large quantities of champagne and gambling freely, Florence was a regular at the Monte Carlo Casino. In complete contrast, Maxine Elliott, another great hostess, never left her villa, the Château de l'Horizon, and intensely disliked it if her guests tried to. Her white villa, gleaming against the brown rocks, was a byword for expensive luxury: each bedroom had a private balcony overlooking the Bay of Cannes, there was an artificial moon to be switched on for moonless nights when guests dined on the terrace, and even the books that did not match her sets of gilded leather had been painted to co-ordinate with them.

As her hospitality was boundless, the house was always full of visitors, all of whom brought either maid or valet and who stayed as long as it suited them. 'She really did think it rude of her guests to go outside the Château de l'Horizon,' said the writer Vincent Sheean, married to Florence's niece. 'I have heard her roundly ticking off those who infringed this rule.' So people came to her, bringing friends and house guests: anything between twenty-five and forty people were at lunch every day on her terrace beneath an awning, fetching what they wanted to eat from a buffet on the side. The food was rich and fattening, as Maxine liked it. In the mornings she would heave her elephantine bulk out to the poolside on size-four feet; here guests had to play backgammon or mah-jong with her. In the afternoon, while they took a siesta, she had tea in the library with hot buttered scones and cakes.

Maxine had built the Château de l'Horizon on an unpromising fifteen-metre strip of land between the railway and the coast road on one side and the sea, to which there was a sheer drop, on the other. She had had the rocks levelled and a superb swimming pool installed with a chute from it into the sea. Planning the width of the chute so that Maxine's enormous rump did not get stuck on the way down required cunning and split-second timing worthy of a French farce. The architect, pretending to see something in the water below, pointed this out to Maxine, who bent slightly forward and down to have a look. Behind her, his assistant whipped out a tape measure and assessed the width of her massive rear. When she turned round, all was bland again – and the correct width of the chute assured.

A certain ennui must have been endemic, as there was little to do except swim, eat and avoid Kiki, the vicious male lemur with needle-sharp teeth that bit almost every woman who came to the château. Adored by Maxine, it was allowed to run free and once bit Maxine's old friend Lady Mendl on a particularly tender spot as she was standing on her head by the swimming pool.

For Chanel, the busy social life of the Château de l'Horizon would have held little appeal. Her closeness to her lover Paul Iribe had increased, so much so that there were constant rumours of their engagement. The other great topic of gossip that summer of 1933 was Elsie Mendl's facelift – it was Elsie who had helped Maxine do up the château.

Elsie was one of the great characters of the Riviera. A tiny woman who liked to wear short white gloves (even while eating) and to carry at least one little dog, she had been in a live-in relationship with another woman for many years. Then in 1926, at the age of sixty and to everyone's surprise, she had suddenly married the diplomat Sir Charles Mendl. One friend explained the match by saying: 'Charles was charming and Elsie was rich,' and that 'they shared the same enthusiasms for people, parties, and the fine art of luxurious living'. Elsie's housekeeper said that Elsie had simply wanted a title. Whoever was right, the marriage was primarily for social convenience: the couple entertained together, but kept separate homes.

At seventy Elsie, trim and fit from years of exercise and diet, reinvented herself, dyeing her hair blue, having a facelift and entering a fancy-dress ball by way of a cartwheel. Standing on her head – often at parties – was a favourite ploy. She had almost singlehandedly invented the profession of interior decorator, introducing simplicity, light, painted furniture, cotton chintzes and plain painted walls in place of heavy, ornate wallpaper. She was also known for her egocentricity: her response to her first sight of the Parthenon was, 'It's beige – my colour!'

Chanel's thoughts too may have been turning to marriage as she and Paul Iribe grew ever closer. Iribe was now virtually a free agent: his American wife Maybelline, fed up with his womanising and under pressure from her parents over his extravagant spending, had returned with their two children to the US. Most of Chanel's friends were horrified at the idea that she and Iribe might marry, as they felt he had gained too much influence over her. Only Serge Lifar remained confident that this would not happen; 'He dominated her and she could not stand that,' he said.

It was not surprising that Iribe was so captivated by Chanel, as a much younger man, Roderick ('Rory') Cameron, then nineteen, described her at fifty as 'irresistible. Absolutely.' When Cameron met her on the Riviera that summer of 1933, she was probably wearing her usual white duck trousers – often teamed with a stripy top and pearls – but what struck him was her jewellery: 'wide ivory bracelets encrusted with a Maltese cross of rubies, and rows of pearls strung with seed pearls instead of knots in between each bead. Wound in with these were blobs of emeralds joined together with heavy gold links. Clip earrings hid her over-large ears.'

As did most people, Cameron found her extraordinarily good-looking. 'She was a bright, dark-gold colour, wide-faced, with a snorting nose, just like a little bull, and deep Dubonnet-red cheeks . . . she lived in a house on the rue du Faubourg St-Honoré. It had an enormous garden with fountains, and something like fifty-four screens shaping these rooms into the most extraordinary effect of charm.' There were also eighteenth-century French gilt armchairs, crystal chandeliers, mirrors everywhere, books bound in black and beige, a pair of gold lions and statuettes of other animals in coral, jade, crystal and terracotta.

'[Here] she received the world,' said Cameron. 'It was a proper society she had around her – artists, musicians, poets – and everyone was fascinated by her.' One of the closest was Jean Cocteau. A slight, angular figure, he was once described as 'the life and death of every party' because he never stopped talking. Another was Picasso, who, said Cameron, 'in those days drove around Paris with his latest mistress by his side in a bright-yellow Hispano-Suiza with a hammer and sickle painted on the side'; and Christian (Bébé) Bérard, fashion illustrator, artist, designer, who,

unlike most of those who took the drug, was an opium addict.
For as the thirties drew on, morphine became more generally
used – opium was considered the 'gentleman's drug', according
to the painter Sir Francis Rose, Bt, who knew this circle from his
training under Misia's former husband, Sert.

'We Europeans of the twenties and thirties only smoked
opium bought in sealed purple tins which was smuggled from
Indo-China, where it was openly sold by the Régie Française in
the same way that Benares opium was sold by the British government in all the tobacco shops in Hong Kong,' said Rose. 'If
we could not get the purple tins we bought the "raw", which
sometimes looks like a great clot of mud or a rounded Hebrew
loaf of bread covered with poppy seeds. It took days of cooking
and filtering through special filters and filled the house with the
strong, rich smell which I love, before we could weigh our kilos.'

At La Pausa, Chanel refurbished the drawing room and entertained. The food she served was simple and delicious but one
kitchen staple was banned – onions ('I don't like food that talks
back at you,' she would tell her cooks). In the summer of 1934,
among others she invited there were the German photographer
Horst, Serge Lifar (now ballet master of the Paris Opéra) and
the Italian Conte Luchino Visconti (then twenty-eight). They had
met two years earlier after Visconti, who had obsessively – and
successfully – bred racehorses for five years, was drawn by his
love of theatre and the arts to Paris. Handsome, talented, rich
and aristocratic, he had been caught up in the Paris scene, and
regularly lunched with Chanel. Chanel found him intriguing, for
his looks, his style and his general air of promise; he in turn
was flattered to be the escort of this chic, sophisticated, and
well-known older woman (Chanel was forty-nine when they
met). By the time he stayed at La Pausa he had met Horst, and
had just begun to embark on his film career. At one of her lunches
Chanel introduced Visconti to Jean Renoir – a year later, he was
working in Renoir's crew.

Iribe, however, had begun to voice criticism of her beautiful Paris
apartment and of Chanel's way of life. 'I don't understand', he

said, 'why you need so many rooms. What's the point of all these objects? . . . Why do you need all these servants? One eats too well at your house . . . I might live close to you, if you knew how I'd be happy with nothing.' At once, Chanel called his bluff, closing the apartment, giving up its lease and renting two rooms in a small house not far from her premises in rue Cambon, taking with her only a heater for each room, her favourite books, a few rugs and of course a Coromandel screen. This was not what Iribe had expected, and when Chanel told him, no doubt with a touch of the irony for which she was known, 'I'm going to lead the famous simple life,' he was intensely annoyed – and even more so when she suggested that he should do the same. There was an argument, and eventual compromise: they both moved into the Ritz.

It was for Chanel a natural choice. The Paris Ritz was one of the most famous – possibly, at that time, the most famous – of the world's hotels, known for its smooth, superbly efficient luxury and elegant furnishings, with big brass beds, exquisite chaises longues and soft lighting. Its clientele was an exciting cultural mix of those who frequented it, everyone from film stars like Marlene Dietrich – who called the Ritz home – and Arletty to statesmen like Winston Churchill, painters and writers; Ernest Hemingway had virtually colonised the Ritz Bar. ('When in Paris,' he said, 'the only reason not to stay at the Ritz is if you can't afford it.') Besides, for Chanel it could hardly have been more convenient, with its rue Cambon entrance only minutes from her couture house and workrooms. Above these she created a four-room apartment, largely used for entertaining, with her beloved Coromandel screens, crystal chandeliers, objets and bronzes.

Once established in the Ritz, in Paris she never lived anywhere else. More than ever, La Pausa became her only real home.

CHAPTER 4

><+>-0-<+><

Love and Glamour on the Sunshine Coast

Chanel was not the only one carrying on an intense and complicated series of liaisons on the pine-scented shores of the Mediterranean. H.G. Wells, the prolific English writer celebrated for his novels and far-seeing science fiction, had for years had a love nest on the Riviera where he entertained a string of mistresses and short-term conquests, while his long-suffering wife Catherine and their two sons remained in England. As he expressed it, in a phrase that seemed to promote this behaviour as a necessary health precaution: 'I wanted a mistress to tranquillise me.'

The most famous of these panaceas was the English novelist Rebecca West, who wrote that the Riviera was 'the nearest thing to paradise'; after this affair had ended Wells began another with a Dutch writer and former Jesuit nurse, Odette Keun. Together they built the villa Lou Pidou, Provençal for 'The Treasure'. Above the fireplace were carved the words: 'Two lovers built this house.' But life with Odette was anything but tranquil. Wells described her as 'addicted to every extremity of emotional exaggeration', and given to slashing her wrists during these crises (as a nurse, she knew how to do this without seriously harming herself).

In 1930 he had just re-encountered an earlier mistress, the mysterious Baroness Moura Budberg, given to appearing and disappearing seemingly at random. By now Wells was ready for a change: Odette's scenes had become wearisome but she was difficult to shed, so he had to move carefully. Moura, then thirty-seven, had always fascinated Wells and their affair was re-kindled, although in secret because of Odette. Moura was tallish, plump but shapely, with grey-streaked dark hair, hazel eyes, a broken nose and wide Tatar cheekbones, the daughter of a Russian nobleman and descended from Peter the Great. Translator and mistress of the Russian poet Gorky, like many Russians she drank a great deal of vodka. Although untidy and given to lying and concealment, especially over her sudden comings and goings, she had a curious and compelling charm.

Wells returned to Cannes at the end of November 1931 for a year of work – and Moura. Before the end of 1932 he had written *The Shape of Things to Come*, which forecast a European conflagration from the flashpoint of a violent clash between Germans and Poles at Danzig in 1940, and the aerial bombing of cities, as well as *The Autocracy of Mr Parham* (1930) and *The Bulpington of Bulp* (1932) – and found Moura's companionship so intoxicating that he wrote: 'By the end of 1932 I was prepared to do anything and overlook anything to make Moura altogether mine.' What he did was finally manage to jettison Odette, of whom he was now heartily sick. Although Moura constantly made it clear she did not want to marry him – she had to remain free – their liaison continued. After Odette's tempests, her serenity must have made it easier for Wells to work, as throughout 1934 books and articles streamed from him, and he planned a feature film based on his earlier book, to be called *Things to Come*.

As Wells never made a secret of a serious mistress (nor did the possession of one stop him pursuing other women), he and Moura were asked everywhere as a couple. After the final break with Odette, they stayed in Menton and Nice and spent a week with Somerset Maugham in December 1934; they had intended to go to Palermo but there was a breakdown in the Italian air service.

On Christmas Day Maugham gave a luncheon party, to which Gerald Haxton had invited a rich American divorcée, Constance Coolidge, a racehorse owner. Soon afterwards, Moura left on one of her mysterious disappearances, this time to England, saying her daughter wanted to see her. The day after she left, Wells, who was by now staying at the Hôtel Hermitage in Monte Carlo, received a note from Constance. She had heard from Maugham that Wells was alone at the Hermitage and, wrote Wells, she 'asked me in a schoolgirl handwriting to dine with her at the Negresco'. To a man like Wells, an invitation from a good-looking woman to dine with her in her suite must have meant only one thing.

The Negresco, on Nice's Promenade des Anglais – so called because it was financed by the English in the 1820s as a way of providing work when the crops had failed locally – is a turn-of-the-century hotel, then known for its comfort. Constance, who had a suite there, could well afford it: she also owned an apartment in Auteuil, wore designer clothes and employed four servants. As a triple divorcée, the first priorities of the patrician Constance had become books and horses; in Paris in the twenties she had become known as the owner of a string of racehorses, and in the thirties she looked at form books and worked out odds regularly every day. She was already an admirer of Wells, having read many of his books and been fascinated by them.

In appearance Constance was a bit like Moura, tall and dark but slim and freckled. The dinner went well – so well that 'after dinner it seemed the most natural thing in the world to take her into my arms and kiss her and for her to kiss me back,' recalled Wells. After that, as he tactfully put it: 'I did not go for an hour or so.'

For Wells, untroubled by conscience over either his wife or Moura, their liaison was the kind of erotic holiday that suited him perfectly – he could maintain his work schedule and yet give himself over to hours of enjoyment. He would work all morning until noon, when Constance's chauffeur-driven Hispano-Suiza arrived to pick him up. The two of them would go to a restaurant up in the mountains or along the coast for an unhurried lunch, then return to Constance's suite at the Negresco. In the evening they would dine out somewhere in Nice.

Suddenly Moura sent a wire saying that she was returning. Wells managed to put her off for a few days, and when she came he introduced her to Constance. All three planned to return to Paris together, but Moura was called away by the sudden illness of her old governess in Estonia. Wells and Constance set off and spent Wells's last night in France before his return to domesticity at Paris's celebrated Hôtel de France. Their last meal *à deux* was breakfast, Wells sitting on the side of Constance's bed and showing her how to eat boiled eggs English-fashion by cutting off their heads – that morning, they had found that they needed more than coffee and rolls to sustain themselves. Then he flew to London.

Their affair, in the early spring of 1935, had lasted only a week but it cast a long shadow of memories. They wrote to each other for ten years – letters often filled with talk of their time together on the Riviera. That February he wrote to Constance: 'I wish I was in bed with you now.' When she wrote to him worrying about the gossip about them that had arisen, and sending him a relevant newspaper cutting, he replied: 'It is nice to be in the same paragraph as you, but it will be nicer to be in the same bed with you . . .'

Of all the personalities on the Côte d'Azur, one of the most notorious was the dazzling Lady Furness, the third wife of the first Baron Furness. Australian-born, Enid Furness, née Lindeman, was already a veteran of two marriages and countless lovers – as a dare, she had slept with all the officers in the battalion commanded by her brigadier husband when he was stationed in Cairo.

Some years before that, as a young widow in Paris, she had caused mayhem among the young officers there: it was said that five men had committed suicide because of her, one blowing himself up, another throwing himself into shark-infested waters when he followed her on a visit home, a third hurling himself under the Blue Train. Or as Enid herself put it: 'They were not able to take the strain.'

She and Furness – famous for his foul language, his temper and his drinking – had married in 1933, when she was forty-one. Hopelessly inefficient with money, she handed over her entire wealth to her son Rory (by her first husband Roderick Cameron, who had left her his huge fortune). Furness in turn showered her with gifts but, unsurprisingly suspicious as to her fidelity, had her watched by detectives more or less constantly. Nor could he bear children near him, so in London Enid had to rent a nearby flat in which to install her three, together with maids and governesses; on the Riviera, they simply lived in another part of the hotel. However Enid, a devoted mother, managed to see them constantly.

A six-foot-tall, silver-blonde beauty with huge green eyes and a stunning figure, Enid was impossible to overlook. Her clothes were superb; Chanel was a great friend, once designing for her a wonderful silk suit in Enid's favourite colour, pale violet, with deeper violet trim. When the Furnesses stayed in the Hôtel de Paris, Enid's style and beauty were such that people stood on chairs in the hotel lobby to catch a glimpse of her as she set off for the nearby Casino – the first time Lord Furness took her to bet at the main table all gambling ceased as she entered, her perfect figure swathed in white lace over violet taffeta.

She was a terrific gambler and usually carried a bag stuffed with £10 notes. In London she would distribute these to ex-servicemen, often helping them to find jobs. She was equally *dégagée* with her jewels, shoving her pearls into Kleenex boxes because they were the nearest things to hand. Wherever she went she caused a sensation, especially when she appeared with her tame cheetah (usually walked every day by the children and their governess). The cheetah travelled with Enid; when she went abroad in Furness's private plane, in her mountain of luggage were a few suitcases into which air holes had been drilled. These contained her pets, including the cheetah, which had been given sleeping pills before setting off.

The year 1935 was perhaps the heyday of glamour on the Riviera of the thirties – that era of bias-cut satin evening dresses, Hollywood films, beach pyjamas, exotic cocktails, harbours crammed with yachts and super-stylish motor cars (which needed washing most days because of the red dust blown in from the Sahara).

From then on, the exotic mélange of film stars, aristocrats, millionaires, playboys and glamorous women on the make – many of them visiting Chanel's Monaco boutique for the 'right' beach clothes – would be diluted by what they would have called 'ordinary' people, and refugees from the turmoil elsewhere. But before this gilded life was touched, the Riviera remained the playground of the Western world – that is, of that part of the Western world that could afford it.

It was on the Riviera that Elsie Mendl gave parties where Cole Porter and Noël Coward played and sang, where Bernard Shaw came first to swim and then to take tea at the Mendl villa at La Garoupe (the beach on the eastern side of the Cap d'Antibes). It was also at La Garoupe that Cyril Connolly wrote his only novel, *The Rock Pool*,* his hero Edgar Naylor summing up its appeal: 'It was his favourite beach, for him the white sand, the pale translucent water, the cicadas jigging away at their perpetual rumba, the smell of rosemary and cistus, the corrugations of sunshine on the bright Aleppo pines, held the whole classic essence of the Mediterranean.'

On the Mediterranean itself Daisy Fellowes was entertaining the Prince of Wales and a then unknown American, Mrs Ernest Simpson, for a cruise along the coast from Cannes – the Prince had taken Lord Cholmondeley's Golfe-Juan villa, Manoir Eden Roc – to Porquerolles. In the close proximity of shipboard, one thing was unmistakable: the Prince was in the early and most obvious throes of passion, 'otherwise, make no mistake, Daisy would have gone for him', observed a fellow passenger who knew of Mrs Fellowes' reputation.

The woman with whom the Prince was smitten, Wallis Simpson, was (in 1935) a slim, elegant, childless thirty-nine-year-old married to her second husband after divorcing her first, an alcoholic American naval officer (divorce, it must be remembered, was then comparatively rare and certainly *mal vu*). It was through Ernest Simpson's sister, Mrs Kerr-Smiley, a society hostess, that the Simpsons had originally met Lady Furness, the American-born second wife of Lord Furness, and the mistress of the Prince of Wales. In the autumn of 1930 Thelma Furness had introduced them to the Prince. Wallis was immediately fascinated. 'His slightest wish

---

* Published the following year, 1936.

seemed always to be translated instantly into the most impressive forms of reality,' she wrote in her autobiography. 'Trains were held; yachts materialised; the best suites in the finest hotels were flung open; aeroplanes stood waiting . . .'

After the Prince had asked the Simpsons to stay at his country house, Fort Belvedere in Windsor Great Park, there had been dinner parties and occasional 'pot-luck' suppers when he dropped in for a cocktail. For Wallis, it was like a dream. Here was the one man the whole world wanted to meet, Prince Charming himself, apparently anxious to have her as a friend. At first, few people noticed this budding relationship; it was well known that Lady Furness was the Prince's mistress, and when he entertained the Simpsons there were always other people there. Gradually, however, Ernest faded from the picture – conveniently busy when the Prince called at the Simpson flat in Bryanston Court, or off 'on business' to America.

Soon the Simpsons were regular weekend visitors at the Fort. Then, in January 1934, Thelma Furness left to visit America for a few months. Before she went, she and Wallis met for cocktails and, according to Wallis, after remarking that the Prince would be lonely without her, said: 'Wallis, won't you look after him?' Wallis promised to do so and, by the time Thelma returned from the US, had supplanted her.

Much of the Prince and Wallis's courting was done on the Riviera, sometimes staying in the villas of friends, when he and Wallis would slip away to dine together alone in a small bistro. One of these villas was right at the tip of Cap d'Antibes and the Prince's popularity was so immense that when a boatload of some of the English who lived permanently on the Riviera passed it on their way to a picnic, everyone clapped. They, of course, did not know that their golden Prince was enthralled by one of his guests. The press was silent and only the small network of upper-crust London society was aware of the new direction of the Prince's affections; his lavish gifts of jewels alone would have given this away – jewels so large and spectacular that when Wallis wore them many thought they were fake.

Sometimes there were brief cruises; they had spent the summer of 1934 cruising there in Lord Moyne's yacht *Rosaura* (without Ernest but chaperoned by Wallis's aunt Mrs Bessie Merryman). In the spring of 1935 the Prince had taken Lord Cholmondeley's villa Le Roc at Golfe-Juan for himself and a party of friends, of whom Mrs Simpson was one. But so little noticed was her presence then that no mention was made of her in any of the press reports of the holiday.

Connolly's novel was not an allegory for a glossy life that continued unperturbed while sinister forces gathered beneath – but it could have been. For in the rest of Europe the threat of war was steadily increasing. That year Britain announced an increase in armament manufacture and the French conscripted military service doubled from one to two years because of a shortage of young men. Hitler declared that Germany was rearming, that he was establishing military conscription, enlarging Germany's army to thirty-six divisions and increasing her air force – all this in violation of the Treaty of Versailles – and the Saar (in a referendum of January 1935) voted overwhelmingly for re-annexation to Germany.

Only Winston Churchill, then in the political wilderness, staying with Maxine Elliott, where he sat by the pool or painted in a red bathrobe over bathing trunks, slippers and a large, floppy straw hat, seemed aware of the danger. Just before he came out he had, wrote the MP Robert Bernays in his diary: 'made a grand speech . . . the last despairing cry of a man who has been ignored and who sees nothing but ruin and desolation in consequence'. Churchill had travelled to the Château de l'Horizon alone. (Vincent Sheean had heard him saying: 'My dear Maxine, you have no idea how easy it is to travel without a servant. I came all the way here from London alone and it was quite simple.' To which Maxine had replied in her deep voice: 'Winston, how brave of you!')

As Churchill only talked about what interested him, at that time he constantly held forth about Mussolini – about to invade Ethiopia – German rearmament, the character of Hitler and the Nazi movement, which bored much of the fashionable company around Maxine's table. One day, recorded Sheean, he said to one of the guests there: 'With Germany arming at breakneck speed, England lost in a pacifist dream, France corrupt and torn by dissension, America remote and indifferent – Madame, do you not tremble for your children?'

Along with these scarcely veiled preparations for war, the tide of antisemitism was rising in Germany, to the alarm of the National Council of Jewish Women in New York City, who saw Hitler as more of a threat than did Britain's government. In September 1935 came the Nuremberg Laws that denied the rights of citizenship to Jews and reduced them to the status of 'subjects'. These laws forbade marriage and extramarital sexual relations between Jews and 'Aryans'. Jews were forbidden from employing an Aryan female under the age of thirty-five as a servant, from shopping in Gentile stores – and Gentiles from shopping in Jewish stores – from going to cinemas, theatres or from strolling in public parks. Most Germans, unaffected by such edicts, simply let them pass.*

Chanel's relationship with Iribe had become complicated. His own emotional make-up was contradictory: while he admired success, he liked to show that he spurned its trappings; while he was drawn to Chanel by her eminence and brilliance, he was also jealous of the fact that she outshone him – by 1935, she was employing 4,000 workers and had sold 28,000 dresses in Europe, the Near East and the US in addition to her jewellery and perfume sales.

As for Chanel, her emotions were more straightforward. This was a man she could admire, who was not dependent on her – nor she on him. She was someone for whom having a man around was a part of life, for fun, for companionship, for sex. But so far, only with Boy Capel had she experienced that powerful fusion of the physical and the emotional felt in passionate love. Yet her feelings for Iribe had steadily grown, so much so that Misia Sert,

---

* Even in 1933, before a number fled, Jews represented less than 1 per cent of Germany's population.

who saw them both constantly, believed that Chanel was, at last, in love again, and that the two of them might marry.

That year, Chanel had decided to spend most of the summer at La Pausa. Iribe came often; when he was in Paris they telephoned constantly and Chanel allowed him to make decisions for her there. At La Pausa, sharing her way of life there, he was so at home that he quite naturally assumed the role of the master of the house.

One day in the late summer, Iribe booked a sleeper on the night train from Paris to join Chanel at Roquebrune, suggesting that they could start their day with a reviving game of tennis. Halfway through the first set, she went up to the net to ask him not to hit the ball so hard; as she did so, he looked at her over the rim of his sunglasses, stumbled and then fell – he had suffered a massive heart attack. He died two days later, on 21 September, in a clinic in Menton, never having regained consciousness.

Chanel felt his loss deeply, grieving over him for a long time. She left everything in her business to subordinates, and did not return to Paris until October. Her sorrow was exacerbated by guilt: although he had said he was feeling faint, she had persuaded him to resume their game. He was only fifty-two, slim and fit, so neither of them had suspected there was anything wrong with him. She never used the court again but let it grow wild with flowers and long grass.

Once again, she had been 'left' by a man, this time by one she truly cared for and with whom, so many of her friends thought, she would have had a future. Grieving, sleepless, miserable, she was in no state to return to Paris, and stayed at La Pausa most of the autumn, dictating what she wanted in the next collection in long telephone conversations. Once again, Misia was with her to support her friend. They also shared drug use; by 1935 Chanel had become a habitual drug user, injecting herself with morphine on a daily basis, a habit she maintained until the end of her life.

That summer, there had been another tragedy. On 1 August Roussy Sert's adored younger brother, Alexis, was killed in a car crash. Roussy was so inconsolable that she lost the will to live, locking herself in her room and refusing to eat or see anyone for a week. When Misia heard of this, she immediately took the train to Barcelona, but neither of the Serts wanted to see her and she was shunted off to a hotel. Sadly, she returned to the only person who did seem to want her company – Chanel – leaving Roussy to overcome her grief as best she could.

When Chanel returned to Paris later that autumn, she found that Elsa Schiaparelli had become more than just a threat: she was now someone who might overtake her. At the root of the problem was the fact that, although both designers had utterly different tastes, they appealed to the same type of woman – one who wanted a crisp-edged, modern, stylish look.

Then, too, fashion itself had changed. The androgynous flapper with her cropped hair, boyish figure and short skirts, for whom Chanel's pared-down elegance might have been created, had disappeared. Girls had become women, with women's figures, curves had reappeared, emphasised and enhanced by the gleam of bias-cut satin, skirts were longer and a newly adventurous note had appeared – and no one was more adventurous than Schiaparelli.

Schiap it was who invented the colour 'shocking pink', and designed clothes that echoed the ideas of the Surrealists she was close to – in particular those of Dalí – offering black gloves with red 'fingernails', brocade ropes that looked like snakes appliquéd onto pink brocade, an evening dress with *trompe l'oeil* rips and tears, and a black gown decorated with a full-length 'skeleton'. Her talent was such that many of Chanel's long-time clients turned to her – though most, like Daisy Fellowes, bought from both *couturières*.

Schiaparelli's appeal to Daisy, for whom the outrageous and the look-at-me was a way of life, is not hard to understand. Immensely rich (she was the heiress to the Singer Sewing Machine fortune), Daisy splashed money about as freely as she indulged in her many caprices. Her huge pink palace was perched on a cliff above the sea but she was just as often seen in the larger of her two yachts, the *Sister Anne*. There was, however, little that was sisterly about Daisy: one of her favourite pastimes was seducing other people's husbands – she described herself as always being 'on the scent' of new conquests. 'It's a thrilling feeling,' she offered, 'like tasting absinthe for the first time. Soon the man asks: "When may I come to tea?" – that's when I sharpen the knife.' In England, she had placed a statue of St Joseph in front of her house, claiming that she was honouring 'the patron saint of cuckolds'.

It was Daisy who was the first to wear Schiap's black suit with (shocking) pink lips for pockets, Daisy who wore the 'Lobster Dress', Daisy for whom diners at the Ritz climbed on chairs to get a sight of her Schiaparelli monkey-fur coat embroidered in gold, and Daisy who had just given up a prestigious and sought-after job as Fashion Editor for French *Vogue* because she was 'bored'.

Chanel fought back by acknowledging this new, more feminine look in her own way. She introduced shoulder pads to emphasise the smallness of the waist, creamy or peachy satins for evening and elegant, gently fitting tweed suits, while her underlying theme remained black and white. At the Monte Carlo Casino, she herself was always seen in the cream or white satin and pearls she had always favoured.

One of those most faithful to Chanel was Diana Vreeland, who lived for fashion. 'You gotta have style,' Diana would say. 'It helps you get down the stairs. It helps you get up in the morning. It's a way of life.' She would go for the endless fittings necessary for a Chanel garment – even a nightgown needed three – to Chanel's private atelier, six floors up in the house on the rue Cambon. 'There was a mirrored staircase up to the first floor – the salon – then five steep flights of stairs. Chanel would crouch at the top of the mirrored staircase watching the collections,' she remembered.

When her husband's job took him back to America Diana moved with him to New York, where she became a columnist and later Fashion Editor for *Harper's Bazaar*. She viewed Chanel as unique. She was 'mesmerising, strange, alarming, witty,' said Diana. 'You can't compare anyone with Chanel. They haven't got the *chien*. Or the chic. She was the most interesting person I've ever met.'

CHAPTER 5

>-◄>-०-<>-<

Socialism and Mrs Simpson

The effects of the Depression had been slow in affecting France but when they did, the country suffered. Unemployment rose sharply from 1932, politics became polarised and anger surfaced. Street rioting, especially that of February 1934, meant that housewives stayed at home as much as possible, keeping baths filled with water in case supplies were cut off.

The left believed a fascist coup was in the making, the right saw revolution coming, while both sides realised there would be active protest. Workers, whose wages had suffered, were beginning a series of strikes, and it was clear that the Popular Front, an alliance of left-wing parties, was gaining ground, in the teeth of opposition from the conservative right.

On 13 February 1936, the tense situation boiled over. Léon Blum, the socialist leader of the Popular Front, was being driven away from the National Assembly by two friends when their car encountered a group of antisemites and royalists known as the Camelots du Roi. These had gathered at the intersection of the rue de l'Université and the boulevard St-Germain for the funeral procession of Jacques Bainville, one of the founders of Action Française, the ultra-right-wing reactionary political group to which the Camelots were affiliated – and to whom, of course, the Popular Front was anathema.

Glimpsing Blum through the car windows, the militants went on the attack. 'Kill Blum!' 'Shoot Blum!' they shouted. They forced his car to stop and began rocking it back and forth.

Blum's friend Germaine Monnet, sitting with him in the back, tried to shield him with her body, while her husband, Georges, who had been driving, ran to look for the police. The militants really did mean to kill him: one of them, who had managed to tear a fender off the car, used it to smash the rear window, and then beat Blum repeatedly over the head. Only the arrival of two policemen saved his life. The police dragged him to a nearby building, where the concierge gave him first aid. The next day pictures of Blum, his head heavily bandaged, appeared in newspapers around the world.

For many in the lotusland of the Riviera the burning of the books, the Italian invasion of Abyssinia, the riots in the streets of Paris might have happened in another world. Life went on as usual, with the same arrangements for lunch and dinner parties, the same organisation of guest lists and, in some cases, the same complaints.

Edith Wharton, missing intellectual discussion and who, despite the rain and wind, had a lot of visitors in early 1936, wrote to a friend on 2 April: 'The poor inner room seems emptier than ever, & if anything were ever needed to teach me to value the precious gift of the *vie intérieure*, it is the old age of some of my English great lady friends, with minds unfurnished by anything less concrete than the Grand National!'

Others, less intellectually inclined, went on exactly as they had before. Elsie Mendl continued to lease the Clos de Garoupe, the villa on Cap d'Antibes belonging to Sir Henry and Fay Norman, which she took for two months every summer; Daisy Fellowes came as usual to her villa.

'The only person I ever knew who seemed fully to understand the accumulating weight and power of fascism, the inevitability of the war and the disastrous slowness of psychological mobilisation on our side was – perhaps inevitably – Mr Winston Churchill,' noted Vincent Sheean, a fellow guest with Churchill at the Château de l'Horizon. For Churchill often stayed with Maxine, sometimes to paint, sometimes to write – his role in politics was then still minimal.

*

For everyone else on the coast, nothing was allowed to hint at a darker world beyond. The illusion of perfection must be sustained. 'I never expect to see a more wonderful sight than the Mediterranean coast from the deck of a yacht on a summer night,' wrote 'Oppy', as E. Phillips Oppenheim was always known, and he was a man who believed that the best of everything was his due.

As a writer, his financial success came from his enormous output: the wordage of the total number of novels, short stories and articles he wrote was estimated to be that of sixteen Bibles. Serialisation was another factor, as most of his novels first appeared in serial form in the US (where fees were higher than in Britain), as did his stories, and he wrote extremely fast. His writing technique was simple: after breakfast he would sit in his large armchair and say to his secretary, 'Where were we?' She would then read out the last half-dozen words from the previous day, and off he would go without faltering until about 12.15, when he went out to play nine holes of golf with Mrs Oppenheim or any available friend. After tea he would write again until about 7.00 p.m. He and his wife, who spent a month at the Hôtel de Paris in Monte Carlo every year, owned a yacht called *Echo*, its small size (and, quite often, his behaviour) earning it the nickname 'The floating double bed'.

Oppy loved going out on *Echo*, especially on summer evenings, of which he wrote: 'The throbbing of music from a dozen dance orchestras of the smaller cafés, even from the casinos themselves, seemed to fill the air with a sort of quivering background of vague yet concerted melody. Past the silent Cap there came into sight the whole semicircle of the far-spreading Nice Promenade – seven miles of lights culminating in the jetty, casino and tailing off then to the harbour itself. In the quieter waters of the Cap, fishermen with blazing torches were catching loup. Pleasure, then, seemed to exist almost as an atmosphere. One acquired the habit of effortless but joyous existence.'

With the Côte d'Azur still the favourite holiday choice of the rich, the Prince of Wales, now King Edward VIII (he had succeeded his father on 20 January 1936) had put in motion plans to rent Maxine Elliott's Château de l'Horizon, for a month of what he hoped would be a secluded and private holiday. 'Invisible eyes will keep a constant watch on the King,' said the newspapers – cars had been forbidden to stop on the road behind the villa and speedboats to approach the little harbour in front; fishermen had been warned to avoid the water nearby. Servants, gardeners, parasols and a powerful wireless receiver had been arranged.

Royalist fervour ran deeply through the English who had settled on or near the coast. 'When the King died, my parents were very upset,' said Dennis Youdale, whose father was the Thomas Cook manager in Nice. 'Mother sewed black armbands on all our coats. All my French friends at the lycée asked why and when I told them, they said, "Who cares about the King?" and mocked me unmercifully. But at home, whenever "God Save the King" was played, we all had to stand up – even if we were at table.'

By this time, all those in the King's circle knew that one of his house guests would be Mrs Ernest Simpson, and that he was in love with her although, as they always appeared in public in the company of other people, no mention of it had appeared in any British newspaper; with the security firewall planned for their coming holiday, it was likely that this state of affairs would continue.

Much of France was preoccupied with the coming elections, at the end of April and beginning of May. Although a rainy day, a record 85 per cent of voters turned up at the polls, which resulted in a victory for the Popular Front, with Léon Blum as Prime Minister. The right was horrified, seeing it as the next step to communism (deeply dreaded since the Russian Revolution), the left greeted it as the harbinger of long-overdue social change.

The election also exposed a vein of antisemitism. Never before had a Jew become Prime Minister; even in the Chambre des Députés Blum was taunted for his race. 'For the first time, this old Gallo-Roman country will be governed by a Jew,' said the right-wing deputy, Xavier Vallat. 'I dare say out loud what the country is thinking, deep inside . . . it is preferable to be led by a man whose origins belong to his soil ... than by a cunning Talmudist,' while a headline in one of the dailies read: 'France under the Jew'.

French antisemitism had deep roots. France was the first country to emancipate Jews and the first to grant political, civil, legal and social equality to them.* 'As a nation (a corporate body) Jews must be denied everything, but everything must be granted to Jews as individuals,' was the famous summing-up by the Comte de Clermont-Tonnerre during the Revolution. Thus Jews could practise Judaism as private citizens but in all other ways were expected to be completely French.

However, the nationalism of the late nineteenth century, coupled with conservative Catholicism, had combined to produce profound anti-Jewish feeling. The tendency to blame Jews, and in particular Jewish financial houses, for many of the nation's woes was emphasised, with the Jew seen as culprit, as in the Dreyfus case.† Although the way in which Jewish soldiers had fought alongside their French fellow-citizens in the First World War had mitigated this, it surged back during the Depression of the thirties, with Jews as convenient scapegoats for the country's difficulties.

In this context, Chanel's antisemitism may be seen in part as an expression of the national attitude, and perhaps also in part of a nature both complex and full of contradictions. She paid her workforce badly (as did most other couture houses) and was furious if any of them asked for a rise, yet she often performed acts of sudden, extraordinary generosity, giving away cars, clothes and cash seemingly almost on a whim. She stayed loyal to her friends but was frequently vitriolic about them behind their backs. 'She was capable of saying horrible things about them,' said the composer Georges Auric, one of Cocteau's circle, who

---

* Through a law proclaimed in September 1791, and provided that they did not found or belong to organisations that were strictly and wholly Jewish throughout.
† Alfred Dreyfus was a French-Jewish military officer, against whom were brought false allegations of passing information to the enemy. He was tried and wrongfully convicted of treason against France in 1894.

had witnessed her turning so sharply on Cocteau himself that Cocteau had cried: 'Stop it, Coco! You're going to make me cry.' Similarly, while she frequently laid the blame for any unpleasant happenings at the feet of the nation's Jews, she had plenty of Jewish friends and clients.

After the election, but before Blum could constitutionally assume office that June, workers impatient for the promises made to them by their socialist administration began to occupy factories and there was a wave of strikes – on the railways, in the steel, construction and mining industries and finally among the textile workers. Then they spread to department stores. With these last two, which touched her directly, Chanel began to take notice, but the idea that she could be affected in any other way never crossed her mind.

Then, one morning at opening time, a young woman employee turned up at Chanel's rue Cambon workrooms and put a notice on the door that said 'Occupied'. Chanel's personal bookkeeper (not an employee of the house), who could not get in, came running across to the Ritz to tell her. Chanel was outraged: *her* workplace occupied! *Her* workers striking! From her point of view, she had given a job to many women who might otherwise have had to live on piecework and therefore they should thank her rather than behave in what she saw as an ungrateful way. Furiously, she dressed with great care in a navy-blue suit with which she wore a lot of jewellery, including her superb pearls. Thus armoured, she went out to face down her workers.

She had always maintained that the wages she paid to her workforce were 'perfectly proper'; she had, in addition, sent the most delicate among them to Mimizan, where she had built workers' hostels in the grounds of the Duke of Westminster's château there (as with all her lovers, the two had remained on good terms). But it was no good. There was stalemate until it was pointed out to her that there would be no autumn collection unless she agreed to her workers' demands. Reluctantly she gave in – but she did not forget.

With more than a million workers on strike, France was grinding to a halt. The eventual settlement between employers and the confederation of the main unions included new workers' rights: wage increases, the right to collective bargaining, an inflexible forty-hour week and *les congés payés* – two weeks' paid holiday a year. These became law on 11 June; and on 31 July every factory in France closed for a fortnight.

'Thanks to you, Mr Prime Minister, workers have been able to have fun with their children on vacation. Thanks to you, Father Christmas will visit even the poorest of our comrades,' wrote the workers gratefully. In addition, one young minister persuaded France's railway bosses to give a 40 per cent travel discount to workers, who otherwise could not have afforded to take a long-distance vacation. Although hedged about with conditions, it was extremely popular. Now, holidays need not be taken at home; now, at last, there was a chance to explore their own country. No longer would the fabled Riviera be solely the province of the rich and fashionable.

But with the new labour laws output dropped, inflation and unemployment rose – and the riots continued. The outbreak of the Spanish Civil War in July, with its influx of refugees from over the border, brought the likelihood of further trouble to the south. King Edward VIII had to cancel his proposed holiday at the Château de l'Horizon on government advice, as an assassination plot was feared.

The King now decided to charter a yacht, first thinking of borrowing the Duke of Westminster's – so familiar to Chanel – but Mrs Simpson vetoed this, saying it was not comfortable enough. Instead, he was lent the yacht *Nahlin* (its generous owner charged no charter fee, only expenses). There were the usual demands by the couple: all the books were removed from the library to provide an extra bedroom; instead of literature there was now a supply of golf balls for the King to hit into the sea.

In August 1936 the *Nahlin* set off for a cruise of the eastern Mediterranean with, as well as the King and Mrs Simpson, a changing roster of passengers that included Duff and Diana Cooper, the Earl of Sefton, a friend and lord-in-waiting to the King, several members of the royal household and various old friends – but not Ernest Simpson.

With a yacht that called at port after port, there could be little question of hiding the identity of those on board, nor did they make any effort to do so. In the eyes of the foreign press, the King and Mrs Simpson were now a couple, the subject of rumour and speculation accompanied by numerous photographs of the two together. The British press, however, led by Lord Beaverbrook, still maintained a blanket silence over their relationship, although Ernest Simpson had moved out of the Simpson flat and into his club. The Simpson marriage, which had once appeared so serene and happy, now seemed in jeopardy.

Wallis and Ernest Simpson had married eight years earlier, in 1928. The following year, Wallis sailed to America to visit her sick mother; during the voyage came the Wall Street crash, and the investments of both Wallis and her mother were wiped out. Three weeks later, on 2 November, her mother died penniless, something that, on top of her impecunious early years, may have influenced Wallis's compulsive quest for all the financial assets she could lay her hands on. However, the shipping business in which Ernest was engaged weathered the Depression successfully.

Despite the idyllic summer life on the Côte, the bronzed bodies, the swimming, the tennis, the healthy local diet, the Riviera had its share of ailments – often those connected to rich living. Elsie Gladman, a young nurse who had accepted a contract to work in the Sunny Bank Hospital in Cannes, a low, white building smothered in purple bougainvillea and set in large gardens, was once sent for by Elsa Maxwell 'to come with high colonic wash-out apparatus' as her house party had been stuffing themselves to the gills with a planeload of food sent out from Fortnum & Mason – steak and kidney puddings, roast beef, Yorkshire puddings. 'I was kept busy with my apparatus for two days,' recalled Elsie. In the summer, the hospital specialised in private patients, from whom no request was too bizarre. Once Elsie had to look after a (perfectly fit) dog, for a weekend; another time she was engaged to sit up all night in the room next to that of a honeymoon couple. The bride's mother, a wealthy American, had engaged her, unbeknownst to the happy pair, to sit up in case the bride needed help . . .

Invalids (wealthy ones, of course) were sometimes sent back to England, usually by the Blue Train, which would put on a special invalid coach, with a bedroom, sitting room, toilet and one attendant. An alternative was a private ambulance.

In England, the romance between Wallis and the King deepened. Ernest, on the sidelines, had turned to an old flame – Mary Raffray, the woman who had originally introduced him to Wallis. In the spring of 1936 Wallis decided to divorce her husband; 'even the outer shell of our marriage had disintegrated,' she wrote in her autobiography. '. . . all in all, I felt it would be better for me to be free to follow my own uncertain destiny'. Her divorce case against Ernest was heard at the end of May, and a decree nisi granted.

Now that Wallis would soon be a free agent, the rumour mills went into overdrive – and on the Riviera, it was more or less the sole topic of conversation. It was unheard of for a king to marry a mistress – let alone one with two living husbands* – yet everyone who had seen Wallis and the King together had realised the extent of his infatuation. By now, as he made clear, he was determined to marry her. Behind the scenes in England there were frantic attempts both to talk the King out of marriage and – by the King – to find a way out of the impasse that would allow him to marry Wallis.

That October Wallis was installed in a house rented for her by the King in Regent's Park. Constance Coolidge (the former lover of H.G. Wells), who had met both the Simpsons through their friends and fellow Americans Herman and Katherine Rogers, heard of the purchase of the house ('Wallis says hers is on the wrong side of the street!', Constance wrote to her father) and also that the King had settled £30,000 on her.

After that, events moved fast. On 1 December the Bishop of

---

* As Head of the Church of England, the sovereign could not marry a divorcé(e).

Bradford (who had never heard of Wallis Simpson), speaking to his diocesan conference on the King's need of divine grace, said: 'We hope that he is aware of his need. Some of us wish that he gave more positive signs of his awareness.' This, taken as the first semi-official comment by a public person, opened the gates to a flood of press headlines and comment – most of it hostile to Wallis.

The idea of a morganatic marriage was mooted, only to be turned down by the Dominions and virtually everyone else. 'In every morning newspaper the King and Mrs Simpson was front-page news,' wrote Duff Cooper in his diary. 'Only the *News Chronicle* quietly supported the morganatic marriage.'

The hostility and the besiegement by the press were such that on the advice of the King's staff, Wallis fled to the Riviera on 3 December with the King's lord-in-waiting, Lord Brownlow, to stay with Herman and Katherine Rogers (she had known Katherine since their days together as young naval wives) in their Villa Lou Viei, a twelfth-century converted monastery near Cannes. She had stayed there on and off since 1929, first under the name of her first husband, Spencer, then with her new husband Ernest Simpson, then in July 1931 without him. In 1934 and 1935 she was accompanied by the Prince of Wales when she stayed with the Rogerses. Now she took refuge with these old and trusted friends after being hounded day and night by the press, who soon surrounded the villa.

Wallis and Perry Brownlow had a dreadful journey across France, trailed by reporters, surrounded when they stopped at intervals so that Wallis could ring the King. As they neared Cannes Wallis lay on the floor of the Buick, covered with a rug, while they drove through a throng of reporters, cameras flashing, outside the gates of Lou Viei to where Herman and Katherine Rogers were waiting inside. For the next few days reporters were everywhere, crawling through the grass, trying to peer through windows, tapping telephone lines, until the police cleared them away. Constance Coolidge invited Wallis to stay with her in Paris if she wanted a refuge, but on 9 December Constance received a typed letter from Lord Brownlow saying that Wallis's plans were naturally in confusion and she couldn't make any engagements.

Steadily the realisation grew that, as the idea of his marriage to Mrs Simpson would not be accepted, the King meant to abdicate. When Churchill, who had a soft spot for Chanel and often visited her when he came to Paris, brought his son Randolph to dine with her in her suite at the Ritz, his emotion over the idea of abdication got the better of him. Jean Cocteau, whom Chanel had also invited, noted that Churchill, who had loyally supported his sovereign throughout all the negotiations, got drunk and, always easily moved to tears, burst into sobs, weeping on Chanel's shoulder as he declared that a king could not abdicate. A few months later Churchill had to help the King with his abdication speech.

On 10 December Edward VIII signed the Instrument of Abdication, approved by Parliament the following day. That evening he made an emotional broadcast, saying that he could not 'discharge my duties as King as I would wish to do without the help and support of the woman I love'. In Lou Viei the Rogerses and all their servants gathered in the sitting room to listen to the radio. Wallis, lying on the sofa with her hands over her eyes to hide her tears, listened to her lover's voice. '[It] came out of the loudspeaker calmly, movingly ... After he finished, the others quietly went away and left me alone. I lay there a long time before I could control myself enough to walk through the house and go upstairs to my room.'

Such was the interest in Edward's broadcast that during it not one single telephone call was made in New York.

Others took it more frivolously. Brian Howard, aesthete, poet and quintessential Bright Young Thing, gave an abdication party in the Riviera villa he shared with his boyfriend and Klaus Mann, the son of Thomas Mann. It featured a gramophone record with Edward VIII's farewell speech, played on an improvised altar with Brian kneeling in front of it. The guests, bewildered and embarrassed, left early; the hosts and their friends stayed on, drinking more and more until they descended on their favourite backstreet Italian bistro. Here a fight broke out, with Brian snatching up a knife, the table overturned, plates of spaghetti al pomodoro flying everywhere and general mayhem until everyone rushed out into the narrow street to collapse into the Café de la Marine, fight over.

For most who heard the news – many of whom were taken completely by surprise – the main emotions were sadness and anger. The ex-King, remembered by so many as an adored Prince Charming, was regarded as having traitorously betrayed his duty; Mrs Simpson was cast as the adventuress prepared to stop at nothing in her efforts to become Queen of England.

'I hear that in Monte Carlo, all the English and French leave as soon as she walks in,' wrote Edward's aunt, Queen Maud of Norway. 'I wish something bad would befall her!' One such episode was witnessed by the English nurse Elsie Gladman, who was having tea in the London Tea Rooms, a chic establishment on the Croisette, the smart seafront road in Cannes. 'An elderly English lady was sitting there, enjoying her tea, but when Mrs Simpson walked in she immediately left everything and walked out.'

CHAPTER 6

>—◆>—O—<◆—<

1937, the Rise of Schiaparelli

For Chanel, 1937 was the year she was temporarily eclipsed by
Schiaparelli, who was now dressing many of Chanel's most faithful clients. With change in the air, Schiap was regarded as the
epitome of modernity, her designs influenced by Surrealist artists
like Man Ray, best known for his photography, and the Cubist
Marcel Duchamp. As the poet Louis MacNeice was to write:

Give me a new Muse with stockings and suspenders
And a smile like a cat
With false eyelashes and finger-nails of carmine
And dressed by Schiaparelli, with a pill-box hat.

Many of Chanel's inner circle had now become part of Schiap's
also, especially those with whom she worked, from Cocteau to
Chanel's ex-lover Dalí. Nineteen thirty-seven was the year of
Schiap's 'Lobster Dress', made of white organza with scarlet
sash and Dalí-designed lobster, made famous when Mrs Simpson modelled it in American *Vogue* (it was rumoured that Dalí
wanted to put real mayonnaise on the lobster but that Schiap
objected).

Schiap's clothes were brilliantly colourful, giving a slight sense
of *déja vu* to Chanel's monochrome palette – although she included a gold lamé evening dress in her autumn/winter collection.
Schiap 'glorified the hard elegance of the ugly woman', wrote
Bettina Ballard, American *Vogue*'s Paris correspondent. Like

Chanel, she had a genius for publicity. Although in public both damned each other with faint praise, in private Chanel referred to Schiaparelli as 'that Italian artist who makes clothes'.

Chanel herself created the costumes for three stage plays by her friend Cocteau (whom she was still supporting at the Hôtel Castille in Paris's rue Cambon, conveniently near her own headquarters, as well as paying for his detoxification cures) and made the wardrobe for Jean Renoir's film *La Marseillaise* (1938). And during long months at La Pausa that summer, she also found time for a brief affair with a rich American, Harrison Williams, ten years older than herself and a self-made man who began life as a streetcar conductor. His socialite wife, a friend of Wallis Simpson, spent most of the year in Palm Beach. He asked Chanel to run away with him but she refused, although, as she said to a confidant many years later: 'He had a yacht and isn't that the best way to start an *amour*?'

After his abdication, Edward was granted the title HRH the Duke of Windsor by his brother, the new king, George VI (on the Riviera, many of the resident English flocked to the English Church in Nice to hear his coronation relayed over the wireless from Westminster Abbey). As for Wallis, it was decreed that when she and the Duke were married she would be styled 'Her Grace' (the form used by non-royal duchesses) rather than HRH. It was an omission that would rankle with the Duke all his life.

Wallis had now moved from Cannes to the Château de Candé in the Loire Valley, owned by Herman Rogers's friend the American multi-millionaire Charles Bedaux, who generously loaned it to her. Here the Duke and Wallis planned to hold their wedding for, fond as Wallis was of the Rogerses, neither their house nor their cook were up to her exacting standards. Also, as the château was surrounded by Bedaux's land, it was easier to keep the press at bay and would offer much more privacy.

Wallis was nothing if not rigorously exigent in her demands, a trait that would become more apparent as the years passed. As it was, from February 1937 onwards, Herman Rogers had been writing constantly to the Bedaux butler on behalf of Wallis and her requirements for the wedding. She wanted an 'important' chef, she wanted two nightwatchmen, she wanted accommodation for a man from the Sûreté and another from Scotland Yard, she wanted rooms for her maid, chauffeur and Mrs Rogers's maid, she wanted a safe for her jewellery and arrangements for her trunkloads of luggage. And she wanted a huge number of extra servants: a pastry-cook, a sous-chef, a scullery boy, a second butler and footman, four maids, two charwomen, five laundrywomen, more gardeners, a telephonist and a number of golf-course workers – all this despite the Bedaux' own considerable staff of twenty-four indoor servants plus grooms, gardeners, gamekeepers and laundry staff. It was fortunate that Bedaux was extremely rich, since all these expenses, up to and including endless telephone calls and postage for the hundreds of letters the couple sent out, would, it was taken for granted by both the Duke and Wallis, be defrayed by Bedaux.

On 3 May Wallis's decree nisi arrived at Cannes, and at once the Duke flew to join her. A month later, on 3 June, Wallis entered the pale green Château de Candé music room with its makeshift altar to the march from Handel's *Judas Maccabeus* wearing a dress of soft blue crêpe with a tight, buttoned bodice, a halo-shaped hat and shoes and gloves all of the same colour, with one of the Duke's gifts, a huge diamond-and-sapphire brooch, pinned to her bodice. The honeymoon was spent in Austria.

To her cousin the twice-divorced Duchess wrote: 'Here I am at last with my king sitting on a mountain in Austria – where it is really lovely and peaceful – we hope here to gather strength for future battles.' They did, however, spend their first married Christmas at the Villa Lou Viei, loaned to them while the Rogerses were in New York.

Writers and artists were coming to and going from the Riviera. James Thurber* and his wife rented the Villa Tamisier on the Cap d'Antibes, a return to the Riviera for Thurber, who had been based in Nice in 1926 in the French bureau of the *Chicago*

---

* Author of *The Secret Life of Walter Mitty* (1939).

Tribune. Much of his work then had consisted of calling in at the big hotels and getting a list of the guests staying there, which he would successfully do; if the list was not long enough, he would invent the rest. Young and poor, when the Depression began to bite he borrowed enough money to redeem his return ticket, which he had pawned, and returned home. By 1937, as one of America's most popular humourists and cartoonists, he was rich and famous and on the permanent staff of the *New Yorker* magazine. 'Nobody could do justice to this blue, purple, warm, snowy mixture of sea, mountains and valleys,' he wrote on his return.

That year Brecht visited, playing his guitar and singing to the German writers gathered there, and Aldous Huxley left, drawn by offers of well-paid work from Hollywood and the lure of the Californian climate. And in August Edith Wharton died, at the age of seventy-five.

For Chanel, 1937 was one of the few years during which she did not have an accredited lover by her side. But her ability to stay on friendly terms with those with whom she had had an affair stood her in good stead: the Grand Duke Dmitri, for example, was someone she could always call on as an escort.

There were the usual house parties at La Pausa – where Chanel, now fifty-four, was as active as ever, climbing the old olive trees clad in a pair of grey flannel slacks. Among the circle around her were old friends such as Bébé Bérard and Jean Cocteau, who remained fascinated by her. 'Her spectacular liaisons, her rages, her nastiness, her fabulous jewels, her creations, her whims, her excesses, her kindness as well as her humour and generosity, all these were part of her unique, endearing, attractive, excessive, and very human personality,' said Cocteau, adding: 'She looks at you tenderly, then nods her head and you're condemned to death.'

That summer, the seclusion of La Pausa was more welcome than ever. The Riviera was changing: this year, the full effect of the *congés payés* could be seen, with almost a quarter of a million workers arriving to crowd the beaches. 'Thanks to *congés payés*,' wrote one journalist, 'the French worker has had a chance to know this paradise long perceived as inaccessible to the common people, the Côte d'Azur.' The special trains on which they came were known as Red Trains – the people's answer to the Blue Train. Some stayed in pensions, others brought their own shelter. 'This morning, coming back with Maurice from a swim in the gulf, we saw thousands of camping tents,' noted Colette's diary for 10 August. 'Laundry everywhere . . .'

Not everyone welcomed them; some shopkeepers, feeling that they lowered the tone, put up signs reading 'Interdit aux congés payés.' Even children noticed them: eleven-year-old Dennis Youdale realised that there were more people, less chic and affluent-looking than the usual *flâneurs* in front of the big hotels like the Negresco and the Westminster on the Croisette. That year, a section of Nice's pebbly beach was monopolised by a crowd of huge German women. 'What fascinated me as a small boy', said Dennis, 'was that these enormous women were all wearing pink corsets instead of ordinary swimsuits.' But after the invasion was over – and for most of the workers it lasted a mere fortnight – life returned to what the Riviera habitués considered normal: that is, luxurious indolence spiced with gambling and parties.

Among the summer visitors was one more typical of the dwellers on the Riviera – a writer with a tangled love life. In July 1937 Vladimir Nabokov, prolific author and later famous for his novel *Lolita* (1955), arrived in Cannes with his wife Vera and son. They had previously lived in Berlin, but as Vera was Jewish had decided to leave to escape persecution, Vera first remaining in Berlin while Nabokov went to Paris to see publishers before meeting in Cannes. While in Paris Nabokov, whose sexual charisma was legendary – he had given Vera a list of thirty of his conquests before they married – began a passionate affair with a pretty, lively Russian blonde, Irina Guadagnini. So serious did the relationship become that Nabokov was contemplating leaving Vera for Irina.

Once in Cannes, the Nabokovs settled in a two-room apartment. Here Nabokov wrote from 7.00 to 10 a.m., then spent two hours on the beach until the noonday cannon. After lunch he began writing again at 3.30, working often until late at night and maintaining a correspondence with Irina.

Nabokov, who loved Vera deeply (their marriage was to last over fifty years), was also very dependent on her: Vera not only typed his manuscripts but acted as his agent, driver, mouthpiece, money manager and bodyguard (she carried a gun in her handbag). Eventually, he confessed the affair with Irina to Vera, who demanded he put an end to it. Realising that there was no other option, and with great reluctance, Nabokov wrote to Irina to tell her that their affair was over. 'She is convincing herself and me that . . . you are a hallucination,' wrote Nabokov gloomily.

Irina was not prepared to give up the man she loved without a struggle. Her reaction was to get on a train and come to Cannes to try and persuade her lover to come away with her. She arrived in early September, walked to the street where the Nabokovs' apartment was, gazed up at the balcony and saw three swimsuits, a man's, a woman's and a child's, hung out to dry on the balcony rail. While she was looking, she saw a woman's hand withdraw the man's and the child's. As Nabokov brought his son Dmitri down to the beach she rushed up to him, to be told she could not stay because of his wife. Irina could not bear to leave; instead, she sat forlornly on the shingle some distance from Nabokov and the child. A little while later, Vera joined her husband and son, then the family all went home for lunch, leaving Irina, alone and ignored, on the beach. It was a sad, brutal and effective ending; Irina and Nabokov never met again.

One who managed to keep both wife and mistress was David Lloyd George, the British elder statesman and former Prime Minister (known to the House of Commons variously as the Welsh Wizard and the Goat for his skill in oratory and penchant for extramarital relationships).

The seventy-four-year-old Lloyd George, an Antibes regular, arrived there in December 1937 with his mistress Frances Stevenson, despatching her home to spend Christmas with their daughter Jennifer before his wife Margaret and son came out to join him for a family Christmas. His habits were simple: he would walk every morning through the grounds of the Hôtel du Cap to Eden Roc, in a cloak instead of an overcoat, his white hair streaming in the breeze. By half past nine at night he would be in bed, where he read a Wild West story for twenty minutes, then slept until six in the morning. Although world politics were dark, his spirits were high.

'It is no use my telling you how I have missed you & still do so,' he wrote to Frances on 22 December. 'You know that well . . . I hated – and resented – more than ever the necessity for your departure . . .' However, he had already started making plans for Frances's return, writing the following day, again from the Hôtel du Cap: 'One word before I leave for Cap d'Ail. Latest news. G [his son Gwilyam] leaves Janry 2nd and Maggie [his wife] arrives January 10th . . . that leaves 8 days for you if you think it worth-while – I certainly do.'

What he did not mention in that letter was that when Margaret arrived Winston and Clementine Churchill were to give a Golden Wedding lunch for the Lloyd Georges, L.G. himself sliding effortlessly into the role of devoted husband and paterfamilias. Churchill and Lloyd George were old friends and had often spent holidays together in Morocco or the South of France. At that lunch, in January 1938, Churchill made a speech saying that Lloyd George would figure prominently in the history of the world, and Lloyd George replied gracefully that there was no one with whom he would rather have celebrated this occasion than Winston and Clemmie.

To some, it seemed as if the Riviera they knew had changed out of all recognition. By 1938 even Colette had had enough. 'The little house was so accessible, so undefended that Colette would find the journalist, the beggar, the autograph hunter in the garden, in the house or joining her on the beach,' said Maurice Goudeket.

None of this deterred the Windsors, drawn back as if by a magnet to the Riviera – the scene of their courting, a place where deference was assured, where the ex-King, unwelcome in his own country, could be certain of being the most important guest at dinner or poolside. That spring they took a ten-year lease of the

Chateau de la Croë, a three-storey building with white walls and green shutters, hidden behind high walls and set in twelve acres of garden and woodland, at the end of a cul-de-sac, reached by a narrow winding road that led up from the port, with only three other villas nearby, one empty, so that privacy was assured. It was built round a huge central hall, off which led large rooms with tall, mirrored doors that were always open; entering the house, one could see straight through to the woodland at the back.

Wallis, with the aid of her friend Elsie Mendl, set about decorating it in the near-regal style the Windsors felt suitable for their position, with the Buckingham Palace colours of white, red and gold everywhere. The dining chairs were of red leather with black and gold backs, the red and white library was dominated by a huge portrait of Queen Mary and its bookshelves filled with the Duke's presentation volumes, trophies and awards. At the top of the leather-framed family photographs was the Duke's crest, in the hall hung his red and gold Garter banner from St George's Chapel, Windsor. Wallis's bedroom had tables and chests decorated with *trompe-l'oeil* images symbolising her past; one was a pack of cards with the king of hearts falling down.

Glass, china, furniture and linen had been sent from Frogmore (where the contents of the Duke's English houses, York House and Fort Belvedere, had been stored when he abdicated). Gold figured strongly: the Duchess's bath was a gold-plated swan, in the first-floor saloon and dining room gold and white cornices decorated the ceilings and surrounded the mirrors that were everywhere – the Duchess loved looking at herself.

Nothing that might make life luxurious was neglected: a hairdresser came daily, a manicurist twice a week, there was a timetable of the day's activities and a strong insistence on royal protocol. Guests were expected to bow or curtsey to both Windsors on first seeing them in the morning, the Duke's secretary had to stand while she took dictation and Wallis herself always referred to her husband as 'the Dook'.

The Windsor monogram, WE above a ducal coronet, featured on everything from writing paper and bed linen to the silver buttons on the menservants' grey alpaca livery and the lifebuoys hanging by the pool. Above the red and white tent that served as a changing room flew the Prince of Wales's standard.

New buildings were sprouting up, not the grand villas of the early part of the century but more modest dwellings that crowded the coastline, so that houses of distinction became rarer.

One that remained suffered, according to its designer, a fatal blemish in 1938. This was the amazing house known not by a name but by a number – E.1027. It was entirely the work of the designer Eileen Gray, aged sixty at that time. She was a well-born Irishwoman known for her elegant and original furniture designs, who lived mainly in Paris. In the early twenties the bisexual Eileen had met a good-looking young Romanian-born architect called Jean Badovici, fifteen years younger than her. They became lovers and it was through him that she gradually turned towards architecture rather than the modernist furniture design for which she eventually became known.

Badovici wanted Eileen to build him a 'little refuge' in the South of France. The infatuated Eileen agreed at once, and early in 1925 they drove down to look for a plot. Eileen explored the coastline and one day she went to Roquebrune. Here, she spotted a rocky patch of land thirty metres above the sea. It was completely inaccessible and not overlooked from anywhere. That was it: 'I knew I was going to build and I was going to build here.'

She found a little flat in Roquebrune and for the next three years worked on the project, refreshing herself only with a daily swim in the wonderful clear water beneath the site. As there was no road, all the material had to be brought up by wheelbarrow. She worked long and hard, pouring all her ideas about living into the house. She believed that a dwelling should be 'a living organism' serving 'the atmosphere required by inner life'. An innovator to her core, she declared that 'the poverty of modern architecture stems from the atrophy of sensuality'.

It was a small house, consisting basically of a large living room extended to a terrace and two small bedrooms, and, though the single-handed work of an untrained person, it was to become a classic of modern architecture. E.1027 was also a work of love; even its name was code for the entwinement of her life with that of Badovici. E. of course stood for Eileen, the J of Jean was the tenth letter of the alphabet, 2 stood for B and 7 for the G of Gray. The two lived there for a while until, in 1932, Eileen designed another house for herself while Badovici kept E.1027 as a holiday home.

Through his editorship of *Architecture Vivante*, to which many of the best-known contemporary names contributed, Badovici had met the great Corbusier, pioneer of the Modernist movement. They had become close friends, seeing each other frequently, going to restaurants together – both loved good food – joking and generally having a good time. And through her lover Eileen too had met Le Corbusier, although, much as she admired him, she rejected his doctrine that a house was 'a machine to live in', believing instead that 'it is the shell of man, his extension, his release, his spiritual emanation . . . human in the most profound sense'.

Although Eileen's love affair with Badovici came to an end around 1932, their friendship did not. Eileen was thrilled when, after she had moved out and Le Corbusier stayed there for a couple of days with Badovici, he wrote to her praising E.1027 in glowing terms: 'I am so happy to tell you how much these few days spent in your house have made me appreciate the rare spirit which dictates all the organisation inside and outside. A rare spirit which has given the modern furniture and installations such a dignified, charming and witty shape.' Praise from the great Corbusier was praise indeed.

By 1935 Le Corbusier had become fascinated with wall paintings, and began to ask various friends if he could paint murals in their houses. Naturally, Badovici was one of those he asked. With Badovici's encouragement, he began to decorate the walls of E.1027. Eileen was appalled and angry. With justification, she regarded E.1027 as her creation, expressing her ideas: she had designed everything, down to the last lamp fitting. To her these frescoes, huge, lurid and frequently sexual in content – she herself was prim and decorous rather than bohemian – were vandalism. There were eight in all, so it must have seemed as if they were everywhere. And when, despite her outrage, Badovici sent a letter to Le Corbusier saying, 'Your frescoes [are] more luminous and beautiful than ever,' it must have seemed the final desecration. She might have been even more outraged if she had known that Le Corbusier had painted them all in the nude.

For other dwellers on the Riviera there were more serious concerns. The first ripples of anti-Jewish persecution had spread from Germany after the Anschluss (in March 1938), when Hitler marched into Vienna and annexed Austria, using as pretext a forged telegram supposedly from the Austrian Chancellor asking for German troops to help to quell unrest. There was already considerable support for union between the two countries, and when German troops entered Austria they were greeted with cheers.

In Vienna the campaign against the Jews began immediately. They were driven through the streets, their homes and shops were plundered. Jewish men and women were made to wash away pro-independence slogans painted on the streets of Vienna ahead of the failed 13 March plebiscite. Jewish actresses were forced to clean the toilets of the SA (the Brownshirts).* The process of Aryanisation began, and within months Jews were driven out of public life.

In Sanary this meant that the German-Jewish writers could no longer rely on royalties or even on finding a publisher. Survival was now harder, with only the best-known and internationally acclaimed such as Thomas Mann and Lion Feuchtwanger secure of a market.

Having money cut both ways in Sanary, as it made the local people suspicious that such affluence came from being a spy. 'They thought many of our friends were Nazi spies,' said Feuchtwanger, who, although well off, was not suspected: everyone knew he had a worldwide following and had been deprived of

---

* Sturmabteilung, a violent Nazi paramilitary organisation.

his German citizenship because of his anti-Nazi views. His wife Marta, a former tennis champion, was equally popular: she was kind, hospitable and paid bills promptly. There was, however, a real spy in Sanary, recalled Feuchtwanger, adding that his name was von Dincklage but everyone called him 'Spatz' (German for 'sparrow'). 'He was an attaché at the German Embassy and he constantly came to Sanary where he was a kind of tennis coach,' wrote Feuchtwanger. 'He wanted Marta to be his partner.'

Later, a Frenchman whom Marta met took her aside and told her that he, the Frenchman, was a counter-spy and that Spatz – who was very popular with the girls – was a Nazi spy. 'We don't want to denounce or expel him,' said this man, 'because we know who he is.' And if Spatz went, the man added, they might get someone they did not know and could not therefore monitor.

What they perhaps did not know about Spatz was that he sent weekly reports to Berlin, which wanted an eye kept on the Jewish exiles in Sanary, influential because of their international prestige. For the sake of his own safety, von Dincklage now took the final step of divorcing his half-Jewish wife Catsy – most of whose fortune he had already spent.

The effect of Nazi Germany's actions on one young American visitor to the coast was profound. Murray Burnett and his wife, visiting her Jewish family in Antwerp, to which they had moved after escaping from Vienna, had gone to Vienna to retrieve as many of the family's valuables as possible – after the Anschluss, Jews lucky enough to leave were prevented from taking any assets with them. To Burnett, Vienna, with its screaming anti-Jewish slogans and tragic stories, brought home the horror of the Nazi regime. After successfully smuggling out as much as they could ('When we got on the train I had diamond rings on every finger and my wife was wearing a fur coat in August,' he recalled), they went for a holiday to the Riviera.

One night the couple visited a smoky nightclub on the out-skirts of Nice, on the road to Monte Carlo, where a black pianist from Chicago, known as Rick, played jazz. The clientele was a mixture of refugees, visitors and military officials (from Germany as well as France), spies, counter-spies and local people. Burnett was instantly struck by the idea that such a club, with its seething political and cultural undercurrents and seedy late-night glamour, would make a wonderful setting for a play. At home, still furious at what he had seen in Vienna, he wrote it, saying to his writing partner Joan Alison: 'No one can remain neutral, God damn it, Joan.' Later the play, *Everybody Comes to Rick's*, was sold to Warner Brothers for $20,000 and became the iconic film *Casablanca* (1942).*

That summer another writer with German connections, the Hungarian-British Arthur Koestler, who had joined the German Communist Party in 1931,† came to Sanary for the summer. The previous year he had been in loyalist Spain as a war correspondent for the *News Chronicle* but was in Malaga when it fell and was captured by Franco's forces. For four terrifying months, until June 1937, he was imprisoned in Seville under sentence of death. Eventually he was exchanged for the wife of one of Franco's ace fighter pilots.

In Sanary, Koestler and Feuchtwanger argued, discussed and tried to thrash out what the intellectuals could do to stem Hitler's onward march. That August, as they and the other German writers met in their favourite cafés and launched short-lived periodicals warning of the Nazi menace or wrote articles or pamphlets, Germany called up half a million troops for large-scale manoeuvres. Koestler, as active as any of the others, and perhaps inspired by the literary atmosphere of that little fishing port which had seen the genesis of several masterpieces, had also begun another novel, the one that would make him world-famous: *Darkness at Noon* (1940).

While the inhabitants of Sanary thought and discussed little else other than the menace of Nazi Germany, which daily cast a longer shadow, the smart set on the Riviera behaved as if the life of privilege, glamour and untrammelled hedonism would go

---

* Quoted from *We'll Always Have Casablanca* by Noah Isenberg (2017).
† Communists were loathed equally by the Nazis and by Franco. Koestler resigned from the Party in late 1938.

on for ever. One of its most ardent disciples was Daisy Fellowes, a woman as demanding and selfish as only the very rich can be, waspish, witty and centre-stage to the point of outrageousness. 'The very picture of fashionable depravity', was how Lady Diana Cooper (whose husband Duff was her lover for seventeen years) described her.

Daisy, or Marguerite Séverine Philippine, to give her her full name, was the daughter of the Duc Decazes* and Isabelle Singer, the sewing-machine heiress, from whom she inherited her immense wealth. By her first husband, Prince Jean de Broglie, Daisy had had three daughters, of whom she once said in her characteristically caustic way: 'The eldest is like my first husband only a great deal more masculine, the second is like me without guts, and the third was the result of a horrible man called Lischmann.' It was only in 1919, during her second marriage, to the banker Reginald Fellowes, a cousin of Winston Churchill, that she became a social icon and fashion leader, a role she played to the hilt – she had been one of the first women to have her nose remodelled, to a classical straightness.

At her villa, Les Zoraïdes, there were leopard-printed carpets and clusters of mirrored glitter-balls filling the stairwell. It was for Daisy that Schiaparelli created the colour shocking pink, Daisy who wore the eye-catching Shoe Hat, created the previous year by Dalí, with the nonchalance of complete self-confidence. If one of the hundred-odd guests she would ask to her thirty-room villa at Antibes appeared in a dress at all similar to hers, she would go up and change at once: one night she appeared in five different outfits.

That August of 1938 Daisy set off on the *Sister Anne*, the larger of her two yachts, for a month's cruise in the Aegean. One of her guests was the young David Herbert, whose father, Lord Pembroke, was one of the many men with whom she had had a fling. Also on board were her daughter Rosamund, two of Daisy's friends and Cecil Beaton, in temporary exile from New York after being sacked by American *Vogue* 'for gravely insulting

* Jean-Élie-Octave-Louis-Sévère-Amanien Decazes de Glücksburg.

the Jewish race on a page-border sketch' – he had put minute but legible antisemitic phrases at the side of an illustration of New York society.

It was not an entirely happy voyage. Soon after the start, the sea became so choppy that all the portholes had to be shut and several of the sailors became seasick; as the yacht rolled, the party felt too ill to keep up their usual standards of grooming. The men remained unshaven, the women left their hair uncoiffed and pulled on their clothes without much thought. Then the steering wire broke – fortunately when they were at anchor, or they would have been rudderless in mid-sea – and took all one hot afternoon to mend, with six splicings. It also meant that the panels in Daisy's cabin had to be removed, which in turn meant dismantling the cabin. This went down badly, to say the least, with Daisy, who predictably took it out on her guests.

'Daisy didn't seem in the best of humours,' remarked Cecil Beaton, adding, 'I believe the game of Monopoly wasn't very enjoyable this morning.' David Herbert, who was winning by achieving a property coup, was rebuked by Daisy with the words, 'That's not a very gentlemanly thing to do,' to which he snapped back: 'All's fair in love and war.' By now Herbert had begun to find his hostess extraordinarily difficult. Captive on the boat, he was a victim of her petulance and whims. 'Whenever we wanted to stop and bathe or go into a little bay, there was always some reason why we couldn't do so. Equally, if there was some island we particularly wanted to visit, we were not allowed to.' By the time they reached Athens, Herbert and Beaton had had enough and, concocting excuses, left.

Chanel spent the summer at La Pausa as usual. She was seen with her former lover, the handsome Grand Duke Dmitri Pavlovich,* attending the ballet in Monte Carlo wearing a white trouser suit with short jacket and heavy jewellery – at fifty-five, her waist was as trim as ever – but this was a deceptively urbane vignette.

---

* Soon after this the tuberculosis from which Dmitri Pavlovich had been suffering meant that he went to Switzerland, to seek a cure in a sanatorium there. He died in the spring of 1942.

At La Pausa the emotional temperature was considerably higher. Staying with her there were some of her friends, including her then lover, Dalí, and his elegant but unpleasant Russian wife Gala (the influential art critic John Richardson called her 'one of the nastiest wives a major modern artist ever saddled himself with'). Chanel, to whom Gala was a loyal client but for whom personal hygiene was a fetish, commented: 'Since she ate sardines, and stuck them in her hair, she stank.'

Though Dalí's life was ruled by the strong-minded Gala, ten years his senior, he was quickly captivated by Chanel. 'Dear beautiful Chanel,' he wrote in one of the many notes he sent her. 'I give you my love and I love you, Your Salvador.' His devotion must have been some recompense for the fact that he was working closely with her rival Schiaparelli, who was now on intimate terms with Cocteau, Bérard and others of the circle of which she herself was so notable a part.

At the same time, the triangular Sert saga was drawing to a close. That summer Roussy and Sert had cruised the Mediterranean in the Venetian fishing boat that Sert had transformed into a black-painted yacht with red and gold sails, named the *Saint Alexis* after Roussy's dead brother. In spite of her constant fever, Roussy would swim for hours. Worried by her ravaged appearance, friends persuaded her to see a lung specialist in Switzerland, where it was discovered that she had advanced tuberculosis.

Misia had been spending most of her time with Chanel at La Pausa, though making constant, unsuccessful attempts to form a triumvirate with her former husband and Roussy. For Misia, not being at the centre of things, not being the one that everyone wanted to see, to be close to, was an experience she found difficult. Her dependence on morphine, hitherto fairly mild, increased, as did her longing to be the focus of the two people she so loved. The trouble was, they did not want her as much as she wanted them. Yet there were contradictory signals. When Roussy returned to Paris, she refused to have a nurse, but often, late at night, she would telephone Misia and ask her to come to her. While Sert slept, Misia would sit beside her, telling her stories and putting out the cigarettes that fell from her fingers – Roussy was a chain-smoker – if she slipped into a doze. For Misia, this must have been some kind of validation that she was needed, at least by one of her two objects of devotion.

By now Roussy too had become a morphine addict and looked terrible, thin and permanently feverish and coughing. Sert, a selfish man who tended to ignore illness, took no notice of his wife's frail and emaciated appearance. It was Chanel, ever practical and who could not bear to watch the young woman's disintegration, who took matters into her own hands: on the pretext of needing a companion while she visited her own doctor in Switzerland, she persuaded Roussy to accompany her. Sert was furious; in the train, Roussy showed Chanel the bruises he had given her in his anger at seeing her go.

Dalí, missing Chanel badly and knowing how wretched Roussy's illness made her, wrote constantly from La Pausa ('terribly anxious about this nightmare you are living through'). One letter to his 'Dear beautiful little bird' told her hopefully that Gala had left. 'While you were here you have truly enchanted La Pausa. One gets used to not seeing this little image . . . one thing is certain is that our meeting is becoming very "good" and very important . . . I give you all my love. Your Salvador.'

But Chanel stayed with Roussy whom, once in Switzerland, she had persuaded to enter a clinic. Roussy was now so completely in the grip of her addiction that she could only survive for brief periods without a fix. Chanel, who must have realised that the poor girl, now mere skin and bones, was dying and that there was nothing to be done, smuggled her in a good supply, concealed in marzipan sweets.

Misia, who followed later, was not allowed to see her. 'Nor did I ever know whose orders prevented me from visiting her,' she wrote later. 'Twice I went back, always in vain. I was told that the smallest emotional upset could be fatal to her.' Misia suspected it was not the doctors, but Chanel, who prevented her. This was quite likely, as Chanel was well aware that Misia's emotional climate was one of turbulence rather than serenity.

Roussy died in December 1938. For Misia, Roussy's death was a body blow. Although Roussy had taken her husband from her, and although Roussy had refused to see her during normal daytime hours, Misia had still loved this waif-like yet determined girl. She had, she believed, 'given' Roussy to her husband, sacrificing her own happiness to that of Sert and the girl she regarded rather in the light of a daughter; now this sacrifice had turned to ashes. She was sixty-six and alone. Although she gradually took over the role of hostess for Sert, they led separate lives and occupied separate apartments.

That September of 1938 war looked all but inevitable. As a friend of the MP Victor Cazalet wrote to him from London at the end of the month: 'The depression was so terrible one could scarcely rise above it. We prayed and worked constantly . . . everywhere people standing dead still scanning the newspapers, sandbags, ARP trenches, the Green Line buses swung with stretchers evacuating the hospitals . . . silent, gloomy groups of men and women, blue lines on the pavement leading to shelters . . .'

In a last desperate attempt to stave it off, the British Prime Minister, Neville Chamberlain, flew to Munich for a meeting that culminated in an agreement signed by Germany, France, Great Britain and Italy that allowed for Nazi Germany's annexation of parts of Czechoslovakia along the country's borders that were mainly inhabited by German speakers, for which a new territorial designation, Sudetenland, was coined. For Czechoslovakia (which was not invited to the conference) it was a disaster, as most of the country's defences, banks and heavy industry were there. The agreement was signed in the early hours of 30 September 1938 (but dated 29 September) and presented as a triumph although, in fact, it had simply met all of Hitler's demands.

In England, Duff Cooper resigned as First Lord of the Admiralty in protest and Churchill, in Parliament, told Chamberlain that he had been given a choice between war and dishonour. 'You chose dishonour,' he thundered, 'but you will have war!'

On the Riviera, the British who lived there noticed a less tolerant attitude, sometimes amounting to hostility. No one wanted war – but was France to be pushed into war by the English or rather, as many of the French viewed it, the City of London and its Jews, and the Germans?

A mere six weeks later Hitler showed his contempt for world opinion in the most widely reported outrage yet. During 9 November until the following day, throughout Nazi Germany, SA paramilitary forces, aided by German civilians, carried out relentless violence against Jewish people and Jewish properties. Hospitals and schools were ransacked, buildings demolished with sledgehammers, while the police and other authorities stood by. Hundreds of Jews were murdered, Jewish-owned stores, buildings and synagogues were vandalised.

Kristallnacht, as it was called because of the shards of broken glass from the smashed windows of Jewish properties that littered the streets, sent shock waves around the world. 'No foreign propagandist bent upon blackening Germany before the world could outdo the tale of burnings and beatings, of blackguardly assaults on defenceless and innocent people, which disgraced that country yesterday,' said *The Times*. Thousands of Jewish men were imprisoned in concentration camps; Jewish children, already barred from museums, public playgrounds and swimming pools, were now expelled from the state schools. Most families tried to flee; some, in despair, committed suicide.

CHAPTER 7

>⬦–◇–⬦<

The Shadow of War

While Dalí was staying with Chanel at La Pausa, he had met Leonid Massine's ballet company. After originally working for Diaghilev as a dancer and choreographer, Massine had finally formed his own company, the Ballet Russe de Monte Carlo, which had just made its debut. Now he asked Dalí to design a ballet for him – and Dali asked Chanel to make the costumes, on which she worked during the spring of 1939. It was to be called *Bacchanale*,* and set to music from Wagner's *Tannhäuser*.

It was a considerable challenge. The storyline traced the mounting delirium of King Ludwig II and was Dalí's attempt at a psychoanalytical ballet. Audiences were confronted by an assortment of bizarre images including dancing umbrellas, a corps de ballet on crutches, dancers with giant fish heads, and Lola Montez in harem pants and a hoop skirt trimmed with false teeth. Dali's set was dominated by an enormous swan, with a large hole in its breast through which the dancers made their entrances. At the same time, Chanel was also working towards her spring collection.

For those on the Riviera, the winter of 1938/9 passed as usual. In the luxurious Château de l'Horizon, Churchill was working on the proofs of his book in bed every morning, and playing mah-jong all afternoon with Maxine – the light was too poor

---

* It received its world premiere at New York's Metropolitan Opera House on 9 November 1939, where it created a sensation.

to paint, and anyway it was dark by 6.00 p.m. One evening the Windsors, now ensconced at the Château de la Croë, were invited to dinner. The great question, already settled at the Villa Mauresque but still in abeyance at the Château de l'Horizon, was how to address the Duchess.

It was discussed at lunch beforehand as everyone knew that the Palace had refused her the title HRH; equally, everyone knew that the Duke was notoriously touchy on the subject and was determined to exact respect for his wife. They agreed that since it was a private dinner party the Duchess should get her HRH and curtsey on greeting.

'From the beginning the Duke of Windsor dominated the conversation,' said Vincent Sheean, also staying at the Château de l'Horizon, describing the Duchess as 'so slim, so elegant, so suggestive of innumerable fashionable shops, dressmakers, manicurists and hairdressers'. Churchill wrote from the château on 18 January 1939 to Clemmie: 'The Windsors dine here, and we dine back with them. They have a lovely place next door to La D[ragonnière]. Everything[extremely] well done and dignified. Red liveries, and the little man himself dressed up to the nines in the Balmoral tartan with dagger and jabot etc. When you think that you could hardly get him to put on a short coat* and black tie, one sees the change in the point of view. I am to dine with him tomorrow night with only Rothermere. No doubt to talk over his plans for coming home. They do not want him to come, but they have no power to stop him.'

The Spanish Civil War was drawing to a close. On the night Tarragona fell, the Elliott party dined with the Windsors and most of the notables from along that star-studded coast. Less than a fortnight later, with the capture of Barcelona by Franco's forces, it was all but over (although hostilities did not officially end until 1 April). When the French frontier roads were finally opened, about 300,000 Spaniards, soldiers, civilians, women and children, all hungry, exhausted and in a panic, swept down on

---

* An old-fashioned expression for a dinner jacket (as opposed to the much longer tailcoat).

the 200,000 French inhabitants of the Pyrénées-Orientales. They were followed in February by the fleeing Republican government.

The soldiers among them were quickly incarcerated, most in two large concentration camps, behind barbed wire, others in smaller ones. 'Although the mimosa was blooming, the air was cold and most draped themselves in their army blanket, the only thing they had brought with them,' wrote Janet Flanner, columnist for the *New Yorker*, on 1 March. 'They ate what they could, sometimes butchering the cows and horses they had brought with them. The French government gave two pounds of bread every day, to be shared between twenty-five men.' In the valleys, they often uprooted vineyards, burning the stocks for warmth on the cold nights.

Yet although the country near the frontier was littered with the detritus of the refugees' escape – abandoned cars, battered trucks, broken bicycles and, much more distressing, thousands of horses and mules left to forage where they could in the inhospitable countryside – the Riviera itself was barely conscious of this wretched influx of humanity. That February Cannes held its annual Fête du Mimosa and Nice its Bataille de Fleurs, and the spring couture collections were shown as usual.

For these, Chanel stepped out of her usual idiom of clean, uncluttered lines in a palette based on black, white, beige and navy-blue, perhaps in answer to the more *voyant* clothes of Schiaparelli. In the spring of 1939 she produced a range of 'Gypsy' dresses, some with lace ruffles on the bodice and as flounces on skirts, others with full, crinoline-style overskirts or broderie-anglaise petticoats and 'the divine brocades, the little boleros, the roses in the hair', as recorded by Diana Vreeland for *Harper's Bazaar*. Or, as *Vogue* put it: 'the provoking gypsy modesty of Chanel's bodice-and-skirt dresses'. On them, here and there, were the colours of the French national flag, *le tricolore* – red, white and blue.

In March Hitler marched into Czechoslovakia, and a few weeks later Mussolini annexed Albania. Lloyd George and his mistress Frances Stevenson were in Antibes, where they heard the news of Hitler's entry into Prague on 15 March. But for anyone living on the Riviera in 1939, with those blue skies, warm seas, pine-scented woods and markets full of fruit, vegetables and fresh fish, the idea of war must have seemed unreal.

Not to Colette, who had begun to think of selling La Treille Muscate (it was bought later that year, in June, by the actor Charles Vanel). Mussolini, said Colette to a friend, was responsible for the bad bargain she had made. The Pact of Steel, linking Italy and Germany militarily, economically and otherwise in the event of war, was signed on 22 May and Colette, unlike many others, foresaw trouble. Her fame was also partly responsible for the sale: the house was only 1,650 metres from the village and tourists and fans would troop up to it, some ringing the bell, others picnicking in the garden, most just gawping. Colette was constantly besieged for autographs or asked to sign one of her books when she emerged to shop.

It was a summer of feverish gaiety, threaded through with rumour and suspicion. There were stories of spies being put ashore at Cap Martin and Cap Ferrat, rumours about German military-intelligence officers in mufti in the casinos. When two aristocratic Spanish women arrived at the Hôtel de Paris, with a suite of servants all of whom disappeared the next day except for the sauce chef and the chauffeur, while the daily bill for food was an unheard-of £2, it was believed that they were secretly sheltering people.

Maxine Elliott, fatter than ever, spent most of her days at the side of the pool playing backgammon. Finding someone to play with was her chief concern, according to her friend Elsa Maxwell, who noted that her 'active mind had become so dulled by reading cheap detective stories that she was not interested in the latest news'. Elsie Mendl would visit the Château de l'Horizon almost daily – at almost eighty she was learning to swim. Earlier in the summer, she and her husband Sir Charles Mendl had been on a yacht that caught fire. Everyone could swim except Elsie, and soon they had all jumped into the sea. Elsie refused, despite all Sir Charles's begging, until finally he lost his temper and shouted: 'Damn you, Elsie, you bloody old fool! Jump!' As he had always been patient and long-suffering with her eccentricities she was so astonished that, holding her nose, she shook her fist in his face and jumped into the sea, screaming, 'Charles, don't you ever dare swear at me again!' But she did decide to learn to swim.

Noël Coward, also holidaying on the Riviera that spring, arrived at the Hôtel Carlton in Cannes in the evening, in time to watch the lights springing up along the Croisette in the growing dusk. To the right, from his balcony were the Estoril mountains, smoky-grey in the moonlight; to the left, the dark, crouching shape of Cap d'Antibes beyond the brilliantly lit Palm Beach Casino. Music from the bars along the Croisette drifted upwards. Perhaps there was still time for some miracle to happen, he thought. As it was, the life of swimming, jaunts to the Casino, lunches of *langoustes*, garlic and French bread on the islands, motor trips to St-Tropez and Nice, *vin rosé*, sunbathing and languorous dinners at one of the small quayside restaurants continued unabated, with motor trips to Nice, Monte Carlo and St-Tropez.

Before he left for London, Coward hired a fast speedboat and went to say goodbye to Maxine Elliott. For once there was no house party; at seventy-one, her health was declining fast and she felt too ill to entertain. As he waved goodbye to Maxine on her balcony from his boat, he realised that he would never see her again and his eyes filled with tears.

That last peacetime summer brought a final burst of the gaiety for which the Riviera was known, with fireworks, balls, open-air concerts, theatres and almost constant parties, and one of the most eagerly expected events, the first-ever Cannes Film Festival, due to open on 1 September. Everyone who was anyone seemed to be there. Chanel, the spring collection over and her work on *Bacchanale* completed, was at La Pausa. Joseph Kennedy had leased the Domaine de Ranguin, which had possibly the finest rose garden on the Riviera. His wife Rose kept her strict eye on their daughters: as good Catholic girls they were not allowed to wear what Rose had seen most other girls sporting on the beach, a brief pair of shorts and a bra top. 'Such a costume is OK for the gals there but not for the Kennedys,' said Rose; for the Kennedys, it was staid one-piece bathing suits only.

Marlene Dietrich, at that time the blonde to end all blondes, her heavy-lidded eyes exuding sexual promise, had no such scruples. She had arrived at Antibes with an entourage of husband, daughter Maria and her acknowledged lover, the writer Erich Maria Remarque, famous for his book *All Quiet on the Western Front* (1929), a glamorous man with a smooth line in introductory conversation. Their love affair had begun on the Lido in Venice in 1937 when Marlene, who even at school had been known for her 'bedroom eyes', turned her blue gaze on him and said: 'You look much too young to have written one of the greatest books of our time,' to hear him answer, 'I may have written it solely to hear your enchanting voice tell me so.'

In the summer of 1939 Dietrich, then thirty-eight, had no cinema work in the offing and therefore no need to shield her famous porcelain skin. So she decided to let herself go brown, bringing to the process of tanning the same obsessive concentration that she devoted to every aspect of her appearance and image, using a special sun oil that was a mixture of the finest olive oil, iodine and a few drops of red-wine vinegar. The sight of this golden-skinned vision in a skintight white bathing suit was a distraction too far for the fifty-one-year-old Kennedy and he and Dietrich, who had dallied briefly the year before, resumed their affair. Since Erich Remarque stayed in his room all day to work, Dietrich could slip off for an after-lunch rendezvous with Kennedy.

Kennedy was not Dietrich's only lover at that time. Known for sexual ambiguity and selective promiscuousness, she had had several affairs with women, all, it must be said, rich or celebrated. As well as Kennedy, 1938 had also introduced one of these into her life. 'Joe' Carstairs, oil and railroad heiress, was well known in the motorboat-racing world and the owner of a Bahamian island called Whale Cay. In the summer of 1939, when she gave all her Whale Cay workers a holiday, Joe sailed to Antibes to see Dietrich.

Dietrich's daughter Maria described her arrival: 'One day

everybody was all "a-twitter". They congregated along the rocks like hungry seagulls, searching the surface of the sea. A strange ship had been sighted making for our private cove. A magnificent three-masted schooner, its black hull skimming through the glassy water, its teak decks gleaming in the morning sun, at the helm a beautiful boy. Bronzed and sleek – even from a distance, one sensed the power of the rippling muscles of his tight chest and haunches. He waved at his appreciative audience, flashed a rakish white-toothed smile, and gave the command to drop anchor among the white yachts.' The 'boy' was, of course, Joe Carstairs – never seen in anything but male clothing – and Dietrich lost no time in embarking on an affair. Fresh from her dalliance with Kennedy while everyone else was having an afternoon siesta, she would part from him for a daily late-afternoon assignation on the Carstairs schooner.

Dietrich had been off the screen for two years when a producer she had known from her early Berlin days tracked her down to the Cap and offered her a part in a Western. She couldn't imagine herself in a saloon-bar role but turned to 'Papa Joe' – as she now called him, to differentiate him from the other Joe in her life – and asked his advice. Kennedy, who had spent many years in the film business, made a series of calls, then advised Dietrich to take it. The result was the famous *Destry Rides Again* (1939) – and the renaissance of her film career.

By July Somerset Maugham was back at the Villa Mauresque, after a long spell of travelling, and expecting guests for the summer, including his daughter Liza and her husband. He had bought this two-storey house twelve years before, along with twelve acres of land. It was a square building hidden among trees on the side of a hill on Cap Ferrat, white inside and out, and it held his collection of pictures, which included several Zoffanys, Picassos and two Matisses, as well as sculptures and bronzes. At the top of the house was Maugham's study, with its famous Gauguin stained-glass window, in which he worked all morning until joining his guests for a pre-prandial cocktail and lunch.

In his garden were pines, aloes, orange trees, mimosas, camellias, hibiscus and avocados: these, the first ever grown in Europe, came from cuttings he had smuggled back from California in a golf bag. The first fruit they produced had been the subject of an attempted theft – and a story that had resounded down the coast for years.

The cuttings, cherished by Maugham and his gardener alike, grew into trees, but no fruit was forthcoming. Finally, the first avocado appeared and Maugham, announcing this to his guests, planned a ceremonial tasting. But when the time came to pluck it, the fruit had gone. Maugham was speculating on its disappearance with his guests at lunchtime when his gardener burst in, holding the avocado, pointed an accusing finger at Cyril Connolly, then staying at the villa, and exclaimed: 'Je l'ai trouvé dans la valise de ce monsieur-là!' Connolly's reply was not recorded.

Maugham also had a lawn. 'The great luxury on the Riviera is grass,' he wrote, 'for it will not bear the long heat of summer and must be dug up at the end of every spring and replanted every autumn. It is a trouble and an expense, but the fresh young green, at once tender and brilliant, has the same moving quality as the look in the eyes of a young girl at her first ball.' High up on one side of the hill was a swimming pool, with a Bernini marble faun beside it.

Maugham was an early riser, breakfasting at 8.00 a.m., but everyone else came down later in pyjamas and dressing gowns. Some would bask by the pool, others would go down to Villefranche, where Maugham's yacht, the *Sara*, a converted fishing boat, was moored, and sail round to a small bay on the other side of Cap Ferrat, where they would swim and lie in the sun until lunchtime. Dinner was on the terrace among the orange trees, looking out to the sea where a full moon blazed a great silver pathway over the water and, from the lily ponds in the garden below, could be heard the croaking of hundreds of tiny green frogs. Afterwards, often, there was bridge; Maugham was a passionate bridge player, although he complained that he had lost hundreds of pounds because of his stammer. 'I may have a perfectly legitimate slam in my hand but I just can't bid it – the "s" won't come out.'

At La Croë the Windsors were visited by many of their old

friends, among them Fruity and Baba Metcalfe and their son David (the Duke's godson), Lord Sefton and the woman Hugh Sefton later married, Mrs Gwynne, one of Wallis's oldest friends, and Commander and Mrs Colin Buist – the Commander had been an Extra Equerry during the Duke's brief reign as king.

The Duke – who seldom ate lunch – would go off to play golf at midday or dig and hoe in the garden. In the middle of August Baba and David went home to England but Fruity, who had been recovering from a hernia operation, stayed on to act as unpaid ADC to the man he regarded as his best friend. On 15 August he wrote to Baba: 'Yesterday afternoon . . . I heard terrible wailings come out of the woods about 5 p.m. & first of all thought that one of the little dogs had got a slight go of rabies but after listening intently I thought I must be – anywhere but where I was – the sun beating down etc. I heard the bagpipes!! Well I knew the worst then!'

Fruity went on to recount the afternoon as friends of Wallis arrived and the Duke appeared. 'His appearance was magnificent if a little strange considering the almost tropical heat. He was completely turned out as the Scotch Laird about to go stalking. Beautiful kilt, swords and all the aids. It staggered me a bit although I'm getting used to blows & surprises now. Then out of the woods rushed what might have been the whole Campbell family – of course very complete with pipes & haggis etc. Women as well as men. I inquired where they sprung from & was told they were folklore dancers (paid for by a society in England & of course Scotland). Personally *I* think that if they get into Germany then I really wouldn't blame Hitler if he attacked anyone and started the European conflict. I felt like helping to do so myself last evening. They piped and danced and made merry until 7.15 p.m. We all had to admire and applaud by order of the All Highest. HRH himself took photos of the merry throng . . .' A week later their pipe major came over to tune the Duke's bagpipes and thereafter, according to the Duke's secretary, 'the Duke practised assiduously. Almost every night I . . . could hear him either on the roof of the château or walking about the gardens blowing robustly with unaffected enjoyment.'

That August, too, Picasso painted *Night Fishing at Antibes*, a painting sometimes described as depicting the end of an era, and of which he said: 'I have not painted the war ... but I have no doubt that the war is in these paintings I have done.'

Churchill, staying with Consuelo Balsan* in late August, as usual went gambling at the Monte Carlo Casino, smoking his cigar most of the time. He lost so much that by 1.00 a.m. the director of the Casino was suggesting to him that he should stop. He had one more bet – on red – but black came up. This time he did stop, saying: 'I'll pay my debt to you tomorrow.' But the next day was 23 August, the day of the Ribbentrop-Molotov Pact signed between Nazi Germany and Russia that turned the likelihood of war into a certainty, and Churchill flew home at once, leaving his wife and daughter to follow later and his debt unpaid. At La Pausa, Chanel heard the news of the Pact as she was preparing to leave Roquebrune for Paris and work on the next collection.

All over France, army officers on leave were gone within thirty minutes and hotels and villas emptied in hours. In Monte Carlo, the mobilisation of the French Army depleted Casino staff to such an extent that the club had to close at once. Everyone who was not compelled to stay was advised to leave immediately. Yet the trains coming to the south were packed (often blacked out, with only a single blue bulb for light) as already people were putting as much distance between themselves and the northern and eastern borders of France as possible.

Everyone in England, and many of those on the Riviera, knew what the Pact meant. The politician Leslie Hore-Belisha, who had been staying in Cannes, left; and many English who had planned visits cancelled them.

On 25 August all British nationals in Berlin and all Germans in England were asked to leave and the Admiralty closed the Mediterranean to British shipping. A squad of Senegalese troops was moved into the grounds of the Château de la Croë, together with

---

* She was the former wife of the ninth Duke of Marlborough, first cousin to Winston Churchill; they had always got on extremely well.

an anti-aircraft battery, to protect Antibes from an attack by sea. Soldiers began to be seen everywhere, their tents in camps in the olive groves and pines. Cap Ferrat had become a military zone, with machine-gun emplacements and an anti-aircraft battery.

In England, special services praying for peace were held and churches remained open all over the country, with people en route for work, home or going out shopping dropping in to pray. The Duke of Windsor sent a telegram to Hitler (whom he had met in 1937) pleading for peace: 'I address to you my entirely personal simple though earnest appeal for your utmost influence towards the peaceful solution of the present problem,' he said, only to receive a brush-off several days later. 'My attitude towards England remains the same,' replied the Führer.

The inveterate party-giver Elsa Maxwell, who had been lent the Villa Lou Paradou, gave a housewarming party for 200 there on the last day of August. Beneath the froth and cocktails, the party so seethed with rumour after rumour that Elsa telephoned the most senior and knowledgeable American on that coast, Joseph Kennedy, to be told she ought to go back to America immediately. As she hung up, someone called from the terrace: 'Something strange is going on. I wonder what it means?' To the left of the house, a blackness was rolling over Cannes, blotting out house- and street-lights. Beneath them, the lights of Juan-les-Pins and Golfe-Juan had already disappeared, and to the east the glow in the sky above Nice, France's fifth-largest city, began to fade.

The French government, which knew that Hitler was massing tanks and panzer divisions on the Polish border, had ordered a blackout.

Maugham and his friends had talked about the possibility of war, but to all of them it seemed remote. Then, suddenly, it was upon them. In the first two days of September most of the remaining Italian servants left for Italy, guns were hidden in the cliffs and the harbourmaster at Villefranche said that all private yachts had to leave the harbour within twenty-four hours: this was so that the French Navy could use the Bay of Villefranche if need be. Maugham and Haxton decided to take the *Sara* to

Cassis, where she could lie up in one of the creeks in safety. At that moment a young English couple who had not seen a paper for days arrived for lunch and refused to believe that war could break out at any minute – it was just a scare, they thought, like the two previous ones, Munich and Czechoslovakia. 'Everyone knew that the French Army was invincible,' said Maugham, and his (French) chauffeur had remarked that they would be in Rome in six weeks. Maugham and Haxton boarded the *Sara* with the tinned food they had bought and sailed down the coast to Bandol.

Maugham's son-in-law, returning from Monte Carlo, told him that everyone was leaving as quickly as possible. There were no places on the Blue Train and cars packed with luggage were filling the roads. Although the Italians had not declared war there was a panicked rush to get to Paris, but the journey, which normally took thirteen hours, now took forty, and people had to wait up to three days at a station before they could squeeze themselves on to a train.

Others were arriving. On the eve of the war around 5,000 Jews came to the coast, some carrying travel guides as if they were on holiday. The well-off and well-known among them, including actors, writers and musicians, took rooms in hotels on the Croisette in Cannes or the Promenade des Anglais in Nice, where scarlet and yellow canna lilies flowered between the palms all summer.

But most of those who lived there took little notice. The Windsors, too, were convinced that there would be no war and that the crisis would 'blow over', so much so that the Duchess was making arrangements to have the new butler's wife brought out from England. And even when told that the Germans had invaded Poland on 1 September, the Duke still refused to believe that Europe was teetering on the edge of war. 'Oh, just another sensational report,' he said impatiently.

Fruity Metcalfe was under no such illusion. Convinced that war would break out any moment, he drove straight away into Nice and somehow managed to reserve a compartment on the 7.30 a.m. train for Paris the following day for eight of the Duke's servants, his own valet and a secretary.

A group of women wearing fashionable beach pyjamas, 1934

Chanel on the beach with Boy Capel, 1917

Chanel with Bendor, the Duke of Westminster

Above Chanel in the garden at La Pausa with her dog, Gigot

Rest of page La Pausa: perched on the clifftop, with its gorgeous internal colonnade, perfect for parties

mi, Sert, Missia et Coco Chanel 1920

Left Misia and Jose Maria Sert with Chanel and Igor Stravinsky, 1920. Chanel's friendship with Misia was turbulent at times but ultimately unshakeable

Below Roussy Mdivani, later Sert, the sculptor-turned-mistress of Jose Maria whom Misia initially fell for as much as her husband did

Opposite page Jean Coctea (*above*) and Serge Lifar (wit Chanel) both of whom sh subsidised, protected and love

This page The Duke and Duchess of
Windsor loved the Riviera and intended
to settle there. They made their villa, the
Chateau de la Croë (*above*), as much like
a palace as they could, and visitors were
expected to treat them like royalty.

Opposite page top The wonderful
modernist villa E.1027, designed by Eileen
Gray for her lover Jean Badovici. Even
its name symbolised their togetherness:
E stood for Eileen, J was the tenth letter
of the alphabet, B the second, and G the
seventh. After Gray and Badovici parted,
Badovici allowed the great architect Le
Corbusier (*opposite below*) to paint vivid
and erotic murals all over the internal
walls of E.1027. The scar on his leg
was caused by the propeller blade of a
yacht that passed over him while he was
swimming in the bay of St Tropez.

Above Lord Castlerosse and Doris Delevigne together. Because of his immense girth, Castlerosse was sometimes known as Lord Elephant and Castle, but his wit and charm made him a hugely sought-after guest. Perhaps the only person who matched him in extravagance was his wife, the beautiful Doris. She would wear a new pair of silk stockings every day – hers cost a guinea a pair. By comparison, a housemaid's average wage was £25 a year.

Left Lord and Lady Furness. Enid Furness, née Lindemann, was Viscount Furness's third wife – her predecessor, Thelma, was the woman who introduced Wallis Simpson to the then Prince of Wales. Enid, a six-foot glamorous blonde, had herself been married twice before. A devoted wife, she nursed her evil-tempered husband to the end during his final illness.

In England, the lawyer Walter Monckton, an old and trusted friend of the former King who had been deeply embroiled in the abdication negotiations, had managed to arrange for a plane to come out the next day, Saturday 2 September, to bring the Windsors home. When he telephoned the Duke late that night to tell him this, the Duke asked him petulantly why he (Monckton) was coming to escort them since (as Fruity's notes record) 'he would take up space that could be occupied by the Duchess's luggage'. Then, when told that on arrival in England the Windsors would be staying with the Metcalfes, the Duke responded that he would only come if his brother and his wife were prepared to have them at one of their houses. The conversation ended.

'Certain people here are *quite extraordinary*. No one could understand how their minds work,' wrote Fruity to his wife, describing the telephone conversation that had gone on that Friday night in the La Croë library. 'I went on reading my book in the drawing room as I did not think anything *could* go wrong. It all seemed plain sailing to me. I have become adviser in chief and the only person who is getting anything done here now & indeed they realise it. I it was who got all the servants off, 8 of them & 1 secretary. It took some doing, I can tell you, as Cannes stn was Hell on earth . . .

'Well, anyhow, they came in to me after about ½ hour & said: "We are *not* going – the plane is for you & Miss Arnold tomorrow." I looked at them as if they really *were* mad – then they started off: "I refuse to go *unless* we are invited to stay at Windsor Castle & the invitation & plane are sent personally by my brother etc." I just sat still, held my head & listened for about 20 minutes & then I started.'

Fruity tore into them, saying among other things: 'You only think of yourselves. You don't realise that there is at this moment a war going on, that women and children are being bombed and killed while you talk of your *PRIDE*.' After what the Duke had said to Walter Monckton on the telephone there was of course no plane.

By 2 September Chanel was back at the Ritz, working on the winter 1939/40 collection. Diana Vreeland's husband returned to America with some American friends, leaving her behind. 'There's no point in taking Diana away from Chanel and her shoes,' he said. Later, a friend told her she *had* to leave and that he had booked her a cabin on the last passenger ship with private cabins out of Europe. 'I'll never forget that afternoon coming down the rue Cambon – my last afternoon in Paris for five years,' she said. 'I'd just had my last fitting at Chanel . . . I was so depressed – leaving Chanel, leaving Europe, leaving all the world of . . . my world.'

That evening, Diana walked up and down the Champs-Élysées with a friend. 'It would be getting dark at six. The weather was balmy, it was quite crowded with people, and absolutely quiet. I can remember exactly what I had on: a little black moiré *tailleur* from Chanel, a little piece of black lace wrapped around my head and beautiful, absolutely exquisite black slippers like kid gloves.' The next day she boarded the *Île de France*, the last ship to leave France before the outbreak of war, departing from Le Havre on the morning of 3 September, just hours before France and the UK declared war on Germany.

In Antibes, it was a hot morning and the Windsors and Fruity had decided to swim in the villa's pool. As they stood beside it, the Duke was asked by one of the remaining servants to go indoors to take a call from the British Ambassador. Ten minutes later he came back. 'Great Britain has just declared war on Germany,' he said. Then there was a splash – he had dived into the pool. In Monaco, the church bells tolled as if for a funeral.

That day Brian Howard wrote to his mother: 'Willie Maugham is at Bandol with his yacht and can't move. I see him every day. Yesterday a new ruling was made that all Germans between the ages of fifty and sixty-five have to go to the camp at Toulon – that means many people from here, including Feuchtwanger, the celebrated anti-Hitler writer.' In Sanary, the German writers were having a hard time. They had less money to spend than before, and with Germany now the enemy the behaviour of those around them changed.

Maugham and Haxton had to buy blue paint to cover the *Sara*'s portholes in order to comply with the blackout, and two of the three (Italian) crew left for home at once. English newspapers were no longer available, all foreigners had to register, bars and cafés lost their staff as men were called up. 'Everyone was full of the defeats that were going to be inflicted on the Axis,' noted Maugham.

Maugham was anxious to return to the Villa Mauresque because he hoped to hear from the Ministry of Information, to which he had written offering his services. Finally, despite all the regulations, he and Haxton simply drove there in a taxi. Once home, he learnt that because of his years in France and the high regard in which he was held by the French and his consequent access to influential Frenchmen he would, the ministry decided, be valuable. They asked him to write a report on the French attitude to the British, and some articles extolling the French war effort. Maugham was delighted at the thought of being useful and left immediately for Paris, where he was appalled at some of the pro-German sentiments he heard expressed.

It was time for the old life of the rich to be put away. In Monte Carlo the Sporting Club and the Casino shut and all along the coast hotels dismissed staff. Railway companies that fed travellers to Nice from Lyons, Avignon and Marseilles, their rolling stock requisitioned by the military, drastically cut services. The first Cannes Film Festival, set to begin the same day as the invasion, was cancelled. Overnight, Nice hotels lost half their business. At the big department stores, sales of jewellery, perfumes and other luxury items dropped 70 per cent.

On 7 September Walter Monckton arrived at La Croë, saying that the King wished the Windsors to return to England as soon as possible, and with the offer of an attachment to the British Military Mission shortly to leave for Paris. The idea of the Military Mission appealed to the Duke, but as both Windsors were terrified of flying the Duke now asked for a destroyer to bring him and the Duchess back. The long-suffering Monckton flew home to arrange this.

Eventually, accompanied by Fruity, the Windsors drove to Cherbourg, arriving there on 12 September and taking with them their three Cairn terriers and a huge pile of luggage. At

Cherbourg they were met by Lord Louis Mountbatten who, on Churchill's instructions, had brought the destroyer HMS *Kelly* to pick them up. They landed at Portsmouth at 10 p.m. on a dark night, in the blackout.

Here, again on the instructions of Churchill, who wished to afford the former King some kind of dignity, they were greeted with a red carpet and a guard of honour of 100 men, with a band playing the national anthem (or rather, merely the first six bars of it) as they landed. It was the last nod to a royal past that they would receive for some time. They were met by Walter Monckton and Baba Metcalfe who, the next day, drove the Windsors to her house at Hartfield. There was no message of any description from the royal family. 'The Duke never once gave the impression of feeling the sadness of his return,' wrote Baba in her diary. 'As with everything else the blind has been drawn down & the past forgotten.' They did, however, prove excellent house guests. 'They both took lots of trouble to be nice to us,' recalled David Metcalfe.

Three weeks after the war began, Chanel closed the House of Chanel in Paris and laid off the staff without warning. Four thousand female employees lost their jobs. Her action was heavily criticised by the trade unions, which begged her to think of the workers, and the government, which talked of the prestige of Paris. But she was adamant.

CHAPTER 8

>─◆>─○─◆─<

'La drôle de guerre'

Various theories have been advanced as to why Chanel shut down her couture business, ranging from a long-held grudge against the workers who had gone on strike in 1936 to a fear that she had been overtaken by Schiaparelli. She herself said simply: 'I had the feeling that we had reached the end of an era. And that no one would ever make dresses again.'

Her doors were not the only ones to close. In the first weeks of the war Paris virtually shut down. Shops, hotels, theatres and restaurants were shut although the Ritz and Maxim's both stayed open, streets were empty and the heat oppressive. The Windsors, who had moved into their house on the boulevard Suchet in mid-October – the Duke had returned to France on 29 September to join the Military Mission – made do with a skeleton staff and limited entertaining.

On the Riviera, although many of the English and Americans had left, a great many also stayed, despite the posters that had been put up in consulates warning that political conditions in Europe were such that all British people who had no urgent reason for staying in France were advised to go home.

It was the start of the 'drôle de guerre' (the Phoney War) and there was in many quarters a belief that the war would be over soon and that anyway this part of France would be safe. 'We had taken a villa at La Napoule, a little *plage* five miles to the west of Cannes,' wrote one Englishwoman. 'When the war came, and

Italy appeared to be content to play the part of an onlooker, I felt there was no reason to leave. Our garage was invaded first by ebony Senegalese who laughed from dawn to sunset, and later by stout khaki-clad Reservists who spent most of their time playing *boules*. But as regards making any preparation for possible invasion, this did not seem to enter into their calculations. Everything remained calm and peaceful; one could hardly know that a great and terrible war was in progress.'

Among such 'stayers' were the Oppenheims, both of whom so loved this part of France that they had bought an old farmhouse, the Domaine de Notre-Dame, in 1938. Now they had a battery quartered nearby, with its sixty-odd horses to be fed and watered every day. For the soldiers they organised a voluntary canteen in an outbuilding, which they made as comfortable as possible, heating it, installing a gramophone and writing paper, and providing hot coffee or cocoa every day at five o'clock. On Christmas Day they handed round hot grog.

Although Italy had already made sabre-rattling sounds in the direction of Menton, Monaco and Nice, which she considered by rights should belong to her, for the next few months the war had little or no impact on the Riviera. People who had made their homes on this delicious stretch of coastline, who loved the place, the people, the climate, the sparkling sea, where living – by which they meant food and servants – was cheaper, and where by now they had put down roots, could not bear the idea of returning to cold, grey England. Their children chattered in a mixture of English, Italian and French, and although Christmas decorations were branches of orange trees, Monte Carlo was on the itinerary of the Royal Navy's courtesy calls and the parties on board HMS *Warspite*, the most regular of the visiting ships, brought gossip from home. Food was still plentiful, Big Ben boomed out as usual to announce the BBC news on the radio; and England was, after all, only twenty-four hours' travel away. Elsie Gladman, who had returned to nurse at Nice's Sunny Bank Hospital, thought herself as secure there as in England. 'France was our great ally and friend.' So placid and normal did everything seem that Dennis Youdale's parents, who had left him in England when war had been declared, decided to bring him back to Nice – to 'home' in Dennis's eyes.

It was during the Phoney War that Maxine Elliott died. One of the last to see her was Elsa Maxwell. 'Maxine was listless until lunch was served,' she recorded. As usual, it was a huge meal that ran heavily to whipped cream and thick, rich sauces, which Maxine tucked into ravenously. 'I've just received my death sentence,' she said casually to Elsa. 'The doctor tells me I've got uremia. He says I must cut out all rich food.' This did not stop her motioning to the butler for another helping. 'You'll kill yourself if you don't listen to him,' cried Elsa, to which Maxine responded: 'There's only one better way to die, and I'm too old for that.'

She died on 5 March 1940. That evening Dr Brès, the devoted companion of her latter years, wrote to Churchill: 'I have in the ears her last words said this morning about you. "Winston knows how to take his responsibilities. Nothing can frighten him – he should be Prime Minister."' Churchill's response, acknowledging his sorrow at his friend's death and his gratitude for Brès's care, concluded: 'In this grim world, the lights are being put out one by one and sunlit days at the Château de l'Horizon are gone for ever.'

Yet life went on much as usual. Within three months the casinos had opened again, the remaining English kept in touch with people at home by sending letters through friends in Switzerland, or via agencies in Lisbon. Every Thursday at noon the air-raid sirens sounded but, as everyone knew, this was only a practice exercise. In Paris, smart women had Hermès leather gas-mask cases, and white gloves were worn at night to help when crossing blackened streets. As every Frenchman had to do military service, women or very old men appeared driving buses and taxis.

But no one was much worried. 'We have the Maginot Line', was the constant refrain. This great fortification ran the entire length of the French-German border; its fifty large forts (known as *ouvrages*), protected by reinforced steel and minefields, were built about fifteen kilometres from each other, each housing 1,000 soldiers and artillery. Between each *ouvrage* were smaller forts with between 200 and 500 men depending on their size, so that the whole frontier was covered.

It was considered impregnable by the French and indeed the rest of the world, so much so that various army chiefs had visited it to study its layout and workings. And for everyone on the Riviera, there was the comforting sight of the Line's first two forts, the underground one on Cap-Martin and the massive creation built into the rocks of the ancient village of Ste-Agnès, almost 800 metres above Roquebrune. Said to be the most heavily armed of all the Maginot forts, it dominated the coastline, its gun emplacements in the rock covering all the bay below.

In Paris, there was a return to normal. The American author and politician Clare Boothe Luce, arriving at the Ritz in mid-March 1940, found the same staff, the same 'smells of fur and perfume, the same sound of high bird-babble voices . . . I saw right away that the guests of the Ritz were the same sort of guests that they had always had.' She was right: among them were Reginald and Daisy Fellowes, Schiaparelli, Lady Mendl and numerous couples from outside Paris whose footmen had been called up and who had then closed their châteaux, sent their children to relations in the country and moved into the Ritz.

Morale, found Mrs Luce, was exceptionally high. 'There was one phrase on everybody's lips: "Il faut en finir".* People said it on the streets. Waiters told you so in cafés. The couturiers embroidered the motto in red, white and blue into the corners of gay chiffon handkerchiefs. Jewellers made gold charm bracelets spelling it . . . It titled the carefully reasoned editorials in every paper. And in the canteens the soldiers sang it lustily and honestly to music.' Elderly bejewelled ladies still sipped coffee or champagne on terraces, some quoting Nostradamus to show that all would be well ('The betrayed lion will unite itself with the cock and then the barbarian will be absorbed') as the chestnuts burst into leaf. The cinemas and shops were open, British soldiers and *poilus* played football in the suburbs.

Then things began to happen quickly. At the beginning of

---

* This time we must put an end to it.

April, Hitler swallowed up Norway and Denmark. The war was coming too close for comfort and Parisians began to leave; at the Ritz, where Chanel was living, half the employees left, often for their home villages. Taxis were requisitioned to take troops to the front, the grass in the parks was no longer cut as there was no one to do it. At the beginning of May Maugham returned to the Villa Mauresque, and the *Sara* was brought back to her berth at Villefranche. It was now very quiet on the Riviera, with petrol rationed, food shortages beginning, no coffee and a blackout.

Yet when the invasion of Holland and Belgium took place on 10 May* most French people, convinced of their country's invincibility, saw these merely as reverses that would, eventually, be straightened out. Even when the first trainful of refugees arrived the same day, followed by many more, often destitute, always exhausted, faith in the country's defences remained.

That day the first sirens sounded in Paris at 4.55 p.m. and in the evening Parisians heard the Minister of Information announce: 'The real war has begun.' Refugees had been passing through Paris, but most Parisians thought that these, many Belgian, were reacting to events in their own country. The Duke of Windsor was taking no chances: on the day the Low Countries were invaded he had driven with Wallis to Biarritz and ensconced her there before returning to Paris.

Then came news of the attack in the Ardennes, north of the fabled, impassable Maginot Line. The Ardennes was considered such difficult terrain that the French believed that, were the Germans even to attempt it, it would have to be with light infantry and would take them at least ten days, especially as all the bridges on the largest river they had to cross had been destroyed.

Instead, it was to prove the 'fatal avenue' to which de Gaulle had referred in 1934.† The traversing of the Ardennes (from 12 May) was a blitzkrieg (lightning war): the Germans crossed the rivers rapidly by deploying pontoons strung along cables to

---

* Their actual surrender took place on 28 May 1940.
† In his book *Towards a Professional Army*.

transport their tanks, which were able to handle rough terrain, emerging from the forest and attacking the unprepared French with heavy weaponry rather than light infantry in a mere three or four days. They had neutralised the wonderful Maginot Line by simply going round it.

The panic began on 15 May, recorded Vincent Sheean, and by the evening of 16 May had begun to turn into a mass migration – mostly into Paris. 'At the stations there were people from Belgium, from Holland, from the bombed cities of Lorraine, from the north and east of France.' Then its citizens began to move out of Paris. The first loaded motor cars appeared on 16 May. A few days later it was unusual to see any car that did not carry luggage, bedding or even furniture lashed to its top, back and sides. One of the largest movements of population* ever to occur in the Europe of historical times was now taking place. Millions of people from Belgium, northern France and Holland were in flight.

The archives of the Ministry of Foreign Affairs were burned in the courtyard and on Sunday 19 May the whole French government, and the British and American ambassadors with their staffs, attended a service at the Cathedral of Notre-Dame to pray for the salvation of the Republic. Their large, shiny limousines were lined up in the side streets to take them away afterwards.

'I decided to have Simone and the children evacuated to Bellac,' wrote Raymond-Raoul Lambert in his diary, 'more because of the danger of air raids than the strategic situation.' The intellectual Lambert, a French Jew and former civil servant, now a captain in the technical section of the Colonial Troops, would soon become the chief link between Vichy and its French-Jewish citizens.

Others were leaving too. The next day Vincent Sheean got someone's cancelled air flight to London, leaving all his belongings at the Hôtel de Crillon. He was unable to return as all visas had been stopped by the French. He never saw any of his effects again, as the Crillon became German military headquarters.

---

* From 16 May to the day the Germans entered Paris on 14 June about two million people left with as many of their belongings as they could pack and transport.

On 18 May, Lion Feuchtwanger in Sanary was told by the Feuchtwangers' maid Leontine that a notice had been posted up outside the *mairie* (town hall), saying that 'all stateless people born in Germany who by the first of January had not reached the age of fifty-six must report to the *mairie*'. A few weeks short of his fifty-sixth birthday, he fell into this category. Feuchtwanger and the three other Germans who were also going presented themselves at the *mairie*, entering what was their gateway to internment under the words *Liberté, Égalité, Fraternité*.

There had been internment camps all over France during the late thirties, most used to detain Spanish Republican refugees and fleeing Spanish soldiers and, on the outbreak of war, communists.* During the Phoney War (which had ended with the invasion of the Low Countries) the Third Republic interned *indésirables*, that is Germans who were found in France, without regard to ethnicity or political orientation, as foreign citizens of an enemy power. Among them were many German Jews who had fled the Nazi regime like Feuchtwanger, who was to be sent to the largest in the area, the Camp de Milles, a former brickworks near Aix.

Each person was allowed to take thirty kilos of luggage. Among them was a Nice hotel trainee, a German-Jewish refugee named Marcel Block, who for some years had been happily learning the hotel trade, confident that a sunny future awaited him. The wise took rugs (for the night) and a folding chair in case there was nothing to sit on. Soon they were divided into three groups: Germans, Austrians and former Foreign Legionaries – some of whom had done twenty or thirty years' service for France, had lost an arm or a leg, and had been decorated. Even the guards felt indignant that France should treat them in this way. Selection seemed quite arbitrary: several people held the Légion d'honneur, one man had four sons fighting for France, many others, including Feuchtwanger, were known as implacable enemies of Nazism.

---

* The Communist Party was banned by the Daladier government after the German-Soviet Non-Aggression Pact.

*

With British troops retreating fast, there was fear of a German invasion of Britain. From the hill between Dover and Folkestone smoke and a constant sheet of flame could be seen over Calais. Roads near the British coast were barricaded, tank traps constructed, signposts twisted to give faulty directions. When news of the Dunkirk evacuation of British troops (between 26 May and 4 June) arrived in Paris, Parisians began to wonder if anything could prevent the Germans from reaching their city, and many of those on the Riviera were looking for the best way to leave the country. 'Some people are trying to get away on a yacht belonging to the Khedive of Egypt,' wrote Brian Howard. 'Furness, the Fellowses . . .' But at the last minute the Khedive changed his mind and refused to lease it.

Yet as late as 24 May the French Prime Minister, Paul Reynaud, was saying in a broadcast: 'France has been invaded a hundred times and never beaten . . . our belief in victory is intact.' Although many of the pillows at the Ritz had already been sent to hospitals in anticipation of the arrival of the wounded, until the last minute people sat in cafés, strolled by the Seine and watched the grass in the Champs-Élysées being watered that hot summer ('They wouldn't do that if they were worried, would they?' thought the French writer and art critic Léon Worth).

Suddenly the false confidence to which everyone had clung gave way and the harshness of reality set in.

When the outskirts of Paris were bombed by the Germans at the beginning of June, Chanel, like millions of men, women and children, fled. She packed her belongings in huge trunks and stored them at the Ritz. Just before she left, she persuaded the Ritz management to give her a two-room apartment on the seventh floor, against her return.

Paying her bill for two months in advance, she left in her chauffeur's car, as her blue Rolls-Royce would have been too conspicuous, taking with her several of her female employees to seek refuge in the south. As well as her chief seamstress and a couple of others, she was accompanied by the employee who probably knew her better than any other, her right-hand woman,

Madame Aubert. They had first met when Chanel had worked as a seamstress in Moulins, and the red-haired Angèle Aubert had been with her during the thirty-odd years since she had launched her business.

They drove out of Paris along with a flood of cars, wagons, lorries, refuse carts, fire engines, hearses (no burials were possible in Paris for several days), even handcarts piled with everything from food and furniture to babies' cribs. People poured out of the capital, in cars, on foot, wheeling luggage on bicycles or prams, piling beds, bedding, cooking implements and sometimes livestock on peasant carts, pushing elderly relatives in wheelbarrows or walking on blistered, sometimes bleeding feet. The great exodus had begun. Civilians were fleeing in their thousands. In the throng were refugees from Belgium, Holland and Luxembourg. In the Paris region alone, almost four million people left their homes. 'It looked as though a gigantic ant hill in the north had been kicked open and all the ants were running away,' said the writer and pilot Antoine de Saint-Exupéry, who saw it from the air. Most of those fleeing were women whose men had been called up. Often they were accompanied by small, confused children. For those in cars, most of the time was spent in traffic jams.

Part of the horror was psychological: until the last minute the confidence in the unbreakable, invincible Maginot Line and France's victory had been such that the sudden appearance of defeat was doubly shattering and many of the French Army had simply fled, often straight back to their homes. As one conscripted soldier, seen strolling along the boulevard de Sébastopol in creased civilian clothes, replied to a friend who told him he would be shot as a deserter, 'First they'll have to find me. And in another week they'll have to shoot half the army. Remains to be seen whether the other half is willing to do it . . .' *

By 9 June the Germans were a mere thirty kilometres from Notre-Dame. The French government left Paris for Orléans on Monday 10 June as Mussolini declared war on Great Britain and France.

---

* Quoted by Arthur Koestler in *Scum of the Earth* (1941).

On Tuesday 11 June Paris was smothered in a thick black fog – the fumes from the oil-storage tanks that had been set on fire from Rouen to Bonnières. 'The sun was hid, the whole aspect uncanny,' wrote Elizabeth Blair Hales in her diary. She and her husband Samuel, respectively sixty-three and seventy, were called on at 6.00 a.m. by her husband's secretary, who told them that there was no time to waste and that she would drive them to Gare Montparnasse where her sister Valentine, a Red Cross nurse, would meet them.

With Valentine's help ('Look ill and old!' Valentine whispered to Elizabeth as they struggled towards the Red Cross waiting room) they managed to get seats on a train leaving for Le Mans. Behind them, on the platform, fighting had broken out in spite of the heavy luggage most people carried. 'As the train set off, we looked on to a sea of faces,' wrote Elizabeth. 'Quickly we reached Versailles where crowds waited in hopes of getting into the train. Terrible cries of "égoïstes" when told there was absolutely no room. But 2 soldiers lifted up 2 young women, mothers of tiny babies and got them in by the window. I held a baby boy of 8 months in my arms . . . People fought and struggled at each little station till Chartres was reached.' After an air raid, changing trains and a long journey in total darkness, they finally reached St-Malo.

On the Riviera, which Mussolini had invaded with 400,000 troops, a large contingent of Italian inhabitants already existed: most of the waiters in the big hotels were Italian and there had been intermarriage of those close to the border. This meant little fighting: a few ancient Italian biplanes flew up and down low over the Cannes seafront, spraying bullets at everyone they saw, and that Thursday the noon air-raid sirens heralded a few real bombs, most of which fortunately dropped into the sea. In Menton some shops closed, some moved their stocks further from Italy.

Until then, the south had seemed immune, so much so that the Windsors had returned to La Croë. The Duke had left Paris overnight at the end of May for Biarritz to collect Wallis, abandoning his faithful aide and friend Fruity Metcalfe without a word. So firm was the belief in France's invulnerability and so far away from conflict was that lovely coastline that many felt daily life would simply go on as before. 'Everything had continued as normal up to this point,' said Constance Newton, a twelve-year-old English girl whose father had settled in France and who was attending a private school that specialised in preparing pupils for the *baccalauréat*. 'It was only when Italy declared war that things changed.'

On Wednesday 12 June, the French government declared from Tours that Paris was an open city* and French radio broadcast a government decree that all male civilians, except the aged and infirm, must leave Paris. 'There seemed to be a desire not to leave Hitler with too many future munitions workers,' wrote Rupert Downing in his flat near Montparnasse. 'Just how they were to escape was not specified. Most of the cars had been commandeered by the military.' Almost all the trains had stopped running; on 13 June the last train left for the south and the gates of the Gare d'Austerlitz clanged shut.

Posters appeared on walls telling people to abstain from hostile acts and remain calm and dignified. But most of them were too busy fleeing to give thought to their deportment when the enemy appeared.

Panic had set in. Cannon fire could now be heard, bringing with it thoughts of that earlier war in which so many Frenchmen had lost their lives, of the bombing of Guernica, of the destruction of Polish villages. Many older people remembered stories of the ancestral enemy, of atrocities, real or rumoured. The newspapers were reassuring and advised people to stay until there was an order to evacuate, but most had already fled. Some women, sheltering in the kitchen of an abandoned house, heard cries that the Germans were coming. 'Rub your bodies with mustard!' instructed one. 'If the Germans try to rape you, they'll burn themselves.'

Chanel and her small party did not go to La Pausa, as the

* A city that, during a war, is officially declared demilitarised and open to occupation, and therefore will not be defended, in order to spare it, under international law, from all forms of attack from the enemy.

Italians had begun bombing the Riviera, but to Pau, where there had always been a sizeable English community, based on that most English of sports, fox-hunting.* It was here, too, in the thirteenth-century château at Pau, to which her first serious lover, Étienne Balsan, had taken her to hunt, that thirty years earlier Chanel had met and fallen in love with Boy Capel.

She did not stay at Pau but drove on to the nearby small village of Corbère-Abères, where she had bought the Château de Lembeye from Balsan for her favourite nephew, André Palasse, and where she had often stayed before with André and his family. André had been called up in the general mobilisation of 1939 and was serving on the Maginot Line; after his departure, Chanel had undertaken the support of his family, which included her great-niece Gabrielle (named after her), another favourite. She had also contributed generously to the support of her two brothers, paying regular stipends, helping them buy cars or small businesses and settling debts.

André was the son of one of Chanel's older sisters, Julia, who became pregnant while at the convent in which all three sisters were brought up. When Julia died the boy was left an orphan (no one knew who his father was, though he was given the surname Palasse). Chanel took on her six-year-old nephew and brought him up as her own, sending him to be educated at the English Catholic public school, Beaumont. She liked what she had seen of the upper-class, public-school-educated men she had met with the Duke of Westminster, once saying drily: 'All Englishmen are well brought up – at least till they reach Calais.'

Soon, other refugees began to arrive, among them some of her most elderly employees. But there was plenty of food – rabbits, chickens, ducks, pigs (much later requisitioned by the Germans).

At 5.30 on the morning of 14 June the first German advance guard marched into Paris and the coalition government collapsed. At 7.00 a.m. a squad of German motorcyclists roared up

---

* The Pau Hunt had started over 200 years earlier, during the Peninsular Wars, when French and British officers decided after the Battle of Orthez to hunt together. The Pau Hunt is still going strong today.

to the Ritz, soon followed by a group of officers, as the forces entered in strength. 'The powerful war machine rolled down the Champs-Élysées,' wrote Rosie Say, an English girl trapped in Paris. 'Gleaming horses, tanks, machinery, guns and thousands upon thousands of soldiers. The procession was immaculate, shining and seemingly endless. It was like a gigantic, grey-green snake that wound itself round the heart of this broken city, which was waiting pathetically to be swallowed up. There was a huge crowd of onlookers, most of them silent but some cheering. As the hours passed and the unending spectacle continued, I thought of my family and friends back in London.'

Misia and her former husband Sert watched the German troops goose-stepping by from the balcony of Sert's flat over-looking the place de la Concorde. That night Sert's secretary, Boulos Ristelhueber, recorded in his diary, 'The troops appear as in a Wagner opera. Ponderous and arrogant, they pass with the sound of an earthquake. Rows of Wotans and Lohengrins in gleaming steel helmets, supernaturally beautiful. Endless lines of enormous horses with long manes pulling cannons with gaping black mouths. At the top of the Arc de Triomphe, half of which is covered with sandbags, an enormous flag with a swastika and a tiny little photographer recording the spectacle for *Wochen-schau*, the illustrated German weekly.'

After the government had left Paris, the Prime Minister, Paul Reynaud, had tried to reorganise it, first in Tours and then, on 15 June, in Bordeaux, where Reynaud settled at the Hôtel Splen-dide with his mistress, the Countess de Portes, whose husband was away in the army. She was a woman who inspired intense dislike: she was called 'a turkey' by General de Gaulle, while Winston Churchill* nicknamed her 'the parrot'. She had become Reynaud's mistress in 1930, the year he entered the Cabinet. Neither elegant nor attractive, she was immensely interfering and a fascist sympathiser, yet Reynaud seemed completely under

---

* Churchill had become Britain's Prime Minister on 10 May 1940 – the same day that the Low Countries were invaded.

the thumb of this 'middle-aged woman, with a shrill voice, and a clamorous, demanding manner, who chattered like a magpie and lost her temper with ease', to quote one description of her.

Once in Bordeaux Hélène de Portès did her best to get Reynaud, who was adamantly opposed to any kind of settlement with Germany, to offer terms of surrender to the Germans, and when he tried to discuss with de Gaulle plans to continue fighting she threw a terrible temper tantrum that left de Gaulle disgusted. She was violently anti-British, with a particular hatred for Churchill; according to his bodyguard, Walter Thompson, she once actually lunged at Churchill's throat with a knife she had concealed within her Christian Dior dress. She even went so far as to try and intrigue with a key diplomat from the US, who later recalled disapprovingly: 'I don't think her role in encouraging the defeatist elements during Reynaud's critical last days as Prime Minister should be underestimated. She spent an hour weeping in my office to get us to urge Reynaud to ask for an armistice.'

'This woman behaved at times like a sovereign, at times like a fishwife, but at all times as if she had some vested right, whether constitutional or divine, in the government of the French Republic,' wrote Vincent Sheean, then a reporter for the *New York Herald Tribune*. Sheean knew that she presided over meetings of the General Staff, prepared state papers for Reynaud, dismissed generals and reproved ambassadors. When a key telegram went missing and was found in her bed, Reynaud was so furious that he threw two glasses of water over her at dinner.

Among those fleeing Paris, there was utter disbelief that France would surrender. 'The most popular rumour – which nobody believed at ten o'clock in the morning – was that the French government was already trying to negotiate a separate peace with Hitler. I bought a drink for the first man who told me that one; such a flight of humorous imagination deserved a reward,' thought Rupert Downing. It was the same on the Riviera. 'Even when the government fled to Bordeaux, no one was seriously worried,' recorded Maugham. 'They were all still convinced that the French Army was invincible.'

Some found it difficult to accept what was happening. Raymond-Raoul Lambert had sent his wife and children away earlier to avoid the air raids on Paris and himself moved with the ministry he worked for to Candé. Arriving at his destination after a struggle, he found that the transport assigned to him had been used instead to move the wine cellar and personal baggage of the colonel in charge. 'Such a mentality on the part of a high-ranking officer explains a lot of things,' he wrote bitterly that night.

On 16 June Hélène de Portes meddled in government for the final time. There had been a last-ditch plan, strongly supported by Winston Churchill, to merge France and the UK into an emergency Franco-British Union. The paperwork needed to create this union was to be presented to the French Cabinet that evening as an alternative to requesting an armistice. De Portes entered the room where the document was being typed, read it, and then left to spread its contents among the Cabinet ministers. It cannot be said with certainty whether or not this advance knowledge increased the leaning towards defeatism already present in the Cabinet.

The eighty-four-year-old Marshal Pétain, idolised as the hero of Verdun, the First World War battle where he turned a near-hopeless situation into a successful defence of that town, had been brought into the government as Deputy Prime Minister on 18 May. His soldierly presence, it was thought, would evoke the true spirit of France, stiffen resolve, and reassure both those around him and the country in general. But, advised by the top French military authorities that 'in three weeks England will have her neck wrung like a chicken', he had quickly been convinced that England was a lost cause, and was insisting on an armistice. He carried the Cabinet with him: a union with Great Britain would be, according to Pétain, 'fusion with a corpse'. The British plan, proposed by Reynaud, collapsed, the government voted for an armistice and on 16 June Reynaud resigned.

The next day Reynaud and Hélène de Portes left Bordeaux, driving south-east, away from the advancing German armies, intending to stop at Reynaud's holiday home at Grès, Hérault, before fleeing to North Africa. Some of the Cabinet who disagreed with Pétain left for Casablanca or towns in Algeria, then a province of France, as Pétain broadcast France's surrender to the Germans.

In London Charles de Gaulle responded the same day with a call to loyal Frenchmen to resist: 'I tell you that nothing is lost for France. This war is not limited to the unfortunate territory of our country. This war is a world war. I invite all French officers and soldiers who are in Britain or who may find themselves there, with their arms or without, to get in touch with me. Whatever happens, the flame of French resistance must not die and will not die.'

So determined was Pétain to yield that he immediately stripped de Gaulle of all rank and sentenced him to death for treason. He also took his revenge on his predecessor: one of the first acts of the Pétain administration was to arrest Reynaud on his departure from hospital – on 28 June, with Reynaud at the wheel, his car had inexplicably left the road and hit a plane tree at La Peyrade, between Frontignan and Sète. De Portes was all but decapitated, while Reynaud* escaped with relatively minor head injuries.

That evening, Ivan Fiddler, an Englishman who with his wife Joyce lived in a small farmhouse near Grasse, growing olives, melons and tomatoes, made a final entry in the diary he kept of day-to-day work. Instead of the usual 'Prepared vegetables for market and watered', or 'Very hot day. Staked tomatoes', it read simply: 'Garden looks lovely but France seems finished.'

At the same time, the Italian Army was invading the Riviera. There was heavy fighting near the border with Italy as the Italians took what they believed was rightfully theirs – an initial zone of occupation, annexed officially to the Kingdom of Italy, of which the largest town was Menton. On the night of 3–4 June, 13,000 Mentonnais left the town in 200 motor vehicles, 130 lorries and various rail convoys, each one with around thirty kilos

---

* In 1942 Reynaud was handed over to the Germans and remained imprisoned first in Germany and then in Austria for the rest of the war.

of baggage, first to Antibes and Cannes and thence further down the coast, wherever room could be found for them, 'Le coeur pleine de larmes, les yeux secs,' as one of them put it. Although some of them had Italian parents or names, they felt themselves French and did not want to live under a fascist regime.

For the Italian plan was that this peaceful resort should become an Italian town. The houses of the departed Mentonnais were requisitioned for colonising Italians, signposts now marked the distance to Rome, Italian identity cards were issued and, from 24 June, the lira became the only legal currency, with all teaching in schools in Italian (some children, with determinedly French parents, crawled under the hastily erected barbed wire to attend a school in nearby Roquebrune). Menton was now Mentone, and Roquebrune the last easterly outpost of the French Riviera.

Monte Carlo did its best, as a neutral sovereign state, to prevent Italian troops entering it, but to no avail. In their olive-green uniforms, they tramped through the streets to a tumultuous welcome from the resident Italian population, the streets lined with cheering girls and young men waving the Italian flag. The Prince ordered immediate confiscation of all Italian flags because such demonstrations were forbidden under Monte Carlo state laws. But most of the soldiers seemed intent on seizing food stores and looking up relatives from the many French-Italian intermarriages rather than fighting. In any case the Germans, who wanted Monaco to remain a centre for German international banking and commerce (something they had been building towards since 1933), soon pushed them out.

Under Pétain's command, the first act of the new government was to agree an armistice with Germany on 22 June. It was signed in the same railway carriage in a clearing in the Compiègne forest in which the French had forced the Germans to sign the 1918 armistice, and was attended by Hitler, Göring, Ribbentrop and Hess.

This agreement divided France into two zones, with the Germans occupying the economically richest part – the north, north-east and Atlantic and Channel coastlines – while Vichy controlled most of southern France. The terms dictated that unoccupied France would be governed by officials willing to co-operate with Germany, France would pay the costs of German occupation, the French fleet would be disarmed and that France would surrender to Germany all anti-Nazi German refugees on French soil.

France was defeated after only six weeks of fighting. When she learnt this, Chanel went to her room and wept.

CHAPTER 9

><+>-O-<+><

June 1940

Unlike Chanel, Elsa Schiaparelli had kept her couture business open after France surrendered, her point of view being diametrically opposed to Chanel's. 'I wonder if people fully realised the importance as propaganda for France of the dressmaking business,' wrote Schiap. Other couture houses took the same line, the need to keep their workers employed, and thus bread in their families' mouths, warring with dislike of dealing with the conqueror.

Chanel also chose the war as a reason, or perhaps an excuse, to cut herself off from her brothers for good. Their lives had become quite separate when their father had abandoned them all, but for years she had supplied generous financial support; now she wrote to Lucien, living with his wife in the house she had bought for him ten years earlier, to tell him that he could no longer count on her. She gave the same news to Alphonse, even, according to one of her biographers, turning away his two daughters when they came to Paris to try and visit her.

It was a sudden and seemingly unexpected decision. Perhaps the closing of her couture house had made her feel that the time was right for a general drawing-in of horns, perhaps she had merely got tired of paying out for men with whom she no longer felt a sense of kinship. What it meant was that she was more psychologically alone than ever, depending for comfort and emotional support on the small circle of friends she saw constantly.

*

On the Riviera, the illusion that in time all would be well had finally been rent away. Pétain's broadcast that France would surrender was at first greeted with disbelief. When, as a child, Constance Newton walked to school that day she found that none of the teachers was there. She and her friends (*la bande*) decided to go to a café opposite where they knew there was a wireless. When they heard that Pétain had signed the armistice the immediate reaction was that this was a piece of German propaganda. 'All the boys thought it was a Boche station. "C'est pas possible! C'est pas possible!" they kept saying.' Finally the group decided to walk to the building that housed the *Éclaireur*,* in the main street in Nice. The offices had a big first-floor balcony to which placards giving the day's headlines would be attached. 'There was a great crowd,' remembered Constance. 'We could see people coming away crying. When you are twelve, it makes a great impression when you see people the age of your grandparents sobbing. The first placard I read said from midnight tonight all hostilities between France and Germany will cease. The last one read, "L'Angleterre continue la bataille".'

The shock, outrage and misery were intense. When Maugham went down to his gardener's cottage to tell him of this, the gardener and his wife wept bitterly. As they had both threatened his Italian servants, he sent them off into the hills to keep them safe from the Italian soldiery swarming around the nearby towns.

Soon there began the search for scapegoats. The corruption and inefficiency at the top did not suffice: with the retreat of the British Army at Dunkirk, many of the French blamed the British as much as the Germans for France's plight.

An atmosphere of mistrust was building: huge numbers of refugees had poured into the south, and those from Alsace and Flanders spoke a tongue that sounded suspiciously like German to the southern French. Strangers appeared overnight, some with money to flash about, others with drawn faces and filthy clothes.

The British Consul in Menton, Arthur Stanley Dean, moved a camp bed and ten dozen bottles of water into his office so that

---

* *L'Éclaireur de Nice* was a daily paper published from 1888 to 1944.

he could sleep by the telephone – his was one of the very few telephones on that coastline, and in mid-May he had been told that an evacuation was almost certain. Within a day or so of Pétain's broadcast on 17 June, all the British nationals, many of whom lived on the Riviera the year round, found themselves told to leave by Dean, who himself left Menton for Nice, first burning all the codes, cyphers and archives. In Nice he was given a small room in the consulate, which he found full of people and full of rumours. 'I was very much astonished when I got to Nice at the number of British subjects still in the district,' he wrote of those days in his diary.

One of those subjects, the Duke of Windsor, telephoned the British Consul in Nice, Major Dodds, for advice. Dodds told him that they should leave, and suggested they join his party to drive to the Spanish border. This time, it was advice the Windsors took. On 20 June the convoy set off: the Duke and Duchess, maid and chauffeur in one Buick, followed by the Duke's aide, Major Phillips, with the Windsor hand baggage in a second Buick, two friends of the Windsors with their maid in a third car, Dodds and Dean in a fourth and finally a light truck with the Windsors' heavier luggage. Although Spain, which did not want a flood of refugees, was only allowing a trickle of cars through, by midnight the party had reached Barcelona – negotiations had been quickly completed when the Duke gave the Spanish Consul his autograph.

Dodds and Dean returned at once to Nice, Dean passing on their return journey a *maison de repos* ('for the ladies of pleasure from Paris and elsewhere who needed a holiday or rest', noted Dean). As the Germans believed the Duke was sympathetic to the Nazi regime and could be manipulated as a puppet king in the event of their victory, there were efforts through fascist intermediaries to keep the Duke in Spain. But after rancorous exchanges with the authorities in England the Windsors finally left for England by ship from Lisbon on 1 August.

Since they had heard of the impending armistice, the consular officials had been making frantic efforts to charter vessels for the escape of the remaining English. Finally they had managed to commandeer two dilapidated coal tankers that had sailed from Cardiff and had just discharged their cargo at Port-de-Bouc near Marseilles. Here, on the first night, before they could return to England, the two colliers were ordered to make for Cannes. One was the twenty-two-year-old SS *Ashcrest*,* 5,652 tons, the other the smaller *Saltersgate*. Now the passengers needed to be gathered.

Dodds and Dean had their work cut out evacuating the remaining English. 'It seemed incredible after the official warnings spread over nearly a year and the events that had taken place that so many chose to sit tight,' wrote Dean. 'For some, advanced old age meant they didn't give a damn, others were too ill to travel.' A number, too, had let their passports expire. Those who remained should group themselves in Cannes, they were told, to await a ship or ships to take them home. Getting the word spread around required considerable effort. 'My father was telephoned at his office,' remembered Dennis Youdale, then twelve. 'When he came home for lunch he told us it would possibly be the last chance to get away. After supper he and my mother went out on foot – we didn't have a car – to tell as many people as possible to be ready to leave from Cannes the next morning.'

The small boy, scarcely able to take in that he would be leaving his home at any moment and worried by the absence of both of his parents, did not want to go to bed. 'I stood at the open window, leaning on the balcony rail of our flat and waited until with relief I saw my mother coming down our street.' His parents packed a suitcase and a local taxi driver volunteered to take them to Cannes, where his father and a friend collected pillows and blankets from the friend's house.

Some residents, like the Oppenheims, had already tried to flee by car. Oppy and his wife, with her lady's maid and their chauffeur, got to within fifty kilometres of St-Malo when they ran into a barricade: the Germans, they were told, were already shelling St-Malo. They tried for Bordeaux but that was even

* She was sunk by a U-boat in December 1940 after a broken rudder caused her to lose her convoy. All her thirty-eight crew were lost.

more guarded, and eventually they had to return to Cannes.

At the consulate all was pandemonium, with people besieging the harassed officials, distraught families, crying children, parents aware that they would be leaving homes, businesses and virtually all their possessions behind them, probably for ever. Oppy was told of the two ships coming in a day or so and put all their names down for a passage. They went to the Carlton, so as to be nearby, and found others also waiting. Many were still in evening dress, some were drunk, a few hysterical.

The instructions were that those who were travelling should be down at Cannes harbour by 10.00 a.m., with enough food for three days and only luggage that they could carry themselves. The Oppenheims, who believed in comfort, made up a superb luncheon basket that included bottles of champagne and a flask of brandy and took their luggage down to the quay, to be watched over by the maid and chauffeur and themselves returned to the Carlton, where they dined and spent the night.

On Sunday 23 June Maugham, who had earlier put his name down for a passage, walked to the harbour. Here he saw a crowd of over 3,000, all laden with luggage, jostling towards a customs desk where two officials were inspecting bags. Some of the queue were on stretchers, others were young and fit. Sometimes the wealthier would arrive in their large cars and because they had, perforce, to leave them behind, would toss the keys into the group of watching locals – one man even drove his Rolls into the water ('I'm damned if those Eyeties will get my car'). Others sold them at knockdown prices (the money received was later confiscated by customs officials as they boarded).

When the Oppenheims went down to the quay and their maid reported that conditions looked terrible and the ship was filthy, they decided against going on it and went back to their house. 'Very soon we sat in the shadow of our cypresses, watched the butterflies, listened to the nightingale and sniffed once more the delightfully mingled perfumes of our mountain pines and the roses with which my wife's balcony was smothered,' wrote Oppy. They ate their picnic dinner and drank their coffee on the flagged terrace, looking at the fireflies, which were everywhere.

It was quite true that the ships were not an enticing prospect. They were black with coal dust, there was no food, water or cabins, only two lavatories on each ship, and no convoy to protect them on the journey home. (They had already had a narrow escape: on the first night the port was bombed and the town was in total blackout, but the port authority had left on the cargo lights round the harbour, leaving the *Ashcrest* floodlit in their glare. Her captain took matters into his own hands and smashed every bulb in the lights until his ship, too, was hidden in darkness.)

With the frontiers barred, the roads clogged and petrol disappearing, these two old, filthy ships seemed the last chance to get away. Maugham, ever pragmatic, was determined to take the opportunity, and tried to persuade his friends the Furnesses to come with him. Planning to do so, they left their villa with Furness, now dying of cirrhosis of the liver, so frail he had to be carried into his Rolls by the butler and one of the footmen. Wilful as ever, once in the car he had a slug of brandy from his hip flask, spilt a drop or two on his shirt and demanded a freshly ironed shirt with matching tie to be brought by his valet before he would set off.

The Furnesses arrived at the Carlton to wait for the boat's departure. Here they saw the pier piled high with luggage and desperate people, terrified of being left behind, camping out beside their cases on the quayside. A German bomber flew over at one point and dropped some bombs on the harbour, upon which two women became so hysterical that they stripped their clothes off as they raced down the street.

At lunch, when Furness's hand shook so much that all the china on the table rattled, he exploded, shouting at Enid: 'That is not a ship, that is a f-ing cargo boat. If you are so worried about your safety you can go with your bloody friends and take that bloody little bitch [Enid's daughter Pat] with you but I am not going.' Enid, determined to care for her dying husband, stayed behind too with Pat.

But most of the English, desperate to get away, piled into both ships, filling them to the gunwales. Customs and passport examinations took most of the day and it was not until the late afternoon that the Youdales were finally embarked. Like them, most of the 1,500-odd passengers were not the glitterati but retired soldiers, civilians and their wives who had worked in India and wanted to remain in a warm climate so had made their homes on this strip of coast, people who ran shops or businesses, elderly governesses, chauffeurs, butlers, workmen. Nevertheless, their leaving gave the Germans a propaganda opportunity that they used immediately. 'The English will fight to the last Frenchman,' they broadcast. 'The English are retreating and leaving the French to face the music.'

For Elsie Gladman and her colleagues the question was whether to stay and look after their patients or close the hospital down and try and evacuate the sick. The answer was decided for them when the English hospital in Nice, on the Italian side of the River Var, shut so abruptly that the nurses did not even have time to strip the beds and hide the sheets, but descended on Sunny Bank with their patients on stretchers. The next step was for the hospital doctor to decide who would be fit to travel in the tough conditions of the coal boats. Those considered able to manage it were given a blanket, a pillow, food and a small case of clothing and taken to Cannes.

The refugees were brought on board by tender, with around 800 on *Ashcrest* and the rest, including Somerset Maugham, on *Saltersgate*. The men were told to go down into the tougher conditions of the hold, where piles of coal dust still lay about, and the women and children allowed to stay on deck. The two toilets, for which there was always a long queue, were reserved for the women; for the men there were latrine buckets behind a curtain at the stern, with orders to throw the contents overboard straight away. No lights were to be shown in any circumstances. Luckily, the sea was flat and calm.

They had to set off immediately to catch a passing convoy, with no time to take on food or water. Slices of bully beef and petit-beurre biscuits were handed round; Constance Newton, on board with her father, her aunt and her little sister, made tea for those nearby. There were no cups or mugs so people used anything from thermos lids to empty sardine cans.

'We had a real mix of expatriates,' wrote William Geoffrey Jameson, *Ashcrest*'s navigation officer. 'I gave up my room to two ladies and two orphans. They all slept in my three-quarter bed. They were lucky, for most had to sleep in the 'tween decks and on the hatches outside.' It was hot and sunny and Jameson, in shirt and trousers and wearing the 'good-luck' beret that had been his mother's, stood at the top of the gangway ladder to greet his passengers. One young woman seemed suspiciously full-bosomed, so Jameson bravely asked her if she was hiding anything, 'as they were only allowed one suitcase each'. She opened her coat and showed him her pet Sealyham terrier. Softened, he looked the other way. He was equally tolerant to a man who ordered, 'Take me to my cabin!' 'Yes, sir!' said Jameson, leading him to a spot on no. 4 hatch and politely refusing the offer of a two-franc tip.

Dennis and his family were billeted in the hold. 'It was literally ankle-deep in coal dust. I had just been discharged from hospital where I had been operated on for peritonitis. The wound was still open, to prevent infection, and Mother had to do my dressings on board, for which she was allowed into the captain's cabin. Everything else was so filthy that this was about the only clean part on my body.' Also travelling were the Duke of Windsor's bodyguard, a piper, much Windsor luggage and two grandsons of the last Sultan of Turkey and their entourage. They left Cannes in a French-escorted convoy but soon had to put in to Port-Vendres – on the French border with Spain – with engine trouble. This gave passengers the chance to go ashore and buy food and carboys of Vichy water, but the delay meant they set off for Gibraltar alone, without the protection of the convoy. There were two lifeboats, on which Jameson had put guards in case of panic, and enough rafts for all the passengers.

On one occasion Jameson came on watch at midnight and was fixing the position in the chart room, seventy-two kilometres south-east of Cape Nao, when the captain came to tell him a submarine had been spotted. 'It was moonlight and the submarine was quite visible,' wrote Jameson in his memoirs. 'He opened fire and so did we. Our gun trainer was our 16-year-old galley boy and the gun layer was a Royal Navy regular. The galley boy was weeping with frustration because he couldn't see the sub, but when I helped him to train on the target he saw it and shouted, "I can see the so and so, let the bastard have it!" We did, and after two rounds at point-blank range the submarine gave up and submerged. I set off a smoke float. He fired three torpedoes at us, but hadn't allowed for a ship in ballast, and they passed harmlessly underneath us.' Nevertheless, the passengers were kept on deck all night, with the women and children ready to be put into what lifeboats there were at short notice; and the captain began a zigzag course to Gibraltar, then hugged the Spanish coast.

Jameson, who had given up his own bathroom and lavatory, described how one elderly lady acted as doorkeeper, handing out one piece of toilet paper to each woman in the queue that stretched up the foredeck. 'After days of sleeping at the gun I wanted to use my own facilities and whispered this to her,' wrote Jameson. 'She held up her hand to stop the queue and in a ringing voice announced: "One moment please! while the officer uses his toilet." She then gave me a whole roll. Was my face red!'

Once arrived at Gibraltar, the *Ashcrest* remained there for two days, during which the crew of a Royal Navy battleship installed electric light in her hold, slung hammocks, improved the sanitary arrangements, provided more blankets and loaded her with meat, vegetables, bread and fruit.

The journey home took thirteen days. German submarines were operating off Portugal and in the Bay of Biscay, so to evade enemy contact the *Ashcrest* sailed due west for several hundred kilometres, then due north. A sing-song every evening, accompanied by bagpipes and a mouth organ, helped cheer the company, many of whom had left everything they owned in France.

The 200 in the *Saltersgate* (designed to accommodate a crew of thirty-eight) had a tougher time. It took twenty days from Marseilles to England and they were so short of water that when they landed Maugham said that four people had lost their minds. They had been rationed to one pint a day for drinking and washing purposes and much of the day was spent queuing in the sun for their sparse rations, a cube of bully beef and four biscuits.

Maugham noted that although everyone was filthy, most of the men managed to shave and the women kept their faces clean with cream. One woman brought her butler to escape with her and he waited on her and Maugham with the utmost ceremony. 'Never by a word, nor by a change of expression, did he give a hint that everything wasn't what you'd expect in a well-regulated household,' recalled Maugham.

An elderly woman died on board and the ship stopped for a minute – not out of respect for the dead but for fear the corpse would foul the propellers. Stopping was hazardous: there were known to be submarines in the area, and unlike the *Ashcrest* the *Saltersgate* had neither lifebelts nor rafts. Maugham, always self-sufficient, read Plato in the mornings, played patience in the afternoons and entertained the passengers with stories in the evenings. 'We had been in that ship for twenty days without ever taking our clothes off,' he wrote when they finally reached Liverpool on 8 July. 'Social distinctions went by the board. Our common dirt did that.'

The *Ashcrest* also arrived safely at Liverpool, with the Duke of Windsor's piper standing in the bow playing his bagpipes. 'The passengers must have been vetted in Gibraltar,' wrote Jameson, 'for there were a number of black marias [police vans] waiting at the quayside.'

Even after these seemingly last departures, some English still remained in France, unwilling to leave the country that had been their home for years. Among them were Ivan and Joyce Fiddler. As their grandson* later wrote, what forced their hand was when a French neighbour warned them that a grief-stricken farmer was roaming the area with a gun, looking to take revenge for his son killed in action near Dunkirk. They went to Cannes, joining other refugees; the mayor offered them a train to Marseilles, where they were told there 'might be a ship waiting'. If not, they could 'walk to the Spanish border', a further 320 kilometres away. Realising that to stay would almost certainly lead to internment, they opted for the train, reaching Marseilles

---

* Mike Fiddler, in the online magazine *Riviera Buzz*.

at night, during an air raid. Fortunately next day saw the arrival of another collier, the *Cydonia*, which had discharged its cargo at Oran.

Brian Howard also managed to acquire a passage on the *Cydonia*, of which he wrote: 'A thick, soft indelible blackness stamped itself on any part of one that touched anything. In fact the dirt and discomfort are so fantastic that it seems unreal and therefore bearable. As for accommodation, there appeared to be nothing but the hold or the deck.' Brian himself slept on deck in a hammock.

The last evening before reaching Gibraltar Howard, smoking a cigarette after dinner on the deck, heard a cry and saw a man and a woman running past him, pointing at the water. 'At first, I thought their child must have fallen overboard. Then I looked beyond them and saw a kind of lane in the sea, as if an invisible iron was smoothing out a long ribbon of water, coming towards us amidships. I realised that it was a torpedo, and I could see it was going to strike a few feet from where I was sitting. For a second or so, I became incapable of thought or action; I simply watched it come. It [seemed to] hit the vessel squarely and I waited for the explosion. Instead, there was a noise like a smoth-ered gong, the ribbon appeared on the other side of the ship and the torpedo made off in the direction of the coast, which it never reached.' An English admiral, on board with his wife, told Brian that the torpedo had missed because the Italian submarine commander had set it at the customary level for cargo ships. The gong-like noise was the empty hold reverberating as the torpedo passed under it.

Brian went to the poop and offered his binoculars to the seamen there, but was told to climb up and rake the sea with them himself. They turned and went as close to the coast as they dared, and when darkness fell they were more or less invisible against the black cliffs. Then came a new danger: the local fish-ermen came out, each boat with a bright flare at the bow. 'They were between us and the land and during most of the night, for minutes on end, we were silhouetted again and again.'

Bread, fruit and cigarettes were taken on board quickly on the coast of Algeria before the ship set course for Gibraltar, where children, the sick and people over seventy were taken off. Gibraltar was already so crammed with refugees that passengers were only allowed ashore in batches of fifty for two hours at a time to buy supplies.

Sybille Bedford had escaped from France via Italy and thence later to America, the goal of a number of intellectuals and artists. The painter Marc Chagall, for instance, was saved by having his name added to the list of prominent artists whose lives were at risk and whom the US should try to extricate. The American Vice-Consul in Marseilles and an American journalist, Varian Fry, ran a rescue operation to smuggle artists and intellectuals out of Vichy France to the US by providing them with forged visas. Chagall was one of between 2,000 and 4,000 anti-Nazi and Jewish refugees rescued by this operation. Salvador Dalí and his wife Gala were also able to escape because (on 29 June) they were issued visas by the Portuguese Consul in Bordeaux.

Some did not want to leave France. Léon Blum, the former Prime Minister, elegant, high-minded, literary, a lover of beautiful objects, literature and music, made no effort to flee his country, despite the extreme danger he was in as a Jew and a socialist leader. Instead, he escaped to southern France. Here he was among 'The Vichy 80', a minority of parliamentarians who voted against granting full powers to Marshal Pétain.

Others, like the Boissevains, were trapped. Laurens Boissevain, of Dutch Huguenot stock, and his wife Vera had been lent a villa at Beauvallon, just outside St-Tropez, as the pregnant Vera had not been very well and it was thought the Riviera climate would help her. They lived both in Amsterdam, where there was a family bank, and Paris. The family was known to be very anti-Nazi and Laurens, highly active politically, was telephoned by the Dutch Ambassador, who told him not to return to Holland. 'Your father and your two brothers are both in prison.' Laurens, feeling it would be safer to keep out of the way, left their seaside villa and took a small house in a mountain village. Just before they left St-Tropez, Vera and a friend, Hélène Vagliano, visited a clairvoyante. 'Your husband will be caught three times but will never be executed,' said the woman. To Hélène she said: 'You will be shot.' Both prophecies turned out to be true.

As for the internees, some 3,500 artists and intellectuals were now detained at the Camp de Milles, including writers such as William Herzog, Golo Mann and Lion Feuchtwanger, scientists such as the Nobel-Prize winner Otto Fritz Meyerhof, as well as musicians and painters such as Erich Itor Khan, Hans Bellmer, Max Ernst, Ferdinand Springer and Robert Liebknecht. More and more were piled in as the age limit was raised to sixty-five. Catsy, von Dincklage's half-Jewish wife, was interned at Gurs, a French concentration camp in the Basses-Pyrénées.

In the camp, a former brickyard, conditions were harsh. As Marcel Block recorded, they rose at 5.30, rushed across the courtyard to queue for one of the seven latrines and the cold tap. The day was spent working – building, breaking stones on the roads, peeling vegetables. The midday meal was taken at eleven, and there was another roll call at two. Supper was at five.

The nights were almost worse. As a former inmate described the building in which they were housed: 'It had several floors, in which the bricks had formerly been stacked on wooden shelves . . . so there was a huge amount of brick dust and masses of fleas. The floorboards fitted badly and there were gaps everywhere, through which anything you dropped fell onto the next floor. On my floor there was one toilet but no water. You could not get to other floors at night as finding one's way to the latrines past rows of sleeping men packed together in the pitch dark was almost impossible so people did their business wherever they happened to be, so that urine and faeces fell to the next floor. Many had dysentery.

'There was hardly any water and nothing with which to clean yourself. There was no paper to be had . . . daily newspapers were forbidden. We cleaned ourselves with grass, sand and empty cigarette packets thrown away by the guards. For the morning wash, there was only one tap, out in the open. Such were the conditions in a French internment camp even before the surrender and armistice, when they were our allies defending democratic values.'

As the German Army advanced in France, fear spread through the camp. 'Among us were forty-two persons on Hitler's death list and we were helpless,' remembered Feuchtwanger a few months later. 'We all prepared to commit suicide by taking Veronal* if the German Army should come. We insisted that the French commander release us or take us away. Finally Hitler's army was only sixty miles away. One writer, Walter Hasenclever, a playwright and poet, committed suicide. He died next day just as we were moved from Les Milles.'

An alternative favoured plan should the Germans arrive was to give all their remaining money to one of the guards, saying: 'I'm going to try and escape, mind you shoot straight.' As Arthur Koestler, another inhabitant, later wrote: 'The camp was run with that mixture of ignominy, corruption and laissez-faire so typical of the French administration.' Eventually the commander agreed to have them moved. As Feuchtwanger remembered: 'We were loaded on a fifty-car freight train, 2,600 of us, sixty of us to a wagon and we had to stand on our feet five days and five nights. The cars were locked and we could not get to the toilets. Four or five days before the armistice we reached Bayonne. There we learnt that the German Army would arrive in a few hours. The French commander told us to stay on the train and he would try to save us.' They wound up in Nîmes, still interned but less stringently.

The Riviera had become more crowded than at the height of the season. Before its service was interrupted by the war, the Blue Train was packed with refugees heading south, mainly Jewish; a Paris newspaper nicknamed the Côte d'Azur 'Le ghetto parfumé', and on the Riviera the antisemitic paper *Au Pilori* jeered that Cannes was becoming Kahn-sur-mer. The rich ones took apartments or lived in hotels, the poorer ones found shelter wherever they could, families sharing one room in a dilapidated hotel with

---

* An over-the-counter sleeping potion occasionally misused for suicide.

children sleeping in the bath, picking up whatever work they could find.

Most, however, had nothing to do but to kill time. Some went on excursions, others spent entire days playing bridge or, if rich enough, gambling and, of course, talking politics. The majority wandered around purposelessly. 'It was the lack of anything to do that weighed most heavily, draining any ounce of energy and resistance,' wrote Françoise Frenkel,* a fifty-year-old Jewish woman who had kept a bookshop in Berlin before fleeing to France three weeks before the outbreak of war.

Almost half of French Jews lived in Paris. Many of those whose families had been established there for generations and had French citizenship, or who had fought against the enemy in the First World War – who, in fact, thought of themselves as entirely French – believed that they would receive the same treatment as any other French citizen, and so stayed in the capital. Others, knowing that they had more to fear from German occupation than any other citizens, quickly joined the flight to the south. The parents of ten-year-old Gaby Schor took her to a small village in the south-west of France; here she had her first sight of the enemy. 'It was very upsetting for a little girl who was anyway frightened and who knew that the Germans were bad people. The farm that we [her family] were living in was requisitioned by German soldiers, who were very young and very happy to have conquered France with so few losses.

'I remember that they settled into the courtyard of the farm and like good Germans they were very clean. They began by washing themselves and singing as they did so, they were so happy. And all the small children of the village watched them from a distance, because even though they were the enemy these young soldiers interested them. We all watched what they did and got the impression it was nothing terrible. One young soldier saw a little girl – me – I looked sweet and he took me in his arms and wanted to put me on a horse and then I screamed terribly. I was very frightened and the German let me go without question.

---

* Author of the acclaimed *No Place to Lay One's Head* (1945).

It was the beginning of the war, the time when the Germans were immensely correct.'

By the time of the armistice on 22 June, approximately 1.8 million French soldiers were in captivity, a figure representing roughly 10 per cent of the total adult male population of France, a proportion on which everything from agriculture to businesses was reliant. One of the terms of the Compiègne armistice was that French prisoners would remain in German custody until the end of the war, which was thought to be imminent.

On 2 July 1940, the French government moved from Bordeaux to settle in Vichy. In the centre of France, Vichy had been chosen primarily because it was only a few hours away from Paris by road or rail and just fifty kilometres from the 2,500-kilometre demarcation line that separated occupied France, which held almost all France's industry, from unoccupied France, soon known as the 'no-no zone' (for *non-occupé*). Everyone believed the government's stay there would be only temporary. In July the Vichy politician Pierre Laval was so convinced of a speedy German victory that he told another minister that a mere six months 'was the time needed for Anglo-Saxon belligerence to be ended, either by the defeat of Great Britain or by a compromise peace'.

Vichy had been made popular in the 1860s, when Napoleon III had built a large villa there so that he could spend time with his mistress on the pretext of taking the sulphurous waters for which this spa town was famous. Since then, fashionable Paris had flocked to it, with around 140,000 people 'taking the waters' every year. It had a lake, a casino, a golf course, a park and over three hundred hotels. Now the wealthy clients were indignantly squeezed out and Pétain took over the town's best hotel, the Hôtel du Parc, with the Foreign Ministry next door in the Majestic and other ministries in nearby hotels.

Anti-British feeling intensified when the British bombarded the French fleet at Mers-el-Kébir on 3 July. In Britain Vichy France was regarded as a puppet state of the Nazis, and with invasion of his country, its back to the wall, seemingly imminent, Church-ill was desperate to keep French ships out of German hands. The admiral in charge was given a six-hour ultimatum of either handing over the French warships to the British or suffering attack. After the French refusal, and the expiry of the ultima-tum, the British attacked, and 1,279 French servicemen lost their lives.

Bitterness and talk of treachery spread; their allies had let them down, said many, or there must have been penetration at the highest levels. Arthur Dean, who had come to Marseilles to help filter residents and escaped prisoners back to Britain, asked the taxi driver taking him to the consulate what he thought of the news. Presuming that Dean was an American, the driver replied, 'Those English, we never loved them, and this is the last straw.'

As Dean noted, 'Many people turned against England and the English as being the cause of all their troubles.' At the same time, many in occupied France were very sympathetic to the British. 'Every single escaped soldier I spoke to without exception spoke of the extraordinary kindness and generosity of the French people, especially the country people, in helping them make their escape into the unoccupied zone,' recorded Dean, who was helping smuggle them out with false papers. Once in unoccupied France, though, they were hunted by French *gendarmes*, so that it was unwise to talk in the streets.

On 10 July 1940, the French Parliament voted to grant full powers to Marshal Pétain, who announced 'the État français' and shortly afterwards engaged in a policy of collaboration with the occupying Nazis. As the government appeared to steady, confidence among his fellow Frenchmen grew that this old and venerated soldier, who had fought so bravely for France in the First World War, would protect her people and keep her spirit alive.

As to the border, people-smuggling was rife. People who lived close to it were the channels through which the line could be crossed on foot, by bicycle, by rowing boat, in carts of manure and in barrels. These illegal crossings were initially carried out by a few isolated smugglers, before becoming increasingly organised by regular networks.

Occupied and unoccupied France were now to all intents and purposes separate countries.

Chanel had soon found that hiding in a quiet country village in the hills was not for her. On 14 July she sent a telegram to a Spanish sculptor friend of Picasso's, Apel.les Fenosa, who had also fled from Paris to escape the Germans, but to Toulouse. Her telegram read: 'Arriving Toulouse Monday afternoon. If not Monday, most probably Tuesday. Please find me somewhere to stay. Greetings Gabrielle Chanel.'

Fenosa, then a good-looking forty-one and filled with the energy that always appealed to Chanel, had had an adventurous life before winding up in Paris, where he met Picasso, who not only bought some of his sculptures but inspired him with a work ethic. 'I didn't begin to work in earnest until Picasso bought my first sculptures,' he said. 'Before that, I'd been a complete idler. I was incapable of doing anything: not only couldn't I lift a finger, I was also overcome by mental laziness and, worse still, I was a spendthrift. If it hadn't been for Picasso, I would never have done anything. Without Picasso, I'd be dead, because since I was a spendthrift, money burnt a hole in my pocket.' Picasso, equally fond of him, called him 'my son of an unknown mother'.

When Barcelona fell to Franco's troops in January 1939 Fenosa, who could not come to terms with the defeat of the Republic, had gone into hiding at his parents' house before finally leaving for Toulon, which he knew well. It was here that Chanel, who had met him the previous year through Cocteau, saw him again. Almost predictably, they soon embarked on an affair – Dalí, Fenosa's fellow Spaniard and also Chanel's lover, wailed that he had been 'left a widow'. For Chanel, this seemingly casual beginning of a new relationship while still in the throes of another was simply one aspect of her general attitude to love and sex. Like food and wine, they were part of life; as an independent being to her very core, she took them as they came along, and, while valuing the companionship of a man in her life and in her bed, did not feel that in any meaningful sense she 'belonged' to him.

Fenosa soon realised Chanel's quality. 'She was highly intelligent,' he said. 'She was good for me. She never left anything to chance.' What came between them was drugs – by now Chanel kept a syringe full of morphine ready by her bed. 'If you love someone who takes drugs,' said Fenosa, explaining what pulled them apart, 'either you take them yourself or the other person quits.' But Chanel, who had never voluntarily given up anything she wanted, was not going to do so now.

CHAPTER 10

>─◆─○─◆─<

The Vichy Government

As soon as Chanel realised that the Germans would not bomb Paris, she decided to return to the capital. She took with her a woman doctor and one of her aristocratic employees, the funny, lively Marie-Louise Bousquet. Marie-Louise, whose husband the playwright Jacques Bousquet had died the previous year, was at the heart of the fashion and literary worlds of Paris. The Bousquets were known for their regular Thursday salon, to which came luminaries like Colette, Jean Cocteau, Marcel Proust and Henri Cartier-Bresson, whom Marie-Louise introduced to the American public through the pages of *Harper's Bazaar*, to which she was attached.

The three women set off at the end of June in a small car in the sweltering heat of the Midi summer, taking with them forty-five litres of petrol (already almost impossible to get hold of, and acquired by Marie-Louise through one of her network of friends). First they had to go to Vichy, to obtain the requisite documentation to allow them to enter occupied France: to travel between occupied and unoccupied France, French citizens had to apply for a laissez-passer, given at the discretion of the Nazis.

Vichy, no longer the quiet spa where the better-off went to take the waters, had become a town stuffed with government officials and their hangers-on, from politicians to prostitutes, with the makeshift offices in the various hotels so crammed with files that many archives were kept in bathtubs. On almost every wall of these crowded buildings looked down the likeness of the tall, lean, heavily mustachioed Marshal Pétain, now the supreme arbiter of life in the 'no-no zone'.

The decision of the Vichy government, by 569 votes to 80, to give all government powers to Pétain on 10 July had ushered in a regime that was authoritarian and rigidly Catholic in its approach. Along with this extreme conservatism went a determination to restore economic power to French businesses and property owners.

In the eyes of the Vichy Cabinet this meant that 'foreigners' would have to be so downgraded that they lost all power and influence. By 'foreigners' or 'non-French' was meant not only those from abroad but also, and in particular, Jews – even those with a fierce loyalty towards 'la Patrie'. This persecution, which would soon become relentless, began within a week, with the denaturalisation law, which resulted in the withdrawal of citizenship from 15,000 people, of whom 40 per cent were Jews. By then, about 150,000 Jews had crossed the demarcation line to seek protection in the south. At the same time, Vichy began to adopt a severely moralistic attitude, implying that decadence and a hedonistic concentration on pleasure were largely responsible for France's defeat.

On the Riviera, the ripple effect of the puritanical new government ethic extended even to the beach: a decree was issued that made one-piece, longer bathing dresses compulsory for women at Nice. 'No more shorts, no more French women disguised as men,' snorted the Marseilles edition of *Paris-Soir*.

For the owners of some of the villas, there was a more unpleasant shock. Originally evacuated to Cannes, they had been allowed to return after the armistice with Germany had been signed, only to find that the exteriors of their houses had been defaced, and the houses themselves looted, with much of the furniture stolen, by both Italian and French troops, particularly at Roquebrune. There was no form of compensation. But as *La Croix*, the strongly pro-Pétain Catholic newspaper, had announced after France had signed its humiliating armistice: 'Victory does not always mean what the common man understands by this word . . . our victory began probably in June 1940.'

Both rich and poor now flooded to the Riviera. Some of the refugees were Frenchmen who had done deals with the Nazis and had been well paid for their services (in French francs printed by the Germans on the Bank of France printing presses). As the cost of food, and living generally, rose, so did a thriving black market. Many of the rich sold their fur coats and jewels to continue with their accustomed way of life – the casinos of Nice, Monte Carlo and Cannes, for instance, began what would be three of the best years they ever had.

For others, food had become scarce and rationing was severe. Oppy thought of shooting wild pigeons, rabbits or the partridges on one of his fields but all weapons had been taken by the *mairie* which, disliking the Oppenheims' extravagant way of life (a dislike perhaps exacerbated by Oppy's Jewish-sounding surname), would not release even his shotgun. Nor was there any petrol allowance for anyone except those on official business, although it was available on the black market, meaning that the journeys of Oppy's Wolseley to Cannes had become so hugely expensive that the Oppenheims took taxis on the rare occasions they went there.

It was even difficult communicating with friends, as the new rule was that all telephone conversations had to be conducted in French. By now everything from silk stockings to cigarettes was disappearing. Living at home was becoming so difficult that towards the end of the summer the Oppenheims moved down to the Hôtel Montfleuri. When Oppy, with his productive vegetable garden, was able to give a sack of potatoes to each of two friends they were greeted with rapture – neither had seen any for several months.

When Hitler came to Paris on 24 June, it was to an empty city. Stores were closed with shutters down, restaurants shut, the fabled nightlife dead and many of the inhabitants fled, some abroad and most to other parts of the country – many French Jews, especially those whose families had been French for generations, thought leaving their country would be unpatriotic.

Going to the unoccupied zone seemed the safest option, especially as Pétain had said in his broadcast speech: 'I have in mind the unhappy refugees who are crossing the country in a state of desperation. I offer them my compassion and my concern.' When news came that life in Paris had returned to something approaching normality – water, gas and electricity supplies had been reconnected, food shops had reopened – many refugees began to return. In the brief window of time before the borderline was finally demarcated, there were few barriers to crossing it. In some cases, refugees were helped by German troops; Hitler had issued orders that they should do everything to instil confidence in those they had conquered and that soldiers who committed 'punishable acts' against the civilian population would face severe penalties.

Jewish families too were among those who went back; with the conquering Germans spending money freely,* those with something to sell – furriers, jewellers, craftsmen, tailors – did well. Deceived into a false sense of well-being by the swirl of money and the correctness of German soldiers, many urged their families and friends to return.

The French had been stunned by the collapse of their army in only a few weeks. Coupled with the innate sense of superiority deeply embedded in the French soul, it dealt a psychological as well as a physical blow. To many, it seemed the end of France as a world power. The corollary to this was that a number soon decided that, since the German war machine was invincible, the only sensible thing to do was to collaborate, and thus become allies with the Nazis, who would soon unite Europe under their domination. But for others, centuries of hatred of the Germans and a tougher fighting spirit prevented them from accepting their defeat.

Chanel, longing to return to Paris, finally arrived there at the

---

* The Germans had lowered the exchange rate, devaluing the franc against the Reichsmark by almost 25 per cent. As their soldiers' pay was calculated in Reichsmarks but given to them in francs, they had plenty of money.

end of August. She found a city with swastikas hanging everywhere, rationing of food, tobacco, coal and clothing, troopers goose-stepping down the Champs-Élysées, the Ritz sandbagged and Nazi soldiers in their grey-green uniforms outside its doors saluting the high-ranking Germans who entered.

She and her party reached Paris after what must have been a nightmare journey. They had to bypass roadblocks set up by the Germans, sit for hours in traffic jams as others did the same thing, and find somewhere to stay in hotels that all seemed fully booked. When they finally found a lodging where hot baths were available, she remembered that her bathwater afterwards was 'so black!'.

Once back in the place de la Concorde, all they could see were German soldiers, with a swastika flying from the Ritz. German street signs, notices and flags were everywhere, as were posters announcing that 'The English and the Jews have brought you to this sorry pass', or showing German soldiers cuddling French children. For on Hitler's orders, his army was going out of its way to seem humane, setting up food depots and soup kitchens to feed people until the economy could be brought back to normal and behaving politely and cheerfully. The conquerors were doing their best to promote not only obedience but friendship with the conquered, to inspire them with the feeling: 'Well, they're not such bad fellows after all!' and show them that they, too, appreciated all France had to offer as the world's leading cultural centre, so that France would collaborate rather than resist,

None of this ersatz warmth stopped the looting of art for despatch to the Fatherland, especially that belonging to Jewish collectors who were, to put it mildly, in no position to complain, although some works were considered too decadent even to steal, including paintings by Picasso, Miró and Max Ernst, and were secretly burned.

With a co-operative France, the Germans knew they could rule with fewer soldiers, so that more were freed for the various theatres of war. They also took the chance of exploiting internal divisions, all with the aim of rendering France an easy-to-rule satellite country after the war, which both they and the French believed they would win – and sooner rather than later. Even the clocks had been brought forward an hour to correspond with German time; a curfew was in effect from 9 p.m. until 5 a.m. (soon to be extended to 11.00 p.m. and then midnight), and the French press and radio contained only German propaganda. The City of Light was now darkened.

Chanel was told that she must seek a permit from the commandant to enter the Ritz, now reserved for senior German officers, with Hermann Göring, the head of the Luftwaffe, in the Royal Suite, which occupied the whole of the first floor. Here he made the most of the luxuries to be found in Paris, ordering a solid gold marshal's baton studded with jewels from Cartier, according to the writer A.E. Hotchner, who later interviewed the waiter and groom assigned to his suite. They also told Hotchner about 'the lavish gowns trimmed in ermine and mink that he kept in the closet, the jewelled sandals, the emerald brooches and diamond earrings'. He wore make-up and doused himself with exotic perfumes, they said, and kept a crystal bowl filled with morphine tablets on a table beside an armchair, alongside another bowl which contained a mélange of precious gems – emeralds, black pearls, opals, garnets, rubies.

Chanel found that her own grand suite had been taken over; although she still had the two small rooms that she had earlier reserved, on the rue Cambon side of the hotel. As a long-time resident, she was able to pay for a small staircase from her two-room suite up to an attic bedroom. All she kept in this tiny room were a Russian icon, a present from Stravinsky, two statues on the mantelpiece and Boy Capel's thick black watch, given to her by his sister and still keeping perfect time.

Entry on the place Vendôme side was reserved exclusively for high-ranking Germans and strict discipline was enforced: everyone had to identify themselves to sentries as they arrived or left, arms were deposited near the entrance and correctness of manner was insisted upon. The Germans paid for their rooms, though at a greatly reduced rate – and the bills were forwarded to the French government.

Odd though it sounds, to Chanel the war was an interruption, rather than a life-or-death conflict in which one had to choose one side or the other. She lived within herself, doing as far as possible exactly what she wanted, untroubled by any thoughts that she might be viewed as a collaborationist by living in the Ritz among high-ranking Nazis.

Although Chanel had closed her couture house, her boutique remained open and here German soldiers bought the famous Chanel No. 5 for their girlfriends at home. About ten couturiers kept their businesses open and fashion shows were now attended by German wives as well as Frenchwomen.

Chanel's main preoccupation was finding a way to help her favourite nephew, André Palasse, who had been a soldier in the Maginot Line fortifications and was now in a German prisoner-of-war camp. She was worried about his delicate health – he developed tuberculosis in the camp – and was determined that he should be freed. When she stopped at Vichy to obtain the necessary laissez-passer, she had tried her best to help him, but without any luck. Back in Paris, and determined to continue her efforts, she quickly learnt that the best way would be through some powerful German official.

The Ritz was the perfect place to find one. Although the officers of the German High Command had their own half of the hotel, the dining room was open not only to them but also to those who lived on the 'neutral' side (the Ritz was Swiss-run, with Swiss staff replacing the French waiters who had disappeared). Many of its guests had, like Chanel, lived there for years and did not wish to search for a new home. In contrast to this semi-domesticity, the Ritz Bar was a swirling mélange of spies for both sides, agents and double agents, American journalists and other neutrals. The familiar Ritz luxury – even the air-raid shelters in the cellars had fur rugs and silk Hermès sleeping bags – was threaded through with plots, intrigues, the passing of surreptitious information and rumours of all kinds.

Along with her deep and abiding love for France, Chanel was vociferously antisemitic, although, like much about this extraordinary woman, even here there were contradictions. Several of her closest friends and best clients, such as Pierre and Hélène Lazareff, Maurice Sachs and a number of the Rothschilds were, of course, Jewish, and she 'adored' her Jewish doctor. In practice, she was indifferent to the fate of Jews and, indeed, that of her fellow Parisians. What mattered to her was survival, if possible in comfort, with the structure of her life depending on financial independence.

When she heard that the Wertheimer family had fled, through Spain and South America to the US, her reaction was to see it as an opportunity. Her hope was that now she might gain control of the business making her perfumes; she had long felt that the contract she had signed with them had given them too much and her too little. The struggle between them had been going on for years; now, with Jews forbidden to own businesses, she thought she saw her chance of achieving a victory by taking advantage of the stringent antisemitic laws.

However, she did not reckon on the ingenuity of the Wertheimers, who had arrived in New York at the beginning of August 1940 and set about building up a perfume business. They had sold their holdings in the parent company at a low cost to a (non-Jewish) plane designer and manufacturer, Félix Amiot, in whom they had complete confidence, and who was now therefore the legal owner of the shares in the Chanel perfume company, so Chanel was unable to oust them through the anti-Jewish laws. (Later, Amiot's firm came under the German aegis and was forced to produce Junkers bombers.) What the Wertheimers needed for real success, though, was Chanel No. 5 – but its secret formula had been left in France. In a covert operation, one of their employees entered unoccupied France with false papers through the Spanish border and got to Paris, where he stayed for four months, leaving after he had managed to get hold of the secret formula.

Chanel was left fuming, and with an unattractive stain on her reputation.

At the end of August, the Vichy government rescinded a decree that had banned antisemitism in the press and this, always

latent in French life, now bubbled to the surface, with espe-
cial virulence in the media. At first, with a French rather than
German imprimatur, it carried great weight; later, there was
a reaction. Even Léon Blum,* twice Prime Minister, who had
refused to leave France, was arrested that September by his
own countrymen, and imprisoned in Fort du Portalet in the
Pyrenees.

In the same month, the Vichy government set up *groupes de
travailleurs étrangers* (GTE), or Foreign Labour Units, supposedly as a method of counteracting unemployment. All able-bodied
foreigners who were 'superfluous to the national economy' were
conscripted into these. The first companies were composed of
Spanish Republican refugees, but later the GTE included units
made up of Germans, Austrians, Czechs, Poles, others from Central Europe and Jews, who were soon grouped into 'Palestinian'
units. They were dressed in drab, brownish-grey uniforms left
over from the First World War and set to work building roads,
breaking stones in quarries, cultivating vineyards, often being
hired out to contractors.

Unsurprisingly, the Jews who sought refuge in the south settled
in the more unobtrusive hotels and apartments, further from the
centre of the various Riviera resorts. For anyone with sufficient
money, and ration cards, living conditions were not yet severe.
'Food was strictly rationed but plentiful,' recorded Arthur Dean
at the consulate. The allowance was 400–500 grams of bread
and five grams of fat a day and 500 grams of sugar a month.
Game and horsemeat were not rationed, and restaurants were
able to produce good meals.

Then came a series of laws aimed at slowly turning Jews
into non-citizens of their country and thus unable to support
themselves. Vichy's definition of a Jew was anyone with three
Jewish grandparents, or who had two Jewish grandparents and
was married to a Jew. It was a policy based on race rather than

---

* As well as leading the Popular Front government in 1935–7, Blum was
Prime Minister for two months, March and April, in 1938.

religion so that, to the Vichy government, if a Jew converted to Catholicism, he was still a Jew.

The first statute, passed on 3 October 1940, banned Jews from the army, press, commercial and industrial activities and the civil service. It is important to stress that this, and the laws that later followed, were promulgated entirely by the Vichy government, without pressure from the Germans. As Pétain's chief of staff later confirmed: 'Germany was not the origin of the anti-Jewish legislation of Vichy. That legislation was spontaneous and autonomous.'

'Racism has become the law of the new state,' wrote Raymond-Raoul Lambert (who had been awarded the Légion d'honneur for his service in the First World War) in his diary for 19 October. 'What boundless disgrace! . . . I shall never leave this country for which I risked my life, but can my sons live here if they are not allowed to choose freely what career to follow? Because of my blood I am no longer allowed to write, I am no longer an officer in the army . . . if I were a secondary-school or university teacher, I should be dismissed . . . Yesterday evening I wept, like a man who is suddenly abandoned by the wife who has been the one love of his life, the one guiding light of his thinking, the one leader whom he has followed in his actions.'

By now many Jews who had been living in safety in Nice realised that danger was threatening. Among them was the Sungolowsky family. They had first fled to a small village near Vichy, where they were welcomed by the French services for looking after refugees, and housed. Then, after the Pétain government was established, with its immediate antisemitic laws, in August 1940 they left for Nice. Here Joseph Sungolowsky's father Aron, a rabbi, was able to take up his religious duties again. Now, with round-ups beginning, it was time to disappear. They hid in the storeroom of a furniture warehouse not far from their flat. They were just in time, as the first statute was followed by a law on 'Aliens of Jewish Race' that allowed for the immediate internment of foreign Jews. Under this law 40,000 Jews were interned in various camps in the unoccupied zone.

One was Lion Feuchtwanger, now in a camp near Nîmes. It

was better than the previous one, but if possible even more unhygienic, and full of mosquitoes, as his diary shows. 'In the evening I get strong diarrhoea. It is almost impossible to shit, because of the many mosquitoes, which immediately settle on the whole body, the inner thigh, the butt. I feel very miserable. I'm getting weaker. There comes a terrible night with the greatest fever, always dragging me to the latrine through the darkness and the uneven ground. Horrible with the many preparations etc.'

A blind eye was turned to prisoners who crawled under the barbed wire and went in to Nîmes for a good dinner in a restaurant and, perhaps, a night in a hotel before catching a taxi back to a spot near the camp and then crawling under the wire again – any further was treated as an attempt to escape, with invariable capture followed by penalties. Life for Feuchtwanger was easier than in the previous camp but, as he wrote: 'The thing to which one could not get accustomed . . . was the profound uncertainty, the apprehension about Clause Nineteen.* It was always there, this apprehension, the fatal question of whether the French were going to hand us over or not . . . Of all the things we chased after in the town of Nîmes, the thing still most coveted was a small quantity of prussic acid.'†

Eventually, Feuchtwanger succeeded in escaping thanks to a daring 'kidnap'. In the heat of that July, the prisoners had been given permission to bathe in the river five kilometres away, once a week in batches. On 21 July, after bathing with two or three hundred men under the eyes of only a few guards, eating, and sleeping in the sun, Feuchtwanger and two or three friends decided to start back for the camp. He was intercepted by a woman who handed him a letter, saying: 'I have news for you from your wife.' He opened it and read, in his wife Marta's handwriting:

---

* This required the French state to hand over to the German authorities any German national on French soil (the 'Surrender on Demand' clause) who could then face deportation and internment in a concentration camp. There were verbal assurances that this would apply mainly to those refugees who had 'fermented [sic] the war', a euphemism for Jews, and especially German Jews, who until then had enjoyed asylum in France.
† Hydrogen cyanide, a colourless poison smelling faintly of bitter almonds.

'Do what you're told ...' A car had drawn up at the side of the road and a young man whom Feuchtwanger knew got out and came towards him. 'Please don't ask questions,' he said in English, 'get in – and I'll tell you everything.' Once in the car he was told to put on a woman's light coat, a shawl and some dark glasses. 'I looked like an elderly English lady, and thus we drove on, very fast ...'

After hiding in the house of an American for several weeks Feuchtwanger and Marta, who had escaped from the Gurs women's camp, crossed the Pyrenees on foot, travelling in the midday heat as the paths were less carefully watched then, and entered Spain with forged papers. It took five days to cross Spain and reach Lisbon, where the American Consul gave them American visas in their real names and they left for the US.

Some inmates of camps came from Germany itself, where the Germans rounded up 6,500 Jews in various German cities, gave them a few minutes to pack two bags, then took them off to an assembly point and thence to the nearest railway station. From there they were sent off on forty-eight-hour journeys to the unoccupied South of France. Many arrived in freezing rain to a deserted empty barracks at Gurs that had housed Spanish refugees. They were interned as enemy aliens but kept there as Jews. Many were elderly and conditions were so appalling that around 12 per cent died during that first winter. Arthur Koestler, who was held at Le Vernet near the Spanish frontier, said conditions were worse than in the notorious German camp, Dachau.

A few days later, on 9 October, after intense propaganda, the Vichy government, through its Commission for Jewish Affairs, ordered the 'Aryanisation' of Jewish businesses. In practice, this simply meant the confiscation of Jewish property. Many Jewish shopkeepers hung their medals of honour, received for service in the French Army during the First World War, next to these signs, in an attempt to emphasise their loyalty to France. Others believed that Pétain, as a soldier himself, would not allow such treatment of old soldiers. They were mistaken. 'I still cannot believe all this is definite, final,' wrote Lambert on 6 November. 'Even in the free zone we are living under German rule.'

Other potential victims had gone into hiding. When betrayed by their Chinese cook, Laurens and Vera Boissevain had to leave the small mountain village to which they had fled when St-Tropez became too dangerous for them in the middle of the night. 'My father was very tall,' recalled their daughter Veracha, 'so hiding was difficult for him. My mother, who was much smaller, and dark, could pass for a Frenchwoman without difficulty. There was a big Resistance network of Dutch in the South of France and they lent escapees money.' Food was now more difficult and the family ate 'endless, endless semolina. Also my father had bought a huge stock of tins of sardines and honey.' Boissevain was caught and imprisoned three times. The third time, when he would undoubtedly have been executed, he was saved by his old friend the Italian Consul, who arranged that one night the gates of the prison were left unlocked so that Boissevain could slip out. 'I knew he would be safe,' said his wife later, 'because the clairvoyante I saw at the beginning of the war told me he would survive.'

In Paris, Chanel was still seeking ways to help her nephew André. He was not among those released that autumn (who were mainly workers needed in France, such as doctors, nurses, postmen and gendarmes and, later, fathers of four or more children). Soon she would meet the man who could help her with this and much else to make life under Nazi rule tolerable.

Spatz von Dincklage had fled to Switzerland when war was declared. Posing as a businessman, his job was to collect military intelligence: would the Swiss fight if Germany attacked France? But his mission failed: the efficient Swiss had realised he was a spy some years back, and all correspondence with his former wife Catsy and his new mistress, Hélène Desoffy, was monitored.

He had returned to Paris in the autumn, and was living in, or, as he called it, 'protecting' the apartment of a woman who had been his mistress until then but who had left France with her husband because she had Jewish ancestry. The city was just beginning to come to life again and nightclubs and the top restaurants reopened, with the difference that now their customers were German, or women escorted by Germans and successful black marketeers. The Germans treated the civilian population well – with the exception, of course, of the Jews.

Although strongly pro-British, Chanel had no moral scruples over seeking help from the conquerors and in Spatz von Dincklage she would soon find it. She was an opportunist with the great gift, not given to all such people, of spotting an opportunity when it was still well below the average person's horizon. Nor, of course, was she the only one of her friends to come to terms with the German authorities. Marie-Louise Bousquet, who had acquired a German lover, the passport to a warmer, better-fed way of life, continued her famous Thursday lunches, inviting 'nice' German officers as well as French socialites, and managing to produce excellent food thanks to her contacts with the black market.

Cocteau was another who kept on terms with the Germans; determined to continue the life he had led before the war, he frequented both intellectual society and the *collabo* salons, where his charm, wit and elegance ensured his continued welcome. (Picasso declared that 'Cocteau was born with a crease in his trousers'; Peggy Guggenheim, who gave him an exhibition in 1938, talked of his 'exquisite hands and tapering fingers'.) He was so successful in ignoring the very idea of war that when its outbreak was declared in 1939 his immediate response was merely to ask, 'How will I get my opium?' and his diary of the war years contains hardly a reference to the conflict.

Picasso himself, like Chanel, did not want either to collaborate or to resist. 'To be left in peace is all I ask,' he said. He was, in fact, disapproved of by both sides: by the French for his communist sympathies and by the Germans for his known anti-fascist views, so he was constantly harassed by the Gestapo. On one such visit, a Gestapo officer spotted a photograph of his painting *Guernica*, depicting the bombing of the city by the German Condor squadron during the Spanish Civil War. 'Did you do that?' asked the Gestapo officer. 'No,' replied Picasso. 'You did.' Picasso was, however, protected by his fame and by his desire for a quiet and unobtrusive life. 'There was nothing to do but work, struggle to find food, see one's friends quietly and look forward to the day of freedom,' was his attitude. (It was the same for Matisse: although German troops were quartered in his villa in Vence, he continued to paint.)

José-Maria Sert was another for whom the war might hardly have existed. Despite being violently anti-German, Sert managed things so that he was never short of food or drink or any of the luxuries of life, many of which arrived by the truckload from Spain. He had been appointed Spanish Ambassador to the Vatican and made full use of the freedom this gave him to buy what he wanted, visit Spain freely and return loaded with provisions. His apartment overlooking the place de la Concorde was beautifully and opulently decorated, its walls hung with tapestries, and with a magnificent tortoiseshell dining table on which he would set heavy gold plates, loaded with delicious food.

Misia, on the other hand, was horrified that Chanel would consider living in a hotel that housed Germans, 'those overgrown homosexual boy scouts', as she described them. 'She is beside herself about the anti-Jewish laws that turn Paris into a prison, the exact negation of what our city is. She is so right!' recorded Boulos Ristelhueber in his journal. Boulos, a pale, aesthetic young man who was always heavily made up, had become a great friend of Misia's and visited her almost every day – apart from conversation, they had music and drugs in common.

After the war, who had and who had not collaborated was to be a question that devastated the national psyche. Yet for the ordinary French citizen, a certain amount of collaboration was impossible to avoid. France, for so long the cultural hub of Europe, still considered itself so. When they invaded in 1940, the Germans not only allowed this belief to continue but seemingly encouraged it as a way of keeping many of the most opinion-forming French 'on side'. Besides, most people in the arts needed to work in order to earn the money to support themselves.

Almost everything required a licence from the conquerors; for those in the arts, refusing or not seeking such a licence meant that a book could not be published, a concert given or a play put on.

And so many of the German officers who attended these plays or concerts were so genuinely admiring of French culture that it was easy to take the path of least resistance, so that the other essential, the omission of any anti-German sentiment whatsoever, was not too difficult to follow. It helped, perhaps, that the new German Ambassador, thirty-seven-year-old Otto Abetz, had a French wife and in his twenties had started a Franco-German cultural group that brought together young French and German people from diverse backgrounds.

The winter of 1940–41 was freezing and the lot of ordinary Parisians terrible. Food no longer came into Paris, as most was siphoned off to go to Germany; only if you could afford the black market could you eat reasonably. Göring had decreed that the French people would have to survive on 1,200 calories a day, with the elderly allowed only 850.* With little or no fuel, the great dangers were hypothermia and starvation. The streets were empty at night save for the occasional Mercedes limousine bearing high-ranking Germans or their guests to Maxim's or other grand restaurants.

Yet the spirits of many Parisians were undaunted. Though they did not actively resist, they did their best to mock and irritate their conquerors in small ways. 'Vive le general de Gaulle' was typed in red letters on the blue-and-white five-franc notes; as nobody could afford to destroy these, this bit of defiance was passed from hand to hand.

There were barely audible jokes about nearby German soldiers, often referred to as 'les Fritz'. V-signs, slogans, threats or jokes were scribbled on walls. When London played the opening bars of Beethoven's Fifth Symphony, the tempo resembling the three dots and a dash of the letter 'V' in Morse code, before every wartime broadcast to Europe, this signal was rapped out everywhere – everyone knew that it stood for 'V for Victory' or 'victoire'. Girls dressed with their usual chic turned their heads away from any admiring Teutonic gaze. 'Why are you so gay

---

* The average man needs about 2,500 and the average woman about 2,000 a day to maintain normal body weight.

when you have lost the war?' the Germans would ask. 'Why,' Parisians retorted, 'when you have won the war are you so sad?'

Many of these remarks and rumours were recorded by Jean Galtier-Boissière, a Parisian editor and writer with an ironic, sceptical turn of mind who frequently wrote for the satirical weekly Le Canard enchaîné. In his journal of the years of occupation, he writes of his conviction, upheld against the views of most of his friends, that the Germans would eventually lose the war. 'Collaboration', he wrote, 'is: "Give me your watch and I will tell you the time."'

Chanel, deeply Francophile, deeply Anglophile, to whom the business world was familiar, was worried by a more abstruse consideration: the Germans, she believed, were infiltrating the entire French economy by buying into businesses – or forcing owners to sell at prices advantageous to them – so that one day it would be almost impossible to uproot or disentangle them. And what, then, would happen to the House of Chanel?

On the Riviera, life was difficult. The hotels were doing badly – one in six of unemployed Niçois was a former hotel worker. Most of the British had finally got away but some, like the Furnesses, still remained. Lord Furness, dying of cirrhosis of the liver, was looked after by a trained nurse, with a doctor in daily attendance; otherwise, life was hard in what had formerly been a luxurious villa. Electricity was often cut and shoes were so scarce that Pat, still growing, usually went barefoot. Enid boiled down candles to make an ersatz soap, bought three goats for milk and made cheese. But she still got thinner and thinner as she saved her food for her husband and daughter; even with the black market there was not much food around. (Carrier pigeons kept in the village of Gaude for the army had already made their last journey – into casseroles and stews.) Nor was it only food: the shortage of clothes was beginning to bite, as later described by Enid: 'Never in living history have women been so badly dressed ... Shoes have disappeared and almost everyone wears wooden sabots, which means that the women have lost a lot of their bearing and carriage. They can't walk, but shuffle along – it's back-breaking.

Where it is possible to buy dresses you must give two old dresses for a new one and pay an exorbitant price. French people are threadbare. There's no dancing. It's strictly forbidden and music is forgotten. Women are banned from wearing shorts or slacks and on the Riviera this prevents them from using up old wardrobes.'

It seemed a long time since the day less than a year earlier when Enid had lain back luxuriously in her bed in the London Clinic after a facelift, her cheetah sprawled across her, seriously disconcerting the famous Sir Archibald McIndoe when he came to see how his patient was getting on. When Lord Furness died on 5 October Enid, now dressing only in black, got still thinner. After her husband's death, she and Pat tended to prisoners from the detention camp near Èze.

Every night the Germans sent up a slow, noisy old aircraft which flew along the coast to check that all householders were observing the compulsory blackout – if a light showed, small bombs and hand grenades rained down.

The Hôtel de Paris walled up its best wines in a secret recess to hide them from soldiers on leave. Refugees unpicked the hems of their coats to retrieve the diamonds they had hidden in them, selling them at a loss to pay for food, now so much more expensive. One of the things that made food difficult was that the Germans had been down to the harbourmaster, got a list of all the fishermen, and taken their daily catch. All the fruit, butter and cheese was also in their hands.

The hotels, many larger ones now run on behalf of German or Italian interests, were gradually recouping. But as Oppy noted: 'Cannes was like a city of the dead, no man or woman smiled, light conversation seemed to have become a crime, the Casino was closed, dancing was forbidden, music was listened to in cold apathy.' (By the following spring, with the reopening of the casinos, business was better.)

Oppy and his wife were now desperate to leave, castigating themselves for having turned down passages on one of the two colliers. They found that the only route out was through the American Consulate in Nice, which as a neutral party had taken over the responsibilities of the British. First, there had to be exit permits, next, money for the trip, then seats booked on an aeroplane (from Lisbon), for which money had to be sent to Bristol, and they would only be allowed to take what they could carry. They also had to bring in and hand over their passports and *cartes d'identité*. It all meant a long wait as their passports first had to be sent to Vichy for inspection before anything could be done.

By now their house was very cold and there was no fuel left except for wood, so they went down to the Hôtel Montfleuri again, where they stayed for six weeks. They spent a quiet Christmas Day, and learnt that wolves had been seen around their property. This elderly couple, now both in their seventies, managed to leave from Cannes station in mid-January 1941 and, after a journey lasting several days standing in crammed trains, with a strip-search examination at the frontier, reached Barcelona. Oppy, who had used both his fame and his wealth to smooth his path, was told he had broken several regulations, but after paying a 'fine' of 500 francs all was well. When they eventually reached Lisbon, it was a case of securing passages on the Clipper, a long-range flying boat* that left daily. Five days later, at 3.00 a.m., they finally departed, in a howling gale. When they landed in England they were greeted by a horde of reporters.

Just before Christmas Raymond-Raoul Lambert wrote, agonised, as he watched those of his countrymen who had Jewish blood being persecuted: 'I am still completely French in my heart, in my mind, as a family man, in the love I had for my mother and that ties me now to my sons . . . in my culture, in my blood, in my inclination.'

A few days later, Misia Sert's friend Boulos Ristelhueber noted in his diary: 'Spent the evening at Misia's with Coco Chanel and François d'Harcourt. Coco goes into a long tirade against the

---

* A fixed-wing seaplane with a hull, allowing it to land on water and float. Flying boats were some of the largest aircraft of the first half of the twentieth century, and by using water instead of expensive land-based runways they became the staple form of transport for international airlines in between the wars.

Jews. The conversation is dangerous given Antoinette's origins [Antoinette d'Harcourt, wife of François, was a Rothschild]. Fortunately she was sidetracked when everyone agreed that Catherine d'Erlanger's emeralds are nothing but bits of green bottles . . . The anti-Jewish laws . . . turn Paris into a prison.'

CHAPTER 11

>◦<

'A German Victory is Certain'

Collaboration started early in Paris. 'Strange lunch at [the ballerina] Suzanne Lorcia's with Serge Lifar and Paul Morand,' wrote Boulos Ristelhueber in his diary for 12 January 1941 (Morand was a rich, upper-class cult French author, collaborationist and later a biographer of Chanel). 'She has a very expensive apartment and offers us enormous amounts of caviar, champagne, and truffles, with great sweetness but in the language of a concierge. Morand . . . tells us that Europe will definitely fall to the Germans. "As of now, the English are already beaten," he says, "and nothing will prevent Hitler's supremacy." I am terribly far from thinking as he does . . . Serge is still in a state of euphoria. He says to me: "The boss is expecting me in Munich soon." It's Hitler he's referring to.'

With the invasion of Britain seemingly imminent in the spring of 1941, Parisian jokes took a different turn. The simplest was the one that had a German soldier asking a Parisian: 'Can you tell me where there is a swimming pool?', to receive the reply: 'But of course. Between Dover and Calais.' Another story doing the rounds, recorded by Jean Galtier-Boissière, was of an elderly rabbi who supposedly knew through oral tradition the method used by the Jews to pass through the Red Sea. This venerable man was sent for by Hitler and promised the freeing of several thousand Jews if he would reveal the mystery. The rabbi replied that the leader of the Jews had a small magic wand that had the power to make a path through the waters. 'That wand! I must have it at any price!' cries the Führer. 'Where is it?' 'In the British Museum,' replies the rabbi.

Chanel's friends Misia and José-Maria Sert took opposite views. Misia scorned any idea of intimacy with the German overlords; Sert, a citizen of neutral Spain, quickly got on terms with the new masters of the French. This allowed someone with Sert's income and German contacts to live in luxury in occupied France. He sent for his gold leaf from Italy, his brushes from London, as though there were no war and no frontiers. He travelled in chauffeur-driven limousines, visiting countries where he had commissions; he ate and drank of the best, and he looked after Misia, whom he now saw daily, seeing that she wanted for nothing. 'Sert took all three of us [himself, Chanel and Misia] to dinner,' wrote Boulos on 5 January 1941. 'Pre-war atmosphere, Russian orchestra, red benches, a lot of caviar . . .'

For others it was very different. Henri Korb had joined the army for his two years of compulsory service when he was twenty-two ('I wanted to get rid of it early in my life'), in 1938. He was posted to Lebanon for thirteen months but there was no fighting there and his unit was sent back to France, to Marseilles, in December 1940. He had been hospitalised, so by the time he had left the army to study electrical engineering in Paris, the war had broken out. 'At my college in Paris, the Frenchmen there were all fed up with the war and with their rulers.' At the college, the fact that he was Jewish was not a problem. 'I never felt like the Jews in Poland who lowered their heads. I felt very equal to anybody else. My best friend in the army was not Jewish.

'Under the French Republic, before Vichy, there was no document, or occasion in life, where religion mattered, because it was considered a private matter. So Jewishness was not a problem. We didn't hide it but it wasn't a problem.'

Suddenly it became one. He was selected as one of thirty for a course, run by the Ministry of Unemployment, to become a topographer. 'Every day there was an hour for a discussion of the reasons for France's defeat. They kept hammering at us – it was the Jews, the freemasons, the communists.' Then came a four-page yellow form that had to be filled in with details of parents, grandparents, religion and so forth. 'This questionnaire was a shock – I considered myself a Frenchman. My Jewishness had never been an issue before.'

While Korb and his fellow students were doing the course, the laws blocking Jews from most professions were passed. 'So when we graduated everyone except the Jews got a job.' But he was now a qualified technician, and the Germans were demanding technicians and designers to go to Germany. Picked as one of these, and knowing what was likely to happen to him, he promptly resigned, which meant he was labelled as *résistant*. Paris was no longer safe.

Although the anti-Jewish laws were even more stringent in Vichy France than in Paris, Korb decided to go to Nice because he had heard there were many Jews there, with a correspondingly greater chance of safety. In Nice, he knew, he would start with several advantages: he did not look like a Jew, nor did his identity card state that he was Jewish, and the only indicator that he was – the lengthy form he had filled in – would, he knew, disappear for a long time as it wound its way through the slow and tortuous byways of French bureaucracy.

There were several ways of getting into unoccupied France. The official laissez-passer, issued by the Germans or the Vichy government, was the simplest – if the most difficult to secure. In some cases, farmers whose farms were split by the border had keys to gates through the barbed wire strung along it. There were also passes, stamped with the German eagle (derisively known as 'the cuckoo') for those who crossed back and forth in buses from Vichy France to their forced labour in the occupied zone, and occasionally an extra worker or two with forged papers could be smuggled in. And there was a network of professional *passeurs*, frequently poachers, who knew the woods by night, who helped people cross while evading the guards. There were about 2,500 of these guards, roughly two for every kilometre; but as they worked in groups of four it meant that most of the line was out of their sight most of the time.

Survival was difficult. Korb had some English wool for a suit

Top The Promenade des Anglais in its thirties heyday. It originated in 1820, when a particularly harsh winter further north brought an influx of beggars to Nice and some of the resident English gave them salaried work constructing a beachside walkway. During the war (*above*), the Germans smothered it with barbed wire and mined the beach beyond.

US soldiers queueing outside Chanel's rue de Cambon store in Paris for her No.5 perfume. If they had no words of French, they simply held up five fingers.

Above The SS *Ashcrest*, one of the two old collier ships that evacuated the British from the Riviera

Right Dennis Youdale and his family in Nice in 1934. His father, shown here, was manager for Thomas Cook in Nice, an important job that required considerable meeting and greeting. A number of English settled along the coast, often because of the climate and low cost of living.

Chanel with Hans Günther von Dincklage, known to all as 'Spatz', her last lover. He left for Germany just before the Liberation, but later re-joined her in Switzerland, where this photo was taken.

Jaques and Ilona Wochiler on the beach in the 1940s, and Jaques' *carte de combattant* from the FFI.

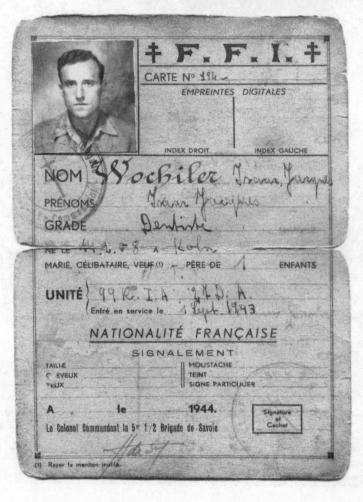

On 27 November 1942, after the Germans had invaded Vichy France – officially neutral – the French scuttled their fleet of Toulon, destroying 77 warships, while several submarines escaped to French North Africa.

Liberation: the residents of Cannes celebrating in the streets following the entry of Allied troops into the city, 29 August 1944

that he sold on the black market, the money from which kept him going for a bit. Being seen to be not working was a hazard, as there were police on the streets who might ask for his papers at any time and find that he did not have the vital *carte de travail* given to all the employed. 'Anyone who didn't have one was suspect. I was desperate. I heard of a town planner in Antibes and went to see him.'

Here, fortunately, he was only asked about his qualifications, and in a country where much of the infrastructure had been damaged by war, a trained topographer was a godsend. Korb was given a *carte*, the necessary equipment and sent to Nîmes. 'When I arrived there it was green with German uniforms. But it wasn't written anywhere that I was Jewish, so I felt safer in the open. I surveyed village after village, for 200 kilometres, for two years.'

He then went into the mountains with his brother and joined the first group of Resistance operatives he met, living in the hills and sabotaging where they could. They were known locally as *maquis*, from the word for the region's dense scrubland dotted with small trees. Arriving in two Citroëns and threatening its guard with a Sten gun, they raided an arms factory in St-Étienne for guns. Sometimes they would put plastic explosive on railway lines when they knew a German convoy was coming. 'That left a bad taste,' said Korb, who disliked the idea of killing people.

During the occupation of Monaco and Nice by the Italian troops, the Jews felt themselves safe in most of the region. Soon others heard of this and there followed an influx of refugees. Some had arrived out of principle: they could not bear to live under the German yoke. Many of France's leading authors, among them André Gide, André Malraux and Henry de Montherlant, had gone to the Riviera to distance themselves from any possibility of collaboration in Paris. Some house-sat the villas left by the hurried departure of their British owners, others stayed in small hotels or pensions.

The Vichy government was losing little time in tightening its grip. All anti-Vichy expression was suppressed – people were warned not to boo newsreels giving details of German victories in cinemas, and even coughing, if it was considered to be exaggerated and subversive, could result in an arrest.

At the same time, there were strenuous efforts to promote a cult of Pétain. There was an *Art maréchal* office, which encouraged the production of any object featuring an image of the leader, from pens, ashtrays, paperweights, mugs and calendars to porcelain busts. He appeared on stamps and there were even tapestries in his honour. A new national anthem was composed: 'Maréchal, nous voilà!'

Marshal, here we are!
Behind you,
The saviour of France.
We swear this,
We, your boys,
To serve you and follow your footsteps.
The nation will be reborn
Marshal, Marshal, here we are!

And so on for a number of verses.

The new anthem was regularly sung in schools. Gaby Fisher, a little Jewish girl who had been sent to stay with her older sister, married to a Frenchman, and was attending the village school, remembered the morning it became compulsory. 'We had a very good, brave teacher. One day she came in and said: "Children there's nothing I can do about it, I've had my instructions. You are all to learn to sing 'Marshal, here we are!'" To console us, the teacher gave a ten [marks out of ten] to everybody who learnt it.'

When Pétain visited various towns in Vichy France, children would be assembled in the main square to wave flags, sing the new anthem and generally show their love for the Marshal. A subtle method of cocking a snook at the regime was for one or two, or sometimes all of a group, to sing deliberately off-key. Another trick was for musicians in a restaurant or café to insert a few bars of the now-forbidden 'Marseillaise' between innocuous tunes.

More widespread was what the writer and literary critic Jean Guéhenno described as 'the battle of the Vs'. The Germans had tried to counter Britain's 'V for Victory' propaganda campaign by splashing enormous 'V's, which they said stood for 'Victoria', on white banners. Guéhenno himself refused to publish anything during the Nazi occupation of France, believing this would be collaboration. Instead, he kept a secret diary of events.* 'The German Vs are not very numerous but colossal; they are spread out over public monuments, on flags, on posters,' he wrote in this subversive chronicle. 'The Vs of the Resistance are tiny but innumerable: Metro tickets folded into a V, matches broken into a V . . .'

Wearing the three forbidden colours of the Republic, red, white and blue, was another sign of defiance: a woman might wear a red check dress and blue scarf or a red jacket, blue handbag and white gloves with impunity, as no one could 'prove' that her attire was anti-Nazi – but everyone knew what she was signalling. For men it was more difficult: perhaps a white shirt and a couple of coloured handkerchiefs sticking out of a pocket, or a patterned matchbox. But these small symbols caught the eye of those of like mind and at the very least gave a sense of fellowship (in her last collection, just before the war, Chanel had added touches of red, white and blue).

Pétain himself, like many others, believed in the certainty of a German victory, and that therefore the only way to preserve what he called 'the soul of France' was to do as much as possible to appeal to the Germans as his view as a conservative, Catholic, French traditionalist would allow. As this meant 'cleansing' France of alien influences, in particular Jewish ones, he was soon, without any prompting from the Nazis, introducing measures almost identical to the Nuremberg Laws, in the hope that this would result in favourable treatment in the future.

Thus, in the second *statut des Juifs*, published on 14 June, Jews were excluded from the few public offices still open to them and from virtually all private careers. This vicious ruling also provided

---

* Published in France in 1947.

for complementary legislation that was to deprive Jews of their occupations en masse and set a quota of 3 per cent for Jewish students in higher education. Veterans of the war did slightly better, as did eminent Jews of the oldest families. As well as its immediate effect of rendering sheer survival, let alone anything approaching a normal life, almost impossible, the psychological impact was immense. 'I no longer know whether to wish to live a long life or to regret not having fallen in the front . . . in the days when all Frenchmen were brothers,' wrote Lambert the day after the *statut* had been published. 'As to the future, I cannot think of it without anguish.'

One of the few who succeeded for a while in earning a living was Isaac Wochiler. Aged twenty-six, he had left Germany for France in 1934, getting a professional forger to change his name from Isaac to Jaques [*sic*; the forger left out the 'c'] on his papers. When the war began he was called up, and became a machine gunner fighting on the Belgian front until it was overrun; then – in his section – it was every man for himself. 'The officers ran, so the men did too.' Once away from the front line, he jettisoned his uniform and put on peasant clothes, making his way across country and hoping to meet his fiancée, twenty-seven-year-old Ilona.

She, meanwhile, had left Paris in the exodus, being given a lift in the car of the doctor she worked for. She got out at Toulon and spent her time asking any soldier she came across if they knew the whereabouts of the 23rd Regiment – the one in which Jaques was serving – and going from *mairie* to *mairie* to see if his name was on any of the lists pinned up in them (these lists were the means by which many people found families from whom they had been separated). Eventually they were reunited and, after first going to Toulouse, where conditions seemed too dangerous, settled in Marseilles and married there in October 1940.

Marseilles was a magnet for Jewish refugees seeking to distance themselves as far as possible from the forces of Nazi Germany or, if possible, to leave France for another country. A favourite route was to travel first to Casablanca or Algiers, thence to Lisbon where, with luck, an onward passage to Britain or America could be found. As an important seaport, its population included elements from all around the Mediterranean basin. In its narrow streets near the Old Port were rival gangs, prostitutes, smugglers, small traders and fishermen and their families. For any Jews, it was at first possible to live reasonably openly there, although the established French-Jewish, like the Marseillais, resented the arrival of foreign Jews, who came in large numbers.

Jaques, who had trained as a dental technician (and therefore did not have to set himself up as a practising dentist, a profession now forbidden to Jews by Vichy), was able to find work. He and Ilona lived first in a hotel, but as this got too dangerous – hotels were always the first targets for round-ups – they moved to a small apartment. As the round-ups started, fellow refugees would arrive to sleep on the floor or in the bath.

In September began the release of most of the 300,000 prisoners of war who had been interned upon the suspension of hostilities in June 1940. Of these, about one-third were peasants, so France's agriculture suffered in those unmechanised days, contributing to food shortages. André Palasse was not among the released.

For Chanel this was a bitter blow. Although she had not seen much of André, he was the nearest thing she had to a child of her own. Financially, she had more than done her duty by him, providing him with an excellent education and a beautiful château as home for him and his family. She had also become godmother to his daughter. Now, determined to secure her nephew's release, she realised the only way was through the conquerors. There were plenty of them around her: as well as Göring, Ribbentrop and Speer, other ministers and various high-ranking German generals lived at this most 'supreme and exceptional' of hotels (as orders from Berlin put it), with frequent visits from others of the Nazi élite.

She decided to approach a man she had often seen in the entourage of von Ribbentrop, perhaps encouraged by the fact that her chosen target not only spoke perfect French but also wore civilian clothes. This was Hans Günther von Dincklage. They dined together and his French, he explained, came from his time at the German Embassy in Paris in the rue de Lille. He asked her to call him Spatz, as his friends did – but alas, he could not help her over the release of her nephew. However, he had a friend he had known since boyhood who might be able to help, Captain Momm.

Theodor Momm, a cavalry captain, came from a family that had been in textiles for five generations and had grown up in Belgium. He was in charge of regenerating the French textile industry, with the aim of using its resources to strengthen the German war effort. Apart from his loyalty to his friend, it must have been flattering for anyone even peripherally in the fashion business to be approached by the great Chanel. He agreed to help her. First, he had a small textile mill reopened in the suburb of St-Quentin. By telling his superiors that its proprietor was the famous Chanel, he managed also to persuade them that her nephew would be the perfect person to run it.

During their discussions over André Palasse, Chanel and von Dincklage grew closer. Soon an affair between them was in full, though not open, swing. Where others dined at Maxim's, Chanel and Spatz met largely in Chanel's rooms at the Ritz or her apartment in the rue Cambon.

It is easy to understand what drew them together. Chanel, always used to having a man around ('I have a horror of loneliness and I live in total solitude,' she had said), saw in this tall, handsome, exquisitely mannered and charming man of the world a pleasing companion of the sort she had become used to. It was several years since the death of Iribe, the last man she had loved, and she had closed her couture house, so she could no longer fill this emotional vacuum with work. 'There is nothing worse than solitude,' she said later. 'Solitude can help a man realise himself but it destroys a woman.'

She was fifty-eight and still glamorous, yet to attract a lover thirteen years younger than herself was undoubtedly a coup and a reassuring boost to her image of herself – it was, after all, Chanel who had said: 'A woman has the age she deserves.' (When chided about the age gap between herself and Spatz she is said to have replied: 'When a woman my age is lucky enough to acquire a lover, she doesn't ask to look at his passport.') Besides, as she never tired of mentioning later, he was half English, from a world with which she was familiar from her years with Bendor. It is even possible that, as a polo player, von Dincklage reminded her of her great love, Boy Capel.

Her fifteen-year-old great-niece Gabrielle, for whom she was able to acquire a laissez-passer to allow her to visit, remembered Spatz as '*sympa*, attractive, intelligent, well dressed, and congenial – smiled a lot and spoke fluent French and English ... a handsome, well-bred man who became a friend. He was the pair of shoulders she needed to lean on and a man willing to help Chanel get André home.'

If nothing else, it must have put paid to the rumour, which began when Chanel installed him at the Ritz, that she was going to marry Cocteau. She had supported him, paying the rent of apartments, for years and they were intimate friends – but he was openly homosexual. Both of them laughed when they read of this proposed match in the newspapers. Only Cocteau's mother believed it, saying to him: 'Why don't you admit it to me, little one, [it must be true] because it's in the papers.'

As for von Dincklage, Chanel must have been a trophy. One of the most famous women in France, supremely elegant and very rich, who could provide all the appurtenances of good living that meant so much to him, from exquisite food and wine in comfortable and stylish surroundings to cultured and interesting friends. It was a life virtually untouched by wartime privations. Judging by his past, he was an opportunist rather than a convinced Nazi.

The life they led together, though luxurious, was discreet. If alone with each other, they often spoke English. They were rarely seen in the fashionable restaurants frequented by German officers and the Frenchwomen they entertained and they saw only a small circle of friends, otherwise dining together quietly on their own. They attended Marie-Louise Bousquet's luncheons, where 'nice', Francophile Germans mingled with Marie-Louise's upper-crust friends. They dined often with Sert and Misia, and about twice a week Cocteau and his lover would have dinner with Chanel in the rue Cambon apartment, often with Serge Lifar, after which she and Spatz would walk across to the Ritz.

For the rest of Paris, however, life was harsh. The winter of 1941–2 was one of the coldest of the century, with temperatures well below normal from the beginning of January until the end of March. There was almost no fuel, coal and gas being scarce and electricity cuts frequent. In the smart hairdressers, current for the dryer hoods was generated by staff pedalling on dynamos. With no petrol, everyone travelled by metro or bicycle. 'For people with time on their hands, the best solution is to stay in bed wearing a pair of fur gloves, a polo-necked sweater, even the kind of nightcap the smart designers are already proposing,' said *L'Illustration*.

Despite the suffering, much of the capital's nightlife still throve. The Wehrmacht so enjoyed seeing half-naked women that often 80 per cent of the audience at the Folies Bergère was German (with whom the can-can was so popular that Offenbach was about the only Jewish composer whose music was allowed to be played).

At smaller, less well-known nightspots, the Parisian spirit of mockery was not entirely quelled, and in the main safely away from German ears – few German soldiers could understand the rapid-fire French peppered with slang and the 'in' phrases in which it was couched. One song used the double meanings of the word 'occupation' in French. Jean Galtier-Boissière tells the story of visiting a small cabaret well away from the beaten track of Nazi nightlife; here the comedian-compère entered with his arm held high in a Nazi salute. Then, his arm still held high, he faced the audience saying: 'Jusqu'à la! Jusqu'à la! Nous sommes dans la merde jusqu'à la!'*

The brothels too had reopened, the most famous – and expensive – being Le One Two Two (at 122 rue de Provence) and the Sphinx. These upmarket establishments held an attraction well beyond their primary function: here German officers, French collaborators, artists, agents and spies could meet on unofficial terms, often merely for drinks or gossip. It was not long before

---

* Up to there! Up to there! We're in the shit up to there!

the girls realised the possibilities and would sometimes ask for a laissez-passer across the demarcation line instead of the customary 'present'.

Rationing had become a matter of privation after privation. Meat was almost never seen and even wine was in short supply, as most of it was sent to Germany. Women ground chicory and barley to make 'coffee', or visited any country relations living not too far away to hope for some eggs or vegetables; pets such as rabbits or guinea pigs went into the stewpan – even potatoes were only available via a ration card. Counterfeit food tickets could be acquired but had to be used with care as they were of course illegal.

'We have ration tickets but we can't buy anything with them any more,' wrote Jean Guéhenno in his diary for January 1941. 'The shops are empty. At home, we've lived exclusively on parcels sent by friends and cousins in Brittany for the past two weeks.' Later in the year, when he rose early to catch the first 5.30 metro in order to be at the front of the queue for a pass to the unoccupied zone, he noticed fishermen in the train. 'They were getting on at every station, with their fishing rods, their landing nets, boxes of worms, folding chairs, and so many hopes. They were all rushing to take their place on the banks of the Seine, and got off at Châtelet.'

On the Riviera, life was more normal. Perhaps because the future now seemed less certain, those who had money often splashed it about. That winter, betting at Nice's racetrack beside the Var broke every record, while Vichy's ban on gambling and dancing meant that those who could afford it flocked to Monaco (still officially neutral).

Listening to foreign broadcasts was punishable by a fine or imprisonment, so thoroughly did Vichy wish to imbue the south with the German point of view, although many patriotic Frenchmen listened in secret to the daily 'Ici, Londres; les Français parlent aux Français!' broadcast from London. Communication of any kind was difficult, especially for families split by the demarcation line. Only prescribed postcards were allowed to be sent from Paris, printed with text that could be left or crossed out ('in good health', 'tired', 'wounded', 'slightly or seriously ill', 'need provisions', 'passed the examination' etc.) but not added to. It was reminiscent, thought Galtier-Boissière, of the classic story of a French labourer sent to work in Germany, who promised to write his impressions; if good, they would be written in black ink, if bad, in red. The letter he sent back in black ink read: 'We are very well. The work isn't hard. The country is good. The people are charming. There is plenty of food. There is only one thing that's impossible to find. Red ink.'

For the many, though, hunger was the preoccupation, so thoroughly did the Germans drain the region of anything that could be bought in a shop. As was the case everywhere in France, it was a cold winter. People queued from early in the morning to buy swedes as even vegetables were in short supply. If a regiment with pack or draught horses happened to pass through or camp in a village for the night, next morning there was a rush and a struggle to collect the manure, a boon for the vegetable gardens.

As a child of five David Pryce-Jones, living with his nanny Jessie and some of his family in Cannes, would bicycle with Jessie into the countryside foraging for food. One memory was being sent through a hole in the wire netting surrounding someone's garden to pull up some vegetables when there was no one about; 'and on another occasion we were reduced to sucking fish bones', while his aunts bicycled up to twenty-five kilometres into the countryside to try and find eggs – the manufacture of bicycles, incidentally, was one of the few growth industries in the 'no-no zone'.

Enid Furness was now installed in the Villa Fiorentina, bought by her late husband, who had also purchased the neighbouring three or four houses to prevent their acquisition by any actual or potential lover of Enid's. With her husband no longer there to care for and now always dressed in black, she had turned her attention to helping Allied prisoners escape: all who had been left in Vichy France once the armistice had been signed had had to give themselves up.

She had been visiting the large detention camp near Èze for

some time, and those who managed to escape knew that they could stay a night or two at Villa Fiorentina before being handed on to another safe house or a courier. Once, she asked her daughter Pat to take such a prisoner into Nice; the two set off on bicycles, with the escapee dressed in one of the gardener's clothes and wearing a beret. Before reaching the back-street address they had been given, there were tense moments when they had to pass patrols on the road, but fortunately were not stopped. It was equally nerve-racking when the Vichy police arrived to search the house during another prisoner's stay; this time, he escaped by being disguised as one of the maids.

Finally, Enid decided that they should try and reach England. When they left she spent a long time pinning up Pat's long hair into curls on the top of her head. In each curl she hid a banknote. Through charm, cash and determination they got to Spain and, eventually, Portugal, after a nightmare train journey. A happy contrast was a fortnight's luxury in Portugal before they were able to get seats on the regular flying-boat service from Lisbon.

Among the Jewish population, money and the prestige of a well-known name undoubtedly helped keep individuals both safe and able to lead as normal a life as was then possible. One such case was that of Baron Elie Rothschild and his childhood sweetheart, Liliane Fould-Springer, both scions of well-known Jewish families, who had become engaged before the outbreak of war.

Elie and his brother, Alain, were serving at the front when Germany overran France in 1940; both were captured and ended up in Colditz Castle, the Germans' most secure prison, after separate escape attempts. From Colditz, Elie wrote to Liliane proposing that they marry by proxy (or *mariage par procuration*, as it was known in France). Her parents were opposed to the idea, pointing out that it was not helpful to bear the name Rothschild with the Gestapo swarming over France, but Liliane agreed. When she went to the *mairie* to arrange this marriage she was asked: 'Vous épousez un Juif?' To this offensive question her response was the proudly spoken answer: 'Non, j'épouse un officier français!'

Their proxy marriage took place and they were reunited after the war.

Pétain did not succeed in gaining any concessions from the Germans, such as the release of French prisoners of war or the departure of German soldiers from this so-called neutral state. But by now the harsh laws he had introduced had a momentum of their own.

CHAPTER 12

><+>-O-<+>-<

The Brutal Antisemitism of Vichy; Italian Protection

Chanel was still battling with the Wertheimers over the right to own and distribute Chanel No. 5, a tussle that continued throughout the war and long afterwards. Her threat to bring out a new and improved version of this famous scent had fallen flat, but it was a struggle that would not end for years. At the same time, she was leading her Parisian life with her circle of old friends. Socially, it was barely touched by the war, but its most important factor, her work, was now non-existent. 'I never made clothes,' she said to Cocteau, when he went to see her at the beginning of April. 'I made fashion. What should I do today? I don't work any more because the women I would dress aren't there.'

Ten days later, Cocteau was reminding her of one of their intimate pre-war dinners (soon after the abdication of Edward VIII). 'We went out with Chanel and laughed a lot,' he wrote in his diary for 17 April 1942. 'I reminded her of a dinner in her room at the Ritz with Winston Churchill and his son. Us four. Churchill dead drunk. He began to cry because of the Duke of Windsor. He wept. His son wept. He said again and again: "One does not put on someone else's costume."' This was a memory she was happy to share, in contrast to those further back, which are a tangle of confusion and obfuscation. To all her biographers or would-be biographers she gave differing accounts of her family, her childhood and her adolescence, so that a clear picture of it is impossible.

What can be stated as fact, though, are the two events that would have felled a lesser personality: the death of her mother and the immediate departure of her father when she was twelve, an abandonment followed almost at once by her incarceration in the orphanage of Aubazine. For seven long years she had been immured in this building with its high stone walls and echoing passages, standing fortress-like on top of a hill, its isolation from the world emphasised by the austere predictability of the daily routine, with the black-and-white clothes of the orphans and the nuns the only colours save for the green of the surrounding forests stretching into the distance.

With such an adolescence, many would have become institutionalised, preferring the safety of what they knew to the uncertainties and dangers of the world outside. Chanel was saved by her unbounded energy, determination to survive, and an originality unbowed by external pressures and constraints.

Yet such conditions leave their mark: for Chanel, it meant learning early on that to survive she had to rely on herself alone, that such reliance was helped by money, and that independence was vital. In the war, which, as she said several times, was nothing to do with her, this will to survive meant that she stepped back from the wider world, living only the life she had constructed for herself, among those she knew well.

She may also have been affected by a disturbing incident that spring. Early one morning two Resistance fighters managed to kidnap her from her room in the Ritz – it is likely they were let in by the manager's wife, who was a Resistance sympathiser. She was blindfolded and taken away; she never knew where to. At this secret spot she was interrogated about her relationship with von Dincklage and told she could face disfigurement or death if she did not change her ways. She stood up to them – one of Chanel's salient qualities was courage – and, surprisingly, she was released unharmed; doubtless the kidnappers realised that if anything happened to someone so well known and looked on favourably by the Germans, they would follow their usual custom and execute a number of 'hostages'. 'You are a Frenchwoman and an important one,' said her kidnappers. 'You are good for France and France has been good to you.' Later that day, German soldiers poured into the Ritz and began to search every room. They found nothing.

In February 1942, the socialist former Prime Minister Léon Blum, arrested on various trumped-up charges in September 1940 by the Vichy regime, was put on trial with other ministers – among them was Paul Reynaud, who had wished to continue fighting – in an attempt to prove that the leaders of the French Third Republic had been responsible for France's defeat.

The trial, supported by the Nazis, had the secondary aim of demonstrating that the responsibility of the war rested with France, with Blum, as a Jew, the chief target. But things did not go according to plan, as all the ministers proved able at rebutting the various charges. Blum in particular made a brilliant speech with such a telling indictment of Vichy, gaining much sympathetic coverage in the international press, that the Nazis stopped the trial. Vichy promptly handed him over to Germany, where he was incarcerated in Buchenwald concentration camp until the end of the war.

That spring, Raymond-Raoul Lambert wrote in his diary: 'I spent a week in Nice with Simone and the two older boys for the Passover holidays. We lunched in royal style in Monaco, where the restrictions are not so severe but at what a price! (twelve hundred francs for four).' It was a brief respite in the growing campaign against Jews – and, indeed, the difficulties and pressures facing non-Jewish French citizens.

At the end of May 1942 all Jews over six years of age in the occupied zone were ordered to wear a yellow Star of David, six-pointed and about the width of a man's palm, with *Juif* or *Juive* stitched across it, over their hearts. It was around this time that Réné Glassman arrived in Paris. Born and brought up near Düsseldorf, where his family had prosperous oil and flour mills, he had left for Holland in 1936 to escape persecution, finally persuading his parents to follow him. In Holland he built up a successful business but decided to flee the country as German round-ups for workers began. He had escaped from Holland through Belgium, with the aid of people-smugglers, frequently hiding under bushes in the dark as the smugglers reconnoitred the border, which was kept under constant surveillance by German sentries.

In Paris, where he was told to wait at a small hotel near the Gare du Nord for the next smuggler, his first act was to remove his yellow star. During the waiting days, he wandered around Paris, later recording his impressions. 'The German oppressor had put his stamp on the city to a horrific extent. Everywhere groups of Germans were strolling, soldiers, officers and civilians, whose Prussian awkwardness stood out sharply in this wonderfully soft, perfectly formed city. Everywhere the swastika, with its aggressive rawness, was wounding the Parisian urban landscape.

'On every corner, with unpleasant obtrusiveness, there appeared a German army hostel, an army restaurant, or an army cinema. On the Champs-Élysées you could hear an army choir singing German marching music, where before the far softer sound of Parisian songs had wafted on the breeze. Almost all the large hotels were occupied by Germans, and many walls displayed strict regulations and propaganda in the unmistakable language of the Third Reich.'

Then came an episode that could have been fatal. He was suddenly hailed by a German soldier with the words: 'Good morning, Herr Doctor, what are you doing here?' This was a man who had earlier holidayed in Holland, where he had met the German-speaking Réné and who obviously thought that Réné was an ordinary German businessman. 'I gave the unwitting Tschoepe to believe that I still lived in Holland,' wrote Réné, 'but was extremely busy with work which brought me to Paris frequently. When you consider that in fact not even the shortest journey from Amsterdam was possible without a permit, it is telling how little troubled the wider German public were about the National Socialist measures against the Jews, and how poorly informed about them.' They had a glass of beer together, chatted, and then Réné 'ended the encounter with the prospect of a second meeting'.

Soon afterwards he left Paris, heading for Nice. 'We arrived at the Cher riverbank, which here formed the border between occupied and unoccupied France,' he wrote of that crossing in September 1942. 'I removed my shoes and socks, and at a signal from Maurice [the people-smuggler] I entered the river. I crossed under the sympathetic gaze of an angler standing in the middle of the river. A few minutes later, only a bit wet, I reached the opposite bank. I put my shoes and socks back on, and with a deep sigh of freedom I glanced at the land on the other side, languishing under the German yoke, and, breathing deeply, greeted the country in front of me, the "free zone", which appeared to me as the land of freedom.'

Over 80,000 Jews obeyed the order to wear yellow stars, to the approval of every Paris newspaper, and from the summer onwards Jews, now easy to pick up in the streets, were deported from Paris – in front of Parisians.

'Never have people been so nice to them,' wrote Jean Guéhenno when the yellow stars were brought in. 'It's because there is no doubt nothing more vile than forcing a man to be ashamed of himself at every moment, and the good people of Paris know it.' It was the same on the Riviera, where sympathy was swinging round to the Jews despite the flood of anti-Jewish propaganda pumped out by Vichy and the antisemitic newspaper *Au Pilori*. The Catholic Church did its best to encourage this sympathy, with the Bishop (later Archbishop) of Nice, Paul Rémond, in particular, helping and supporting Jews and encouraging his flock to do so.

By now even those most fervent in their original support for Pétain, as the patriotic and gallant general of the 1914 war, were beginning to question not only his attitude but his motives, especially when on 2 June Laval (who had returned to power in April) announced the latest edict from Vichy, the *relève*. This was a form of human exchange: in return for every three workers who volunteered to go and work in Germany, one prisoner of war would be released. It was the first time Vichy had actively encouraged workers to go, rather than just allowing the Germans to recruit. It was a scheme that entirely benefited the Germans, who acquired labour but released sick men of whom they were anxious to rid themselves.

Laval then made perhaps the most notorious statement of his career: 'I wish for German victory because, without it, tomorrow Bolshevism will be installed everywhere.' This desire for German victory, and effort to fall in with the will of the conquerors, was apparent in the telegram to Eichmann that he sanctioned: 'Laval has proposed that children below the age of sixteen be included in the deportation of Jewish families from the free zone. The fate of Jewish children in the occupied zone does not interest him.' Many French agreed with him; although others thought differently. As Lambert recorded: 'On the 14th of July I saw, in the streets of Marseilles, the first mass demonstration against Laval and Hitler ... 100,000 people in the street cheering de Gaulle and singing the "Marseillaise".'

On the Riviera also there were disturbances and riots, caused by the lack of food, and even wine. In Nice, tea, if available, cost around £20 per pound and the precious leaves went through several incarnations. 'We boiled a little in a saucepan to draw out all the strength, drank this liquid and dried the leaves for the next day,' remembered Elsie Gladman. 'We repeated this three times then finally gave the dried leaves to one of our helpers, who gladly took them home. She gave her husband one drink made from them, then dried the leaves for the last time, for him to smoke in his pipe.'

As for cigarettes, when available the ration was nil for women and a very small, varying number, for men. Butts were now never seen on the streets. A few managed to grow their own tobacco; others dried cabbage and potato leaves, crumbling and rolling them into cigarette papers. There were queues for everything. Where rations could be obtained, and of what, was announced in the daily papers, with long lines of people forming immediately.

Then came an episode so barbaric in its cruelty that when reports of it reached the Riviera pity was stirred up among the Niçois and the Church became vocal in defence of the victims. 'We are witnessing a cruel scattering of families where nothing is spared, neither the aged, nor the frail, nor the ill,' said Cardinal Pierre-Marie Gerlier in an open letter.

This was the *grand rafle* of 16 July 1942, when about 13,000 Jewish men, women and children were rounded up and confined in appalling conditions in the Vélodrome d'Hiver, a Parisian bicycle stadium. The *rafle* was Nazi-directed but carried out by the French police, acting on the basis of lists they themselves had drawn up. It was primarily concerned with deporting all non-French Jews, such as the refugees from Poland, Belgium and Holland, as well as those who had been rendered stateless.

In the stadium the heat was intense, increased by the dark-blue paint on the glass roof (to avoid attracting Allied bombers) and the screwing-shut of the windows. There were no lavatories: of the ten that should have been available, five were sealed because their windows offered an escape route and the others were blocked. There was one sole water tap and the only water and food was brought by Quakers and the Red Cross. A few doctors and nurses were allowed to enter. Those who tried to escape were shot on the spot. Some took their own lives.

As a young social worker wrote to her father: 'When you come in, you can hardly breathe at first because of the stench. Each person has a bit more than a square yard of space on which to lie down. The handful of toilets are stopped up and there is no one to fix them. Everyone is forced to go to the toilet along the walls. As for water, since I have been there I have seen only two outlets, like the ones on the sidewalk, to which someone has fitted rubber hoses; the crush around them is beyond description. There are three doctors for 15,000 people. They went into hospitals and took even people who had operations the day before, so some are disembowelled, haemorrhaging, etc. . . .' After five days, the prisoners were taken in sealed cattle trucks to the internment camps of Drancy, Beaune-la-Rolande and Pithiviers, and thence to the Nazi death camps.

'Will Germans who travel after the war have to wear a red star?' wondered Galtier-Boissière acidly – he himself had never ceased to believe in an eventual British victory.

*

In the unoccupied zone, the Vichy regime was busy painting Jews as living the high life while Frenchmen suffered, feasting on black-market food while everyone else went hungry. Notices went up saying, 'Down with the Jews', in Nice street names commemorating Jews, such as rue Rothschild, were changed and, of course, the remaining Jewish businesses were shut down.

The French authorities began to segregate the Jewish from the non-Jewish in the *groupes de travailleurs étrangers*. Seven such 'Palestinian' groups were created, subject to much stricter discipline than the other GTEs. More and more were interned in forced-labour camps in order to facilitate deportation. One of these was Marcel Block, who had been moved to an internment camp near Carcassonne and was working in a vineyard. In August 1942 came the order that he and his fellows were to be arrested but, to their credit, the local police refused. It was a time, thinks his son Peter, when he could have gone underground. 'My father was totally bilingual, and the population hid people.'

Despite local sympathy, the deportations continued. 'At the entrance and exit to railway stations, in front of ticket counters, on platforms, at the main bus stations, at the toll barriers on the outskirts of town, travellers were interrogated by *gendarmes* and their papers inspected,' wrote Françoise Frenkel. 'On the trains, German police in civilian clothes would pounce on people . . . on the roads every vehicle was pulled over, from expensive cars to carts pulled by donkeys.'

Many of these arrests took place in small stations in the Provençal countryside in order to avoid the wrath or horror of local people. 'The deportees' roll call begins in the courtyard under the cruel sun,' wrote Raymond-Raoul Lambert, who as president of the Committee for Assistance to Refugees was able to save some of those caught. 'The departure takes place next day at dawn. We can see the camp station with the railroad cars, black like hearses, waiting on the siding . . . I cannot watch each group leave the camp, I hide where I can weep. I have spent the night in the camp and managed to obtain grace for a few from the police inspector: certain war veterans, old people, political refugees . . . but I have the feeling that their fate has only been deferred.'

Occasionally prisoners escaped from detention camps and hid until they could contact the Resistance, which had begun organising escape routes out of the country. Others were concealed by French families, who hid them at the risk of their own lives.

So far Pétain had refused to hand over the French Jews. Pierre Laval had persuaded him to let the foreign Jews go in order, so he said, to save their own. Foreign Jews were in fact a cunning target, as to most native French – including French Jews – they seemed alien, speaking foreign languages and had different customs and appearances. Once the decision had been taken to deport all foreign 'Israelites' (a word that sounded more foreign than 'Jews'), including those more recently naturalised, and detailed instructions had been given as to how to catch, arrest, concentrate and load people onto trains to the occupied zone, 600 of them were rounded up in Nice on 26 August.

Families were seized in their houses, or captured after manhunts across the countryside. 'The police', wrote one Jewish survivor, 'surrounded hotels, villas, whole blocks of houses and dragged out of their beds terrified Jews who had come to France after 1936. The shouts, the wailing and the groaning broke the stillness of the morning.' Most of the Niçois were horrified.

Five days later the captives were bundled into trains, with children as young as three separated from their mothers and the *gendarmes* using batons and hoses. Under French guard they were shipped to Drancy, a huge apartment block built round a large square, in a poor working-class suburb near Le Bourget airport and heavily guarded by French police. It was a place that became notorious as the departure point for the death camp of Auschwitz.

The voluntary departure of workers from France to Germany, in the shape of the *relève*, was not working as Vichy hoped it would, with the quota of men demanded by Germany unfilled. With most German males now fighting on different fronts, foreign workers were needed to keep German factories going. So on 4 September, Pétain and Laval signed a new law requiring all able-bodied men aged eighteen to fifty and single women aged twenty-one to thirty-five to 'be subject to do any work that the government deems necessary'. In other words, this was forced labour coupled with enforced departure to Germany if told to do so. This *service du travail obligatoire* meant that French forced labourers were the only nationality to have been required to serve by the laws of their own state rather than by German orders.

This was a heavy blow to the cult of Pétain. By now most people in the unoccupied zone had realised that the head of their government was little more than a figurehead, and that Vichy jumped to the Nazi tune. A new nickname had been coined for him – 'Pétoche'. It sounded like an affectionate diminutive ... but everyone except the Germans knew that 'avoir la pétoche' was street slang for to be scared stiff.

On 8 November 1942, in Operation Torch, the Allies* invaded French North Africa (the French still held the territories of Algeria and Morocco). At 7 a.m. on 11 November, German troops crossed the demarcation line and Italian troops invaded south-eastern France. There was no longer an 'unoccupied zone' – it was immediately renamed the southern zone. The Riviera, now not even nominally free, was under the jurisdiction of the Italian Fourth Army. For the Italians, parading slowly along the Promenade des Anglais, it was a triumph – Nice was now theirs again, as they believed it should always have been. The cheers of the onlookers (many of whom were of Italian extraction) seemed to confirm this.

The arrival of the Italians, with their demand for food, meant that living was becoming daily more difficult for the Niçois. Elizabeth Foster, an elderly American confined for health reasons to her apartment in a smart part of Nice, had to rely on her cook to shop and market for her. When the cook left, she placed advertisements for a replacement, and found that 'all the cooks enquired if I used the "marché noir" and refused to come when

---

* America was now in the war, after the attack on Pearl Harbor in December 1941.

told I did not'. It was something her upright American conscience would not allow her to do. 'The reign of cheats and corruption is unimaginable,' she wrote in her diary. 'Every day long lists of arrests and fines for marché-noir dealings, cheating, stealing and illegal price rises, and yet cooks refused to enter your service unless you run the risk of fine and imprisonment and let them buy on the marché noir.'

But for the Riviera's Jews, far from adding a fresh layer of persecution, the Italian invasion proved a lifeline.* The Italian *carabinieri* protected them, especially when they were hounded by the French. When French antisemites marched on a Nice synagogue, the local Italian commander threatened to arrest them. The general in command of the Fourth Army ordered that no Jew in the Italian-occupied zone should be interned by the Vichy authorities, and when Vichy police continued to arrest French and foreign Jews, the Italian authorities released many of them and prevented further arrests. They also prohibited the stamping of the word *Juif* on ration and identity papers; this in turn meant that any Jew not noticeably Jewish in appearance could blend into the local population more easily.

News of this humane treatment spread far and wide. Jews emerged from hiding – among them the Sungolowsky family from their warehouse den. As the holocaust raged in Germany, Jewish refugees flocked to the Riviera by train and boat, filling the small hotels, apartments and boarding houses. Thirty or forty thousand of them crowded into thirty kilometres of coast. Nice in particular was their goal; here they were received by the Refugees' Aid Committee and issued with temporary identity cards that marked them out for 'forced residence'.

This 'forced residence' was a safety measure. Jews were sent to villages near the Alpine border with Italy, where they were protected by Italian soldiers; when some French *gendarmes* tried to snatch a couple of the women, the Italians prevented them.

---

* It was true that Mussolini had introduced severe anti-Jewish laws in Italy as early as 1938, and when he declared war foreign Jewish men in Italy were rounded up and interned. But there was one crucial difference: the Italians did not deport Jews.

Provided they registered with the local garrison twice a day, and stayed inside the village, they could live a normal life. Families remained together, Jews sat drinking coffee in cafés or strolled the streets; there were even synagogues and schools.

'St-Martin in the Italian zone was like paradise,' said Adam Munz, a refugee from Poland aged sixteen at the time, who had survived by being disguised as a non-Jew in a boarding school near Montpellier ('the constant fear during the German occupation of France is something difficult to describe'). 'There were so many Jews living peacefully and openly there! *Carabinieri* and soldiers would smile and say hello. We invited them to our parties and concerts, and they came.'

Another boy, Alfred Feldman, whose mother and sister had already been caught and deported, arrived at about the same time to join his father, who had escaped from a labour camp. 'I saw something I had not been accustomed to seeing for a long time: Jews were passing peacefully through the streets, sitting in the cafés, speaking in French, German, some even in Yiddish.' Thousands were smuggled into Italy after Italian generals said that 'no country can ask Italy, cradle of Christianity and law, to be associated with these Nazi acts'.

The chief of the Gestapo's Jewish Office in France, Heinz Rothke, complained: 'The attitude of the Italians is and was incomprehensible . . . in the last few months there has been a mass exodus of Jews from our occupation zone into the Italian zone. The escape of the Jews is facilitated by the existence of thousands of flight routes, the assistance given them by the French population and the sympathy of the authorities, false identity cards, and also the size of the area, which makes it impossible to seal off the zones of influence hermetically.' Even those holding plainly false papers, lamented this officer, enjoyed Italian protection.

A large part of what Chanel had constructed for herself exactly as she wanted was La Pausa, the house she loved above all others. Rather as one might draw a cloak tightly around one's shoulders and body to keep out cold and unpleasantness, Chanel drew the comforting ambience of La Pausa around herself. For most of the summer of 1942 she and von Dincklage lived there. The sea, the sunshine, the tumbling geraniums and the liquid song of the nightingales were still the same. Life, even for those without Chanel's special privileges, was still a little easier on the Riviera than in Paris.

For Chanel and von Dincklage, insulated from the hardships surrounding them by his connections, free to come and go across the demarcation line thanks to his laissez-passer and unaffected by food shortages, this summer at La Pausa was not dissimilar to those of pre-war years, save for the lack of large house parties.

When there, Chanel often ate at the Roquebrune restaurant of Madame Imbert. With her husband away at the war, Blanche Imbert had opened the restaurant as a way of supporting herself and her family. Her regional specialities of *langoustes* and *lapin à la moutarde* so impressed Chanel that soon Madame Imbert was being asked to come up to La Pausa to help Chanel's own cook when she had a few friends to stay. 'Chanel ate very little but she wanted her guests to have plenty,' says Blanche's granddaughter, Patricia Marinovich. What was also obvious to the Imbert family was that, though not exactly mean, to Chanel, as the saying went, 'un sou est un sou'. Careful with money, what she hated was the idea that anybody was taking advantage of her.

She was, however, capable of extraordinary and unexpected acts of generosity. From 1928 onwards, after being solicited to do so by Princess Ghika,* she had become the leading benefactress of the Asylum of Ste-Agnès, an orphanage devoted to the care of children with birth defects. De Pougy's memoir, *My Blue Notebooks*, is sprinkled with references to Chanel's large and numerous donations. 'Gabrielle Chanel a été spontanément et magnifiquement généreuse,' wrote the Princess, and again later: 'Gabrielle Chanel a envoyé cinq mille francs . . .' Friends seldom turned to her in vain.

One of these friends was Robert Streitz. Whether Chanel was aware that Streitz was now a member of an important Resistance network is not recorded; what is interesting is that he asked her

---

* The former courtesan Liane de Pougy.

for help. Serge Voronov, a physics professor, of Russian-Jewish ancestry, had been arrested by the Gestapo, and Streitz begged Chanel to intervene; she in turn asked Spatz. Spatz, supposedly involved in the field of German intelligence, much of which involved rounding up Jews or enemies of Germany, such as Russians, did his best to intercede but was unsuccessful (Voronov was eventually released through someone else's intercession).

Why would a man answerable to senior officers try to help someone who was either an enemy alien or a member of a race those officers were trying to eradicate? This curious episode underlines Spatz's ambivalent attitude to those he worked for, and perhaps helps explain why Chanel believed him to be more sympathetic to the British cause than his own. As for Chanel, her antisemitism largely took the form of words.*

What neither of them knew was that Robert Streitz, who had designed La Pausa and therefore knew every inch of its capacious cellars, had installed a transmitter in an alcove in one of them. Concealed there, he would use it to facilitate the escape of a number of Jews. Often these would come to the villa itself before being 'forwarded' into friendly hands.

One way this happened was through Blanche Imbert. Often Blanche would send her daughter to La Pausa to help or to carry up supplies for the kitchen. 'There was a German guard in a small lodge by the gate,' says Patricia Marinovich. 'My mother and my grandmother both had laissez-passers and by now the guard knew them quite well. Often my mother would go up with some Jewish girl she said was her helper. They would walk together up the path to the villa and round its side, when the Jewish girl would slip out of a small gate, invisible from the lodge, and continue up a path into the mountains, or to a village where arrangements had been made to receive her. Of course Mademoiselle Chanel knew nothing of this!'

*

---

* Her attempt to wrest control of her business from the Wertheimers was not because they were Jewish but because she felt they had cheated her. Equally, she believed that their Jewishness would give her an advantage in the struggle.

At the end of the year the Nazi/Vichy campaign against the Jews was stepped up. In December 1942, Berlin issued orders demanding the immediate arrest and deportation of all Jews in France, while the next day Laval ordered all Jews to report to the nearest police station to have the word 'Jew' stamped on their identity and ration cards. The Italians, who felt that their authority over the Italian-occupied zone was being challenged, bristled. It was immediately pointed out that it was the Italians, not the French, who were running the region . . . and the stamping did not take place.

But although the Italians were running the southern zone, there was still a strong German presence in Marseilles, largely to prevent Jews and others escaping by sea. The German Army took over several of the largest hotels and all French flags were removed; most of the newspapers ceased publication and French radio was silent. After Operation Torch, Admiral Darlan (formerly Vichy's deputy leader) promptly defected, ordering the French forces there to join the Allies with him. 'Wildly exciting . . . "The writing on the wall" indeed,' thought Elizabeth Foster.

To prevent the seizure of the French Navy in Toulon the Nazis attempted to take it over, but the main German force got lost in the arsenal and, behind schedule by one hour, gave the admiral in charge a chance to warn the fleet to prepare to scuttle. So when, at 5.25 a.m. on 27 November 1942, German tanks finally rolled through, the order 'Scuttle! Scuttle! Scuttle!' was given by radio, visual signals and dispatch boats. The French crews evacuated, and scuttling parties started attaching demolition charges (to destroy armament and ignite the fuel stores) and opened sea valves on the ships.

In all, the French demolished seventy-seven ships, including all the major warships, leaving only thirty-nine small ships, most sabotaged and disarmed, to be captured while several submarines, ignoring orders to scuttle, slipped away to join de Gaulle's forces in French North Africa. Some of the destroyed ships were ablaze for several days, and oil polluted the harbour so badly no one could swim there for two years.

*

Jaques and Ilona Wochiler had left their apartment in Marseilles as it was too dangerous, and moved to a small hotel. It was run by a former madam who had good connections with the Préfecture. But now the threat of a *rafle*, or round-up, was always there. The Gestapo would focus on boarding houses and small hotels, because that was where refugees were usually found, and the dreaded knock at the door was generally around 5.00 a.m. One quick-witted man saved himself by shouting furiously and loudly in German, 'Leave me in peace!' and the Germans left. In November, the madam warned the Wochilers that they were on the list for the next round-up. Straight away, Jaques and the eight-months'-pregnant Ilona fled inland to a small village.

By now Germany had established quotas for deportation, but when the Vichy French tried to impose these the Italian Fourth Army prevented them. As the nurse Elsie Gladman pointed out: 'The people most to be hated and feared were the French who collaborated . . . These comparative few were noted by the patriotic French and they received menacing letters and small black wooden coffins, a threat of what would happen to them at the end of hostilities.'

On 15 December 1942 came the demand for a further quota of 250,000 men to be sent to Germany by mid-March 1943 (300,000 German workers had been transferred to the German armed forces). To fulfil this, Laval ruled that all males over twenty were subject to the *service du travail obligatoire*. Theoretically, the STO also applied to young women, but, for fear of the reactions of the people and the Church, women were not generally called up.

As both the German and the French police grabbed young men where they could – coming out of a cinema or a metro, working in the fields – to fulfil their quota, thousands fled to join the Resistance. The demarcation line had been abolished in February 1943, so there was one less hazard for those wanting to put distance between themselves and possible pursuers. In the countryside behind the Côte d'Azur, young peasants and farm workers melted into the woods or the mountains when they heard of a forthcoming search for conscripts, returning only when the coast was clear.

In Paris, a priest pinned a yellow star to the baby Jesus in a crib at Christmas.

The New Year of 1943 opened with the Casablanca Conference. This convened from 14 to 24 January to plan the next stage of the war. Both the US President, Franklin D. Roosevelt, and Winston Churchill were present and the conference concluded with the Casablanca Declaration. This announced to the world that the Allies would accept nothing less than the 'unconditional surrender' of the Axis powers. It was the expression of the Allies' implacable determination that the Axis powers be fought to their ultimate and total defeat. But in certain circles it was felt that the war had already gone on long enough, and that it was time for peace. Perhaps thoughts like this, revolving in her mind, were the genesis of the extraordinary proposal Chanel was to make a few months later.

CHAPTER 13

>─┤◆>─○─<◆├─<

Escapes, Captures and
Starvation Rations

Both Vichy and the Germans were unhappy with the Italian approach to 'the Jewish question', so much so that on 14 January 1943 the Prime Minister, Laval, grumbled to the Italian Ambassador in Vichy that the Italians were protecting not only Italian Jews but foreign ones as well.

Less than a fortnight after Laval's complaint, however, the Gestapo and the French police took matters into their own hands. Twelve thousand French police sealed off the Old Port in Marseilles and searched every building, herding out the inhabitants for identity checks. Locksmiths were requisitioned to open doors, women were taken away in police vehicles without having time to dress, sick people pulled from their beds and parents separated from children. As each building was cleared, it was dynamited. On the same day, cinemas, shops, buses and trains in greater Marseilles were also searched.

In Cocteau's words: 'The amazed Germans saw emerging whole farms with cows and dairies. When they threw in tear-gas bombs out appeared Chinese with tons of opium, intoxicated blacks, forgers of dollars, queers, lepers, and a camp of English aviators.' And of course, refugees and those trying to escape from France. In all, it is estimated that 40,000 identities were checked. Around half of those arrested were released, but not the Jews – almost 2,000 found themselves on the death trains.

In Paris, permission was granted for three more trains to leave the internment camp of Drancy for Auschwitz. Drancy, it should be said, was run by the French, with French *gendarmes* loading the internees onto the death trains. When the French police heard that these would include French citizens, they offered to save them by substituting foreign Jews instead. Those they caught were mainly the old, and children and the sick from the Rothschild Foundation Orphanage and the Rothschild Hospital, torn from their beds. It made no difference: two days later, the French Jews were also deported – accompanied by French police to the frontier.

On the Italian-dominated Riviera, Jews still felt comparatively safe, so much so that on 3 January 1943 Lambert was writing from Nice: 'When I am old, I shall retire to the Côte d'Azur. There, between eleven in the morning and dusk, the pure blue sky and the sun's vigour, in the middle of winter, dispel one's bodily woes and moral anxieties.'

So perhaps it was not surprising that the beginning of 1943 saw a new and sinister force called into being, the 'Milice française' (usually called simply the Milice). This was a political paramilitary organisation created on 30 January 1943 by the Vichy regime, with German aid, to help fight the growing French Resistance. One reason for this expansion was the bitterly re-sented enforcement of the *service du travail obligatoire* for all men of conscription age (between twenty-one and twenty-three), resulting in the 'disappearance' of almost 200,000 of them, many of whom became full-time members of the Resistance. As Jean Guéhenno wrote: 'All young men in the classes of 40–42 have to leave for Germany on 1 July. The panic of a crushed anthill. Some are thinking of crossing the border into Spain, others of hiding in the mountains. But most will resign themselves to it and leave. Many are already talking about the difficulties they will cause their parents if they leave . . .'

Fascist in outlook, the Milice went in for summary executions, used torture to extract information and helped round up Jews for deportation. Its formal head was Pierre Laval. It was more dangerous than the Gestapo because, being composed of native Frenchmen, there were no language difficulties, many of its members had intimate knowledge of the local towns, streets and countryside and were frequently close to local informants; and it operated outside civilian law. Some of the Milice were petty criminals, told that their prison sentences would be commuted if they joined; others became members because this exempted them from deportation to Germany as forced labour.

The Milice set to work at once. One morning the Wochilers saw a Milice man in the distinctive blue uniform making his way to their house in the small village in which they had taken shelter – they had been denounced by a neighbour. Jaques hid and Ilona greeted the Milice man warmly and offered him a glass of wine. His response, like that of any Frenchman offered a glass of wine by a pretty girl, was prompt acceptance. Ilona refilled his glass, telling him that her husband was out. After a few more refills the atmosphere grew noticeably friendlier, with the Milice man saying, 'I'll call back tomorrow.' The Wochilers took the hint and left with their small baby for Grenoble immediately he had gone.

There they were able to contact the Resistance and were smuggled across the border to neutral Switzerland, hiding under a load of hay in a haycart with another couple. 'If the baby makes a sound we're finished,' they were told. Fortunately he was silent. Once over the border the Wochilers* were safe, as at that time the Swiss allowed in families with children under a certain age; the couple with them, who had no child, were turned back.

For any Jew who could manage it, escape was now essential. Françoise Frenkel, who had tried twice to reach Switzerland, where friends had obtained her a visa, only to be turned back at the last minute, realised that now was her last chance. The wire on the border was impossible to climb over but there were gates at intervals, often unlocked so that farmers with land on both sides of the border could pass through. The trouble was that there were also watching sentries.

Françoise reached such a gate – only to find it jammed after

---

* Jacques Wochiler returned to France to join the FFI. After the war the Wochilers settled in Paris.

heavy rainfall the night before. As an Italian soldier rushed towards her, she managed to climb over it and fell to the ground on the other side. She heard a shot, then saw another soldier running towards her. This one raised her up, telling her that the Italian had merely fired in the air and that she was now in Switzerland. 'I was saved!' She burst into tears as she watched the Swiss soldier walk ahead of her carrying her small bundle of possessions. 'In it was everything I had taken from France, save my grieving and deathly tired heart.'

Colette Halber was also lucky. Her father and six of his eight children had already been deported to Auschwitz. Colette, then a toddler (she was born in 1939), had been put in a home in the avenue de la Plage in Cannes. It was mainly for children whose parents were in the colonies and run by the Protestant Madame Charpiot.* Madame Charpiot also took in a number of Jewish children, some sent by the Bishop of Nice, others by people she knew. The Jewish children would be given falsified identities and ration cards and new, French-sounding names, as similar to their old ones as possible so that they would not betray themselves in front of the Gestapo. 'Teaching them to remember these was the main difficulty,' recalled Madame Charpiot's daughter Françoise. Colette's new surname was Auber.

When the beach was forbidden for the children's walks and games, the home was moved to a neighbouring hotel, the Château St-Georges. One part of the hotel had been requisitioned, first by the Italians, then by the Germans, so that sleeping under the same roof were French, German and Christian and Jewish children with, some nights, men of the Resistance.

'Unlikely though it seemed, this togetherness helped us,' recalled Françoise. 'From the moment the Nazis settled in the hotel, the searches were no longer a menace. It didn't cross their minds that Jewish children could seek refuge in their midst. However, the occupation, as the days drew on, became very invasive. I remember one Christmas Day. We had decorated a tree

---

* Madame Charpiot was recognised as Righteous Among Nations at Yad Vashem in 1982.

in the dining room and organised a little party for the children. Suddenly the door opened and some German officers came in and mingled noisily with us. I saw officers give a friendly pat to the cheek of a Jewish child. The children went on singing a carol but we were in an anguish of apprehension.'

While Colette was there, her mother was picked up at the St-Charles railway station in Marseilles in May 1943 and sent to Drancy. On 29 July she managed to write a letter one piece of toilet paper and slip it to someone outside. With her family scattered, none of them knowing what had happened to the others, it was rather like putting a letter in a bottle and throwing it into the sea.

'My dear ones,' she wrote, 'It's a long time since I've given you my news . . . My health is really very good. I haven't got thinner. I have seen two major departures and now I know that I shall be on the third, which leaves tomorrow or the next day. Don't be sad. You would be astonished to see how calm I am in the face of this. All my companions are cheerful, of good morale, and certain that we will all be together again soon. Our departure doesn't resemble the others – we think we are not going far. What torments me and gives me anguish is that I know nothing about what's going on at home. I have several times advised Papa that the children need a change of air.' Two days later she was deported to Auschwitz.

Many years later, Colette was to write: 'I knew nothing of this. For forty years, I thought I was a war orphan.'

Now comes one of the most curious episodes in Chanel's life – a seeming attempt to act as intermediary in a peace settlement between the Allies and the Axis powers. Whether she really thought she had a chance of success, or whether she merely reckoned it was worth a try, is not known. It is also possible that, with no work to fill her days, boredom might have had something to do with it. She had decided to try and initiate peace talks between Churchill and the German High Command, a plan breathtaking in its audacity no less than in its belief in her own powers. Churchill was due to visit Madrid after the Tehran

Conference,* and she later stated that he had said he would see her there, on his way back to England. Or was it, as has been claimed,† an attempt to obtain information for the Germans?

She had clearly been thinking about it for months. Her first step, in the spring of 1943, was to send for the man who had organised the return of her nephew, Captain Theodor Momm, and outline her plan to him. Stupefied, he listened to her telling him her idea, adding that in order to get along with the British you had to know them well, over a long period of time, as she did. Carried away by her own words, she began to act out the conversation that would take place between them, as she paced up and down her drawing room in the rue Cambon. Gazing at Momm as if he were Churchill, she said: 'You foretold blood and tears and your prediction has already been fulfilled. But that won't give you a name in history, Winston. Now you must save human lives and end the war. By holding out a hand in peace you will show your strength. That is your mission.'‡ Almost hypnotised, Momm wondered: 'How could anyone resist this woman?' (Years later, he described her effect as 'the force of a unique personality'.)

She was, of course, not the only one who dreamt of a cessation of hostilities. Von Dincklage, who had been to Berlin in the early winter of 1943 and must have seen the devastating bombing of the city by the Allies, returned to Paris convinced that Germany would lose the war and that it was only a question of time – something he must have talked about with Chanel – and among the German High Command were those who privately felt that this would be the best solution.

Momm set off for Berlin, with the risky task of acquiring permission to go to Madrid for such a meeting, which would take several months to set up. The first essential was to meet

---

* A strategy meeting of Stalin, Roosevelt and Churchill from 28 November to 1 December 1943, after the Anglo-Soviet invasion of Iran.

† In *Sleeping with the Enemy* by Hal Vaughan (2011).

‡ Quoted by Edmonde Charles-Roux, who became Editor of French *Vogue* and who interviewed Momm for her book *Chanel: Her Life, Her World, and the Woman Behind the Legend She Herself Created* (1975).

the right people. It would have to be someone in the office of Heinrich Himmler, the only person whom Hitler really trusted and who, as head of the SS, reigned over that dark, mysterious and all-powerful body.

Momm was directed straight away to Walter Schellenberg, the thirty-three-year-old head of all Germany's foreign spies. Though Momm did not know it, Schellenberg himself was broadly in favour of ending hostilities with the Allies, largely so that Germany could concentrate uninterruptedly on the Russian front. The final defeat of Germany in the Battle of Stalingrad, which had ended in February 1943, was the clearest signal yet that the tide of war was turning – had turned; even Schellenberg's superior, Admiral Canaris, had been receptive to the idea of peace feelers.

So Momm was told that Chanel would receive the necessary permissions to travel to Madrid, the whole exercise to be undertaken in the utmost secrecy. It was not the first time Chanel had been to Madrid during the war; there is an account of an earlier visit during August 1941, when she was (according to Hal Vaughan) a German agent supposedly gathering information. Also, undoubtedly, she was hoping to increase sales of Chanel No. 5 in the Spanish market. Then, she had travelled with an associate of von Dincklage, the Spanish-speaking Baron Louis Piscatory de Vaufreland. Once in Madrid, the pair separated, Chanel moving into a suite at the Ritz.

Yet the record of an evening spent at a dinner party during this trip does not give the impression of her being a spy. A British diplomat, Brian Wallace, attending the dinner, sent a long and detailed report of her conversation to London. 'She talked for nearly three hours very frankly about Paris and deeply impressed me with her sincerity,' wrote Wallace. 'She is a friend of the PM and obviously very attached to the Duke of Westminster. She would like to go to England but cannot bring herself to abandon France.' Among the many points recorded in his report was her view that in the occupied zone people were not pro-British but anti-German, and that the Germans were buying themselves into French businesses and interests. The French, she said, still did not realise that they had lost the war. '"You wait till we have got rid of these swine," they say.' Soon after this Chanel and her Spanish-speaking German escort returned to Paris. Now, all she had to do was wait while arrangements for her Spanish venture were set in place.

On the Riviera, food was harder to come by than ever. Trainloads of fresh vegetables and fruit left daily for Germany. People cut the stems and leaves off potato plants so that the Germans did not spot them and uproot them, and collected the pods of broad beans that the conquerors had discarded. So scarce was food that the elderly patients in Sunny Bank even left their occasional rations to other patients in their wills. 'The old lady in the next room may have my sugar that is left and you, Sister, can have my bread and my rum ration,' one terminally ill old man told Elsie Gladman.

For her birthday, Elizabeth Foster was given 'all the things one can't buy . . . a toothbrush, matches, soap, paper and to crown it all, honey which no one has seen for a year. Also four eggs arrived last night; and yesterday we ate meat for the first time for twelve days – we are supposed to have it three times a week. We get no substitutes, only vegetables and half a pound extra of macaroni. Carrots are almost unfindable, we must have eaten many acres of turnips, boiled, sliced, mashed. We have seen no butter for two months until today, no eggs and no milk for six months but one of our worst afflictions has been no salt for ten days. Then the *femme de chambre* got a little present of salt from a friendly waiter in a restaurant and shared it with us.'

Leather had disappeared all over France – sent to Germany for soldiers' boots – and twenty-four million pairs of wooden shoes had been sold. 'Shoes and stockings', wrote Elizabeth, 'are far-off divine events towards which everyone yearns.' Hair-dressers were even ordered to sweep up and save hair that had been cut or trimmed, these clippings to be forwarded to slipper manufacturers.

Textiles were in such short supply that the government offered coupons for rags. Those taken to hospital often had their clothes stolen and had to be returned home naked and wrapped in a blanket, and careless swimmers were often robbed of their garments while they were in the water – clothes could be exchanged for food in the barter system that had arisen. Such thefts were doubly serious as no one could buy, say, a new pair of trousers without handing in the old ones. If someone died, after the funeral friends would ask the family if they could buy the deceased's clothes.

Small currency disappeared, and post offices gave change in stamps; brass door and drawer handles were removed from banks and other institutions to help the German munitions industry; the small ration of coal due was seldom delivered and gas was only available at certain times.

'The worst moment of my day is the dismal hour before sunrise when I try to do a little washing in an icy-cold bathroom with a tiny pitcher of hot water prepared for me before the gas is suppressed,' wrote the seventy-five-year-old Elizabeth Foster. 'The truth is we are all equally grimy and battered from cold water, lack of soap and constant fussing over stoves. We are all increasingly shabby. There is more skin than fur in coats, capes and collars. We are also hungrier and hungrier. The cough syrup which substituted sugar for my friends has given out and they are now using children's laxatives such as Syrup of Figs, Syrup of Apples. The consequence is that all but the most robust are now suffering violent diarrhoea.'

Those French who had a bit of land cropped it as hard, and as secretly, as they could. If they grew corn, they threshed it inside their houses at night, before creeping out with it to the miller to grind. So long were the queues at the almost-empty grocers' shops, with priority given to pregnant women, that some of the less scrupulous housewives would stick cushions under their dresses to ensure they were first for whatever was going. When this trick became known, other women would sometimes prod a swelling stomach to see if the bump was real or not.

The only thing that kept many people going was the radio. 'How I should have endured these grim years without the BBC I do not know,' wrote Elizabeth Foster on 23 July. 'Big Ben has been my steadiest friend and in hours when it seemed a little lonesome to be the only hopeful person of my acquaintance, Big Ben sung out "Lift up your hearts", *Sursum Corda*, and did lift mine vigorously and how many millions in occupied territory listening furtively or in lonely outposts longing to join in the fight must have felt as I did.'

Listening required secrecy and watchfulness. Windows had to be closed so that neither the enemy nor possible denouncers could hear; whether or not to close shutters was a moot point, as though the radio was less audible when they were closed, when they were open the approach of an alien authority was more visible. For sheer daring, little matched the bravery of the manager of the Negresco in Nice, headquarters of the Gestapo, who had installed a radio receiver high up under the hotel's pinkish slate dome, and who managed to disseminate its news among trusted friends (one of whom was Dennis Youdale's father). If caught, he would undoubtedly have been shot.

For anyone else caught listening to the crisp BBC tones the penalties were severe: confiscation, a heavy fine, deportation to a concentration camp and possible death (in July, when she left her window open because of the heat, Elizabeth was warned by a friend that her radio could be heard). But the news of the growing number of Allied advances was so exciting and gave such hope that people clung to the news bulletins. As one French girl wrote after the victories in Africa: 'I was so excited that I did not even shut the window when I turned on the radio. I took an extra slice of bread and an extra lump of sugar in my coffee!'

Elsie Gladman and her colleagues kept their radio in the cellar, with one nurse at the top of the stairs to keep watch while the others listened. The English nurses left in the hospital had to go regularly to the *mairie* to have their fingerprints taken and sign their names. In July 1943 they were told they had to leave the coast – no English person was to be allowed within 100 kilometres of the sea. As many traces of the English as possible had been removed: their churches closed, their libraries ransacked and many of the books burned, and there was a rigorous curfew. A large number of English residents in Cannes were sent to a concentration camp in Grenoble.

*

As summer 1943 drew on, attitudes and convictions hardened and polarised. The tide of war appeared to be turning and German victory no longer seemed certain, so the idea that France would be better off in the future by collaborating with Germany was steadily losing ground. To a population already nearly starving, the continuing sight of quantities of food daily being despatched to the enemy country increased hatred for the Nazi regime. Then, too, many French were horrified at seeing the arrest, now more open, of Jewish fellow citizens, often friends and neighbours for years, and by the callousness with which these round-ups were carried out.

In one of these was Marcel Block, sent first to Drancy and then, three days later, to Auschwitz in Convoy 25 in conditions of hideous brutality. As one anonymous survivor wrote: 'Piled up in cattle trucks, unable to bend or budge, sticking to one another, breathless, crushed by one's neighbour's every move, this was already hell. In daytime, a horrid heat and a pestilential smell. After several days and nights, the doors were opened. We arrive exhausted, dehydrated and with many ill. A newborn baby, snatched from its mother's arms, was thrown against a column. The mother, crazed with pain, starts to scream. The SS man hit her violently over the head with the butt end of his weapon. Her eyes haggard, with fearful screams, her beautiful blonde hair tinted with her blood. She was struck down with a bullet in her head.' On arrival, seventy-seven women but no men were selected for labour. The rest were gassed.

This had its effect on the French police. As Heinz Rothke, chief of the Gestapo's Jewish Office in France, reported: 'We can no longer count on the collaboration of the French police in the arrests of Jews en masse – unless the German military situation clearly improves within days or weeks.' On the Riviera these raids were still rare, although the Germans and Vichy officials bombarded the Italians with demands for the arrest of foreign Jews in their area, in which up to 30,000 Jews lived openly and legally. However the Italians, while declaring they were doing all they could, not only refused to co-operate but actively protected the Jews. 'The attitude of the Italians is incomprehensible,' said Rothke on 21 July. 'In the last few months there has been a mass exodus of Jews from our occupation zone into the Italian zone.'

The memories of one Italian soldier, twenty-four-year-old Arturo Finotti, posted to a small village not far from Nice, explain where many of those soldiers' priorities lay. 'We were paid very little, and badly,' he later told his son Federico. 'I saved what I could – money would always be useful in an emergency. Another way of paying us was with cigarette "sticks" [cartons of ten packs of cigarettes], which were sometimes also given to us as a bonus. In the barracks we often used them as currency. Outside the barracks and military life, most soldiers preferred to invest their money in the local women'.

But the months of comparative safety for the Jews on the Riviera were soon to end, although the Italians continued to protect them until they could do so no longer.

The Italian Army had already been defeated in Russia and, with the German forces, was crumbling in North Africa. On 10 July 1943 the Allies invaded Sicily and just over a fortnight later Mussolini and his fascist regime fell from power, although this made no difference to the protective behaviour of the Italians towards the Jews on the Riviera, where most of them were living in Nice or Cannes.

Lambert and his family were not so lucky. Working openly in the UGIF (Union générale des israélites de France, the body set up in 1941 by Vichy, at the request of the Nazis), he was now arrested and sent to Drancy, as part of the German plan to curtail the UGIF's effectiveness. Simultaneously, as the war looked as though it would soon end for Italy, there were huge efforts to save the Jews in their area. As arrangements for an armistice between Italy and the Allies were being drawn up, go-betweens made approaches to the British and American Ambassadors to the Vatican.

Finally, on the morning of 8 September 1943, an agreement was reached: the Italians would provide four ships and the British and Americans would allow 30,000 Jews from Italian-occupied

France to land in North Africa, which was now under their control.

Organising all this would take two or three weeks, but as the projected armistice was understood to be taking place in October it looked as though there would be just enough time for rescue. The Italian Army hastily began to move the Jewish refugees who had been housed in 'safe' villages closer to the border in readiness for a flight into Italy, sending some to Nice, whence they planned to transport them by ship.

But events proceeded too fast for them. The armistice, which had been signed secretly on 3 September, was announced by General Dwight Eisenhower on 8 September, the same day on which plans for rescue of the Jews had been finalised, catching the Italian Army off guard – many of its commanders were taken completely by surprise. The result was chaos. Without any clear instructions the Italian Army headed home, but many were too late: as soon as the armistice was announced, Germany promptly attacked Italy, occupying most of it.

For the Jews whom the Italians were protecting on the Riviera it was even worse, although some Italian commanders did manage to bring Jews with them when they returned to Italy. The Italians guarding one forced-residence village set up a route across the Alps into Italy, helping its inhabitants with food along the way – only to find that the Germans had anticipated this, and arrested both Jews and their Italian escorts when they arrived.

In Nice, so strongly Italian, there was jubilation at the thought that the Italians were no longer part of the hated Axis. Church bells rang, women kissed Italian soldiers, accordions played and couples danced in the streets. But this celebration did not last long, as within two days the Germans had rushed down to fill the void left by the Italians. Here is Raoul Mille, who had lived in Nice since the age of sixteen, describing their arrival in his novel *Les Amants du Paradis* (1987):

'From the west, where the sky glowed with a faint, milky light, rose the distant murmur of a panting beast. Its moan grew into a throbbing. The soil, the foundations, the walls, the beach itself shook in slow, heavy spasms. The day dawned, grey and pink, like the belly of a fish pulled from the sea. A mist blurred the horizon. It was against this surreal and quavering backdrop that the first tank appeared, then cars and trucks. The Germans were on the Promenade des Anglais.'

The difference between these new invaders and the Italians, with their haphazard, happy-go-lucky approach to military life, was striking. 'I can easily imagine a mass surrender of these troops to anyone for the taking,' wrote Elizabeth Foster presciently of the Italians. But of the German newcomers she said: 'I have just seen two companies of tough-looking customers march past our house singing at the top of their lungs a horrid song. The real invader, this, and no mistake.'

Soon the sunlit coast was a scene of horror and repression. Almost immediately the streets were filled with German soldiers, patrolling day and night, and a curfew was put in place; there were rumours and stories of arrests and executions. For with the Wehrmacht arrived Alois Brunner,* senior assistant to the Nazi Jew-hater-in-chief Adolf Eichmann. With his team of fifteen highly trained SS police, Brunner established his headquarters at the Excelsior and with cold efficiency immediately set about his chief's ruling passion, the capture for extermination of as many Jews as possible. Other troops requisitioned Nice's schools and most of the hotels.

Borders were quickly sealed, bus and rail terminals occupied and harbours blocked. Then, as Jews in the Italian zone had not been required to register, Brunner's men cruised the streets in their black Citroëns, picking up anyone who looked remotely Jewish. Men would be taken to the synagogue, made to drop their trousers and, if circumcised, seized (they included, of course, some Christians and Muslims). One French Catholic nurse was arrested simply because her name was Esther.

Other police raided hotels and apartments, and took away whole families – French collaborators would check names on mailboxes to see if they looked Jewish. Sometimes the Germans

---

* In the eighty days from Brunner's arrival to the day he left Nice over 2,000 Jews were rounded up, brought to the Hôtel Excelsior, registered there, and then sent to the death camps from the nearby train station.

were helped by French police, who still resented the Italians over-ruling them and who also thought that getting rid of foreign Jews would ease the situation over food for their own citizens. The concepts of nationality or mixed marriages, the age of children or the infirmity of people stood for nothing. They would be brought in trucks to the Excelsior, where Brunner would watch them arrive from his second-floor balcony. If found to be Jewish, their money and jewellery were confiscated, supposedly to reimburse the hotel for food and lodging during the days or weeks before they went to Drancy.

Many were tortured for information about brothers, parents and children not yet caught in the net. One begged an attending physician for a lethal injection; when this was refused, he threw himself from a window. Some young Jewish women, it was rumoured, were kept at the Excelsior, sterilised, then shipped out for the pleasure of the soldiers on the eastern front.

After the first successful sweeps, Brunner's quarry became more elusive as Jews were caught or disappeared into hiding. Those who went out at night might return to find that the Germans had invaded their apartments and stacked some of their goods, ready to take away; more often Brunner had to rely on informers who – paid 100, 1,000, even 5,000 francs per Jewish head – would come to the Excelsior to report, and collect. 'The people most feared and hated were the French who collaborated with the occupying troops,' said Elsie Gladman. To von Dincklage, who returned with Chanel from La Pausa at the end of the summer of 1943, the *maquis* sent word that he was now on their death list. So was Serge Lifar, who openly consorted with the Germans.

At this point Lifar moved into the Ritz and lived intermittently with Chanel, who took great care to keep this secret, never being seen anywhere in the hotel with him. The only person who knew was the wife of the manager, who heard it from the floor maid, deeply envious of someone who had not one but two attractive men to herself.

CHAPTER 14

>·→·◇·←·◇·←·<

Trying to Survive

After the Germans invaded the Riviera in the autumn of 1943, life for its inhabitants became a question of fear and survival. Families lived in terror: anything from a Jewish great-grandmother to an early membership of the Communist Party might trigger that dreaded knock at night. When Henriette Scortecci turned the mattress on the marital bed one day and found a number of Party leaflets (most *résistants* then were communists) that her husband distributed in the hospital where he worked, she lived from then on in a permanent state of terror that someone would betray him.

At the same time, cinemas, and even the opera, were packed. The black market was flourishing more than ever, although those who could not or would not afford it had seen no butter or fats of any kind, including olive oil; the monthly bread ration was constantly being halved; and the chicken or rabbit supposedly allowed every three months had not been seen for years (cats had disappeared, caught and sold as rabbit on the black market for high prices).

It was possible to tell those who used the black market by their silhouettes: they were the only people who were not skinny. Malnutrition had become so severe that teeth broke and finger- and toenails fell off. Two of Elizabeth Foster's teeth snapped in half while she ate her morning slice of bread, and the nails on the *femme de chambre*'s left hand came off. 'La maladie à la mode,' said the doctor who inspected it. Adding to demand were the women who had had, or were pregnant with, babies by German soldiers.*

Vichy Radio's only response was to castigate the black marketeers. An angry French Cabinet minister declared that it was commonly said: 'Les Allemands prennent tout et les Français volent le reste,'† adding that 'When the *camion*s of the Banque de France are used to transport tons of stolen food, and an organised band of schoolmasters of the secondary schools form an organisation to steal cigarettes from the prisoners' parcels, dishonesty and corruption are going too far.' An anecdote going the rounds, wrote Françoise Frenkel, was: 'Jean has just died!' 'Was he ill, then?' 'Not exactly, but you know, the poor man was only living off his ration coupons!'

Theft – of anything that could be sold to provide money for food – was constant. Patients stole thirty bottles of wine and most of his sheets from Elizabeth Foster's doctor; Elizabeth herself had various household articles stolen as well as kitchen pots and pans. Thieves would dress up as policemen and order the householder to open up, or disguise themselves as harmless-looking postmen saying they had something that had to be signed for, so could they see Madame? In both cases they would enter and ransack the apartment, tying up the owner if necessary.

With no petrol, any form of transport was at a premium. It was not safe to leave a bicycle anywhere as it would disappear almost instantly: doctors wheeled theirs into the apartments of their patients rather than, as formerly, leaving them in the halls of buildings. As the Germans requisitioned cars at random, some people 'buried' theirs, digging deep holes, putting the car on boards inside and covering the trench with a sheet of corrugated iron disguised with topsoil and growth.

The German invasion had taken many of the refugees, accustomed to the comparative safety of life under the Italians, by surprise. Some, however, were more prepared than others.

---

* By the middle of 1943, around 80,000 Frenchwomen were claiming support for children resulting from liaisons with the enemy.
† The Germans take everything and the French steal the rest.

The Klarsfeld family, who had been living in Nice, had prepared a hiding place. They had placed a cupboard in front of the opening to a small room and inserted a panel that opened into the back of the cupboard, the whole thing hidden by clothes hanging in front of it. When the Germans pounded on their door at midnight, the two children, eight-year-old Serge and his sister Georgette, and their mother quickly made their beds and climbed behind the panel. This took only a few moments – the sort of time anyone would take when woken out of a deep sleep. When their father Arno opened the door to the Germans he told them that his family was in the country. Looking at the empty, made-up beds, the Germans believed him, taking only Arno with them. That October he was deported to Auschwitz, where he died, having saved his family.

The Sungolowsky family also decided to leave their apartment when the round-ups began; one deciding factor, said their son Joseph, was the increasing number of denunciations. It was the start of a series of moves, keeping them barely one step ahead of the Gestapo. Their first hiding place was with an elderly widow who put her tiny apartment at their disposal, but as she knew the Gestapo could search her block of flats at any moment, she could not keep them long. Through the Bishop of Nice, Monseigneur Paul Rémond, a man who worked bravely and indefatigably on behalf of Jewish children and adults, despite knowing that the eyes of the Gestapo were on him, Joseph and his younger brother were sent to a villa called Cottage Bellevue, which was in the Cimiez quarter of Nice, run by a Madame Lemas.

Officially, it was a nursery for young children whose parents were away, usually living in a French colony. They took in other Jewish families and furnished a cellar for those fearing a round-up. The trapdoor leading down to the cellar was covered with cement (rather than being left wooden), and the entire floor of the room above was covered with carpet, so that there was no sign of the occupants cowering below ground. But when the Gestapo entered, their boots would ring through the cement, warning everyone to keep quiet.

'In the month of October 1943 we were woken in the middle

of the night by Madame Lemas, who told us that Gestapo agents had come to this area to pick up families who were hiding, and said we must pretend to be fast asleep,' remembered Joseph. 'We were very frightened. A few moments later, the Gestapo strode in – I saw them from under my eyelids. Madame Lemas accompanied them, holding in her arms a little Gentile girl who was in floods at having been woken. She told the Gestapo that we too were her children and must not be touched. They shone their torches on us, opened the door of the pavilion that gave onto the road to assure themselves that no one was there and then left, without looking for any other verification – which would have been disastrous for us. We were saved! A miracle had taken place!'

The German grip was steadily tightening. Bicycles were now banned from the Promenade des Anglais, and in December cement barriers nearly four metres high were built. The round-up raids were regular affairs and more difficult to evade, with informers everywhere.

Sometimes, though, the safest place was under the enemy's nose.

One Resistance leader, Colonel Gallizia, sent to Nice, left his men at Grenoble and installed himself in a villa in the rue François-Aune belonging to a sympathiser. As he ran a network he needed an office, and this was provided for him by Robert Streitz, Chanel's architect, who for some time had been an active Resistance worker while carrying on his practice. The room he offered was tucked high up under the attics of the seven-storey Palais Marie-Christine.* 'Here I had an office that only Cambours [his superior] knew of,' recorded Gallizia.

Just beside the Hôtel Celtic in Cannes, where Gestapo officers were quartered, stood the convent school of Ste-Marie. Here a brave nun called Mère Irène welcomed seven young Jewish girls, despite the fact that the Gestapo could see all the paths and alleyways in the garden and the various comings and goings from

---

* Now the Préfecture, Nice.

their windows. The primary-school inspector, who was aware of the situation, was frightened for Mère Irène's life and was always telling her to take the utmost care; he would also warn her when a round-up was coming.

The children had been sent there by the Bishop of Nice, who had managed to obtain false papers for them, as well as false baptism certificates. When they arrived, Mère Irène immediately gave them new names – but she had another, more tragic duty to perform: she had to tell them that their families had been caught in a round-up. 'I will never forget the scenes of despair when I had to tell them this terrible thing,' she said. 'I told them I would never abandon them.' Nor did she. All of the children spent the school year 1943–4 there, until Cannes was liberated in 1944. Only when all eight little girls had found lodgings or a family did they leave.

Gaby Fisher, now eleven, entered a dangerous and lonely period. She had been staying with her elder sister, whose marriage to a Frenchman had given her a French name, and attending the village school. Now old enough to go to a *lycée*, it was a question of Gaby, too, changing identity and living as a non-Jew. She had of course to attend school, or suspicions would instantly have been aroused. It was an unhappy time. The meals at the *lycée* were appalling, and so scarce that everyone was always hungry. Parents and relations often sent the girls food, which they tried to keep safe in locked boxes, but it was frequently stolen. Gaby had to sleep in a dormitory of fifty, so freezing-cold at night that the girls often slept two in a bed. 'This was strictly forbidden but we couldn't understand why the supervisors had such fear of letting us sleep two by two in a bed.' Gaby herself often slept with another Jewish girl called Miriam, sometimes both crying themselves to sleep as they confided how much they missed their parents. 'Once I told a Gentile friend that I was Jewish, it was a secret too heavy to keep to myself.'

Schools were a favourite target for the Gestapo. They would notice if a child did not immediately answer to its name – a sign that it might have been given a new, non-Jewish one to disguise its origins. At boys' schools they simply looked to see who was circumcised. To avoid detection some Jewish children pretended to be Catholic. Those who refused because they did not want to go to Mass were told to say they were Protestant, which excused them, but still allowed them to pass as Christians. Sometimes a child would be held back from the all-important *baccalauréat* exam because militiamen would invade the exam room checking the identities of pupils – they knew the importance of the exam, and that hidden Jewish children were therefore likely to sit it.

Occasionally a child cast as Catholic to save its life would remain in that faith. Miriam Selz and her brother were both baptised Catholic in the first year of the war in order to escape persecution. When Paris fell, her father brought a lorryload of children under the Red Cross to Cannes. He and her brothers left to hide in the Dordogne and Miriam was put into a religious school. Here she made her first Communion and was confirmed by the Bishop of Nice, Monseigneur Rémond.

When the Germans arrived in 1943 her mother left at once for Monte Carlo. One day the headmistress called her in, aged twelve, and said: 'I'm terribly sorry but I can no longer keep you here because the Germans came yesterday to the boys' school to see if any of them were circumcised. Here at Ste-Marie we are hiding a dozen young Polish-Jewish girls and it's too dangerous for us to keep you.' She left the same day for Monte Carlo, where she found her mother and her aunt. Fixed up with false papers giving her name as Marie Sellier, she was sent to a convent deep in the country. Here she stayed, lonely and miserable ('from time to time I had fits of uncontrollable weeping'), missing her family and wondering how they were and if they had survived, an almost unbearable burden for a young child. With a changed name and a new faith, keeping a sense of her own identity was extraordinarily difficult.

Not everyone succeeded in escaping the invaders. Raymond-Raoul Lambert and his family were arrested in Marseilles and deported via Drancy to Auschwitz on 7 December, where they were gassed.

*

For her proposed trip (which became known as Operation *Modelhut*)* Chanel again wanted a companion, so much so that she refused to travel without one – she had never travelled alone in her life, she told Momm – and the one she wanted was Vera Lombardi, her old friend from the Duke of Westminster days, whom she had last seen four years previously. Although Vera had left Chanel's employment in 1930 to work for the designer Edward Molyneux, the two had remained friends.

This was an added complication: Vera's Italian Army husband Alberto had fled into the hills to escape when the Germans invaded Italy after the 8 September armistice. When a German officer called on Vera with roses and a letter from Chanel ('I'm going back to work and I want you to come and help me. Do exactly as the bearer of this letter says . . . all my love') Vera refused at once. The last thing she wanted was to be away from the possibility of seeing her husband.

A few days later, on 11 November 1943, Vera was arrested and put in the Roman women's prison, among thieves and prostitutes. It was somehow understood by the Nazis that she was a British spy, but when they learnt of her social connections they believed she could be useful to them and she was released and told she must go to Paris to join Chanel. With the Allies advancing up Italy, her brother with the British Army and her husband hidden nearby, she was reluctant, but realised she had little choice. To Paris she was taken, much against her will, and in the Ritz she met Chanel, who told her that she was going to open up the House of Chanel in Madrid.

Each kept a secret from the other. Chanel did not tell Vera that the moment they reached Madrid she was going to call on the English Ambassador to arrange the meeting with Churchill, and Vera did not tell Chanel that she herself planned to visit that same English Ambassador, to see if he could arrange for her to travel to the part of Italy where the Allies were now securely entrenched. Once there, she was certain, she could contact her

---

* Operation Model Hat – perhaps a reference to Chanel's early career as a milliner.

husband (now in hiding with a family she knew) and he would be able to join her. All they talked about, though, was fashion.

They arrived in Madrid in late December 1943 or early January 1944. Once there, the inevitable happened. The two women, who both headed for the British Embassy when they found themselves on their own, came face to face in its doorway as they were leaving. According to Edmonde Charles-Roux, it was Chanel who first recovered from the shock. 'Well, this is a fine thing!' she is supposed to have said. 'Are we going to stand here for ever staring at each other like a couple of cats?'

Vera had been to the embassy not only to try and reach her husband but to denounce Chanel as a German agent. Chanel cannot have known this at the time, as she wrote to Churchill (who had become seriously ill in Tunisia and cancelled his visit to Madrid) on behalf of Vera. Her six-page handwritten letter, handed to a senior British diplomat at the embassy, asked Churchill if he would put in a word that would smooth out all Vera's difficulties and allow her to go back to Rome and her husband without fear of prison (as Vaughan records, there is a copy of this letter in the Churchill archives at Chartwell, along with a note saying that it was seen by Clementine Churchill while her husband was away). It ended: 'Always affectionately, Coco Chanel.'

After writing it, Chanel returned to Paris, leaving Vera in Madrid. She also wrote Vera a letter showing that she had now become aware of Vera's denunciation. 'In spite of the frontiers, everything travels quickly! I know of your betrayals! You will gain nothing from them except having hurt me deeply,' although one of her concluding sentences was less accusatory: 'I hope with my whole heart that you find your happiness again.' In Madrid Vera stayed with various people she knew and earned her living by painting equestrian scenes until she was finally able to escape.

Then came Chanel's most extraordinary move: a visit to Berlin to report to Schellenberg the failure of her peace mission. When Schellenberg was interrogated by the British after the German defeat, he indicated that he had hoped Chanel might at least give Churchill a message that senior German commanders were at odds with Hitler, and were seeking an end to the war.

They met in his office, fortified against every possible contingency. 'There were microphones everywhere, in the walls, under my desk, in every lamp,' wrote Schellenberg in his memoir *The Labyrinth* (1956). 'My desk was like a miniature *blockhaus*. Two automatic weapons were built into it, which could fill the entire room with repeating fire at a moment's notice . . . another button set off the alarm signal ordering the guards to surround the building immediately and block every exit.'

There is no record of the conversation between the pair, so why Chanel went to see him has never been fully explained. Perhaps it was simply to draw a line under that particular episode.

How much or how far Chanel collaborated is still a matter for conjecture. There are certain incontrovertible facts: she was on the files of the British, the French and the Germans. The Germans clearly thought she could be of use to them; to the British and French she was a person, as were many others, to be watched.

What is certain is that while she was both pro-British and pro-French, she was above all pro-Chanel. Having hauled herself up from a background of which she appears to have been ashamed – why else would she so obfuscate her early years? – to achieve the life that she had designed for herself, she was not prepared to see it obliterated if she could help it. In addition, her view of the world was profoundly solipsistic. She did not feel part of the war; all she wanted was to go on living as she wished, seeing her lover and her friends – if this meant meeting German officers in the drawing rooms of the Serts or Serge Lifar, so be it; and she attended events and dinners given by friends who themselves worked with or for the Germans. Otherwise, she ignored the enemy.

Certainly, she was an enthusiastic 'horizontal collaborator', with a German lover (whom she never tired of saying was half-English). Yet although since long before the war Hans Günther von Dincklage had been known as a spy, in Sanary, where his wife lived and where he frequently stayed, it is difficult to believe that Chanel's pillow talk contained anything of real value to Germany. Without access to either the British or the

Resistance, she could not have known much that was useful militarily, although perhaps she hinted that she knew more than she did in her efforts to secure the release of her nephew.

Could the visit to Madrid be described as working for the enemy? In one sense yes, as it was what some in Germany – who knows how many? – wished. Yet Chanel's belief in her own powers, and wish to see peace again, coupled with Schellenberg's anxiety to make tentative approaches to the Allies to negotiate an end to the war, is not exactly treachery as most people would count it. The record of her conversations with diplomats discloses nothing more than the French attitude to their German overlords.

As to her affair with von Dincklage, he was a man of great physical attraction and Chanel was used to having a man both by her side and in her bed. She was sixty and could no longer count on having a pool of suitors at her beck and call. As always, she was determined to lead her life as suited her and she would not have wanted to pass up this fine specimen because he happened to be the wrong nationality. Although for both it made life easier, there seems little doubt that they loved each other.

CHAPTER 13

>-◆>--O--◆-◁

Dubious Activities

The Paris that Chanel returned to after her Madrid visit had become known as 'La capitale de la faim', so desperately hungry were most of its inhabitants. Everything possible was sent to Germany; German soldiers received forty francs a day to spend on French goods and shopkeepers and farmers were required to sell to them.

Restaurant meals consisted of three courses only, and on certain days neither meat nor alcohol could be served. To survive, most restaurants had to have recourse to the black market, somehow disguising the extra (illicit) price customers had to pay. The commonest method was by giving two bills, one with the legal cost of the meal and a second, supplementary one containing the extra costs which was destroyed immediately after payment. As on the Riviera, food was the constant topic of conversation.

None of this applied to the lucky few, of whom Chanel was one. From the start, the Germans allowed controls to be ignored on restaurants they favoured. Determined to enjoy the best of the world-famous French cuisine as victors' perquisites, they classified certain restaurants as *hors catégorie* (all others, from the cheapest to the more expensive, had to keep accurate written records to prove that they were sticking to the rules). Although by March 1944 most Paris restaurants closed for two or three days every week, at these HC restaurants, where the clientele was composed of German officers, French nouveaux riches, collaborators and black marketeers, meals were as

237

elaborate and delicious as before the war: Maxim's customers were said to drink more than 10,000 bottles of champagne every week.

Social life was flourishing. 'The two high-spots were Maxim's and the Racing,'* wrote Serge Lifar. 'There everyone who was "anyone" in Paris went to see and be seen.' They also walked or took the metro, as other transport had become almost impossible, to some of the favoured hostesses. Perhaps the most famous of these was Florence Gould, already one of the best-known figures of the Riviera. Soon after the occupation, Florence had hurried back to Paris, leaving her husband leading a life cushioned by his wealth in his Juan-les-Pins villa. As the couple's boulevard Suchet apartment had been requisitioned by the Wehrmacht, Florence went to live at the Hôtel Bristol, where she began to entertain lavishly.

It was not long before one of her friends, Marie-Louise Bousquet, popular for her regular luncheons where upper-class French society figures and certain selected German officers met, suggested that Florence host a literary salon. It was an idea that appealed to her: as she once said, 'I may not know much about literature but I know a lot about writers.' She bought a spacious apartment in the avenue Malakoff, furnished it well and expensively, and in April 1942 opened her doors to high-ranking members of the Wehrmacht and German officialdom as well as literary Paris. It was an immediate success. She was rich, hospitable and at forty-seven still extremely good-looking. One of her most frequent guests, the blond, Teutonically handsome Gerhard Heller, took her for thirty.

She and Heller had met at one of Marie-Louise's parties, of which Heller had written: 'Her apartment in the Palais Bourbon was filled with the sense of past centuries. One felt one was in a treasure house, filled with manuscripts and books with precious bindings. The first time I penetrated her sanctum, at the end of spring 1941, was for a concert, so crowded I sat on the

---

* Racing at Longchamp went on throughout the Second World War, with many German officers in the stands.

floor, At the reception afterwards, I was introduced to Florence Gould . . .'

Heller was a guest worth having, the man in whose hands lay the power to allow or ban all publications, and to whom every manuscript had to be submitted for approval. The thirty-three-year-old Heller, head of the Literature Section of the German Propaganda Department, was a man who genuinely admired French culture, although his seemingly liberal approach belied his core belief in both Nazidom and the superiority of German cultural achievement.

In his journal of those days, he describes the luxury of Florence's entertaining (the salon took place around lunchtime so that it was not interrupted by the curfew): 'nothing was lacking at her table. Some of the guests . . . had difficulty managing these opulent meals with their refined wine, champagne and – rarest of all – coffee, because their stomachs had become so unaccustomed to those things'.

Thanks to her German lovers, Florence's life and entertaining were as extravagant as in pre-war days. As most of Paris, including the literary élite, were cold and almost starving, Florence's apartment, heated by the truckloads of coal she was allowed to purchase (anyone else was lucky if they managed to acquire a kilo or two) and her black-lacquer dining tables loaded with sumptuous food were an irresistible draw to all but the most determinedly anti-collaborationist. One writer handed a 'doggy bag' of leftover beef felt that he would now be able to eat for a week; food had become so scarce that some Parisians had even begun to breed rabbits in their apartments as a source of meat.

Another who had left the Riviera in the autumn of 1940 was Colette, who had returned with her Jewish husband Maurice Goudeket to their apartment in the Palais Royal. Here she had begun to write again, in German-approved weeklies. She needed the money and she stuck to her favourite, apolitical subjects – cats, the intricacies of love, the comfort of a well-arranged interior. Her fame not only ensured a lively social life, it also secured the release of Maurice when he was arrested in December 1941. To save him, she had appealed to all her famous friends who might help, from the actor, playwright and screenwriter Sacha Guitry to José-Maria Sert, both of whom had come to terms with the Germans; but it is thought that her countrywoman, the French wife of the German Ambassador Otto Abetz, who loved Colette's work, was the one who clinched it, managing to persuade her husband to order Maurice's release.

Maurice returned at the beginning of February 1942, his first act being to strip off his clothes in the hall of the Palais Royal apartment (so as not to bring in any insect infestation) and demand a bath to rid himself of the smell of the camp. With false papers, he left briefly for St-Tropez; the letters he wrote to Colette were signed with his host's (French) name. Colette, whose health had begun its disintegration, remained in their apartment where, in the summer of 1942, she wrote one of her best-known works, *Gigi*. Maurice returned at the end of 1942 and, because Colette was so worried about the possibility of his rearrest, thenceforth spent every night in the small maid's room above Colette's apartment, coming down at 9.00 a.m. (Gestapo arrests were usually much earlier).

Though Chanel spent most of the time living quietly with Spatz, she would quite often attend the parties and events given by friends who either worked for or with the Germans, such as the novelist Paul Morand, much admired by the upper echelons of Paris society, Serge Lifar (ballet evenings were popular with German officers), or the Serts. Lifar would also pass quiet evenings with Chanel as she played the piano and sometimes sang – a reversion to her early beginnings as a café singer.

Others at these gatherings might be Cocteau and Sacha Guitry. Guitry, a strongly patriotic man who had managed to smuggle a replica of the Enigma code-breaking machine to Bletchley Park in August 1939, had continued to work on both stage and screen under the Germans; although this enabled him to help compatriots, it also brought accusations of collaboration. Another guest, the immensely popular actress Arletty, made no bones about having a German Luftwaffe officer lover, reputedly saying: 'My heart is French but my ass is international,' when later charged with the crime of treason.

*

In January 1943 restaurants and cinemas in Nice were closed and the Promenade was off-limits. It was announced that if anyone failed to observe the blackout completely, the Germans would shout, 'Lichter aus!' (Lights out!), and if this command was not instantly obeyed, fire shots at the offending window. One day the entire population was ordered to remain in their homes from 7.00 a.m. until the all-clear siren sounded because Rommel and various dignitaries were visiting.

The cold and the lack of heating were such that Elizabeth Foster dressed daily for her indoor life in several pairs of thick stockings, a heavy winter dress topped by a fur cape and one of her two overcoats. Her apartment was becoming barer by the week as she sold various of its contents to obtain the money to survive. 'Not to be cold, nor hungry, nor dirty are worth a Te Deum, and yet I have had these blessings all my life without noticing them.'

The Germans seemed to be everywhere. Soldiers, their chests bare as the spring sunshine arrived, built gun emplacements, dug trenches and laid mines in the beach, stripped the Jetée-Promenade of its copper, bronze and zinc and took over the top hotels in Nice for their different commands, or could be seen marching along country roads camouflaged with branches of mimosa in full bloom. Only those with some access to a clandestine radio could discover what was going on outside. In country villages, often the only news came through the town crier beating his drum to get attention and then reading out the news; otherwise people relied on the 'pavement radio' (gossip).

People were already fleeing Nice, a process speeded up when the order came that all foreigners living in hotels had to depart. For Elizabeth, unable to leave her apartment, this news was a horrible shock, especially when it was reported to her that the French police had refused to accept her doctor's certificate to this effect, merely replying, 'What does it matter if she dies a few days sooner rather than later? She is an American, and must leave.' After days of anxiety she found she could stay, as did a number of others. The evacuation in any case was a slow process, as no one was allowed to go until they had got a permit from some department prepared to receive them, and more and more of these refused. It was generally only small towns or villages which would take in evacuees, who had to bring all bedding, even mattresses, with them.

Barbed wire appeared on the Promenade des Anglais, the windows of the majestic Hôtel Negresco were boarded up and trenches dug in parks and flower beds. Next came a government order that all householders must hand over a specific amount of copper, or be fined. Brass or nickel could be substituted, but then more was needed. Doctors took down their brass plates, door knockers and doorbells were wrenched out, stair rods and curtain rings removed and brass candlesticks, fire dogs and fenders sacrificed.

There were an increasing number of rules and regulations. The small bread ration now always had to be bought from the same baker, which resulted in long queues; often the bread ran out halfway through and the rest of the queue was told to return later – something difficult for working people. Elizabeth continued to sell possessions to obtain the money to survive: 'My latest sale was my large Vuitton wardrobe trunk, a present from Uncle George one Christmas. This brought 2,500 francs – pretty good after twenty years' service. Vuitton bought it back.'

Even when the Germans realised that they might lose the war, they pursued the Jews with unrelenting ferocity.

'There is a terrible little notice that appears almost daily in the Nice Éclaireur headed "Avis" and giving the names of men shot by order of the German High Command,' wrote Elizabeth Foster on 3 December 1943 in her daily diary. 'It does not mention whether Nice or the Riviera in general but it makes my blood run cold as does the roar of huge trucks dashing through our streets, for I know that means the arrests of Jews or suspects. The Gestapo make people open up in the middle of the night and show their papers to prove they are not Jews. A pug nose is an asset nowadays.'

Some older children were saved by being put in boarding

schools. As stories of families that had been killed in air raids could not be disproved, since archives in their 'home cities' were also destroyed, such children were often described as orphans which, lonely and miserable, they must have felt like. But the search continued, with German thoroughness and persistence, fanning out into the countryside and remote villages. Here it was often easier to hide someone: not only was there a strong sense of community, coupled with the general niceness of country people everywhere, as well as hiding places and paths unknown to 'les Teutons', but also the fact that it was more likely that any betrayer could be identified.

All the same, extreme caution was needed. 'When did you last see your father?' might be asked of a small child, who would automatically answer truthfully. 'People were traced to even the most obscure hideouts,' wrote Paula Tattmar, who had been living in the small town of Lagrasse after being released from Gurs detention camp. Anything might give them away. One Jewish woman being hidden in the village of Annot, where several villagers had been deported and others shot and the Germans were ever present, had been tucked away in a small attic at the top of one of the houses, where food could be brought to her but where the big problem was emptying the chamber pot she was obliged to use. Only under cover of darkness, when it was certain no one was about, could it be taken down and surreptitiously emptied into the gutter.

Paula herself was among these survivors, living in constant fear that the next few days would bring death. She had rented a small house in a village and in October 1943 she offered the shelter of its barn to a young Jew named Martin, who had escaped from a forced-labour camp. Soon the two were in love, when to her horror Paula learnt that both the Gestapo and the Vichy police were now looking for Martin.

'On Christmas Day 1943 a Jewish woman from a neighbouring village told me that there was a warning of a big manhunt to be carried out in the next three days. I knew very well what this meant: a warning to look for a hiding place for these three days. But where to seek refuge? Most of the villagers were in church.'

Paula threw herself on the mercy of the district's chief of police, who promised he would not give her away. 'I understood that we had nothing to fear from the local police, but this was not so with the Gestapo and the Vichy police.'

She was fairly sure that her village friends would not denounce her, but giving shelter was another matter as it was punishable by death. She went to see the local baker, Monsieur Bertrand, who delivered bread in his little van twice a week to the nearby hamlets, thinking that if anyone would know of somewhere she and Martin could hide, he would. She also knew that although leaving by day would be dangerous, by night it would be suicidal, because of the German soldiers patrolling the region.

The brave Monsieur Bertrand said he would give her shelter. 'We have a room in our house just above the oven,' he told her. 'It's very hot but we'll bring you water to sprinkle on the floorboards. At night you can open the window a little and during the day you can put up a blanket to hide this. It is a loft, in line with all the houses all round and we don't want anyone to see you.'

He stressed the need for total secrecy. 'You know what can happen to us if I'm denounced to the Germans. They will burn down my shop, deport my wife and children and shoot me in the village square. My wife will bring you food whenever she can. Our bakery is open all day and my parents, who don't live far away, come visiting all the time. Nothing must change. And by the way, our three daughters must not know you are here. Come tonight and bring what you need.' Madame Bertrand added timidly: 'I hope you'll like my cooking. We haven't much, what with all the shortages and rationing, but we can sort things out.'

Paula was so overwhelmed by their kindness and courage that she burst into tears and managed with difficulty to express her gratitude. She then explained she was not alone, and the Bertrands agreed to take them both, refusing any offer of payment either then or later ('If we can help save you, that will be our reward'). Paula was told to come by herself, followed a few minutes later by Martin, dressed as a woman and with a scarf round his head.

They put out the fire in Paula's cottage and cleaned the ashes away so that no one would see any trace of someone having lived there recently, then slipped over to the Bertrands' to be greeted by a spotless room with a bed smelling of fresh linen. There were towels on a shelf and a mirror had even been fixed to the wall. A heavy blanket covered the window and a lamp gave a feeble light. Nothing could have been more welcoming. As Paula later wrote: 'From the moment we were in this marvellous house, they treated us as welcome visitors or very dear friends. I have never experienced such warmth and goodness. As the door closed behind us we both cried, both because of the terrible day just passed and because we had forgotten that people like the Bertrands still existed.'

They stayed there for three months, after which time Martin was able to get in touch with the French Resistance, and in August was one of those who marched in to liberate the village.

The *Éclaireur* was shut down, despite its pro-German stance and constant use of phrases like 'Our magnanimous victors'. All bookshops and libraries were closed, with every English book and those written by Jews confiscated. Any travelling now meant changing trains several times, often walking a few kilometres between stations.

In the villages behind the coast, life was a little easier – or rather, a little less difficult. It was in any case a peasant economy, poor and basic, with everything geared to scratching a living from the farms, smallholdings, or a few square metres in the valleys that threaded the hills running down to the sea. Here life went on as it had done through the centuries, according to both superstition and custom: within living memory, for instance, potatoes were only planted on the night of a new moon, preferably around 3.00 a.m.

Education was rudimentary. Children went to school aged seven or eight, with a three-month-long summer holiday at harvesting time. In the winter, recalled Yvonne Simon, an elementary-school teacher from Le Cabbe who taught in the back country, children would arrive at school clutching their packed lunches and a log. 'These logs kept the stove, our only form of heating, going,' said Yvonne, who lived in a room above the classroom.

Most children left at the age of twelve to help their parents, she remembered. There was the vegetable garden to dig and harvest, hens and rabbits to feed and, if goats were kept, these to watch over and milk; the cheese could be sold at the market. With enough land, a few vines could be planted, from which was made the local rough red wine. If anyone was lucky enough to catch one of the wild boars that lived in the woods nearby, the village was sure of meat that night. Clothes were basic, patched and re-patched, with heavy, home-knitted long woollen stockings in winter and potato sacks draped over the shoulders if it rained.

Those with family in Nice or one of the coastal towns would sometimes make the journey down with vegetables or eggs, carefully concealed because of the theft or confiscation that was rife; one man, a worker at the Pasteur Hospital in Nice, given the wonderful present of two eggs by a colleague who owned a small farm, put one in each pocket for concealment when he left the hospital that night. He was stopped by the Gestapo, who thought the suspicious bulges might be grenades. The discovery that he was unarmed and carrying the correct papers did not stop them from taking the eggs.

In 1944 the *baccalauréat* was to be taken in March, not as usual in June, as the Nice authorities feared an Allied landing and disruption. One of those taking it was Simone Jacob.* Her father, an architect and veteran of the First World War, had moved to Nice in 1924 because he realised that building on the Côte d'Azur would expand. His foresight enabled him to establish a successful practice and the family were comfortably off.

'At first the war seemed but a distant echo,' wrote Simone, expressing the feelings of all those around her on the Côte. Then came the Jewish statutes, as a result of which two of Simone's teachers had to vacate their posts in December 1940; then, in 1941, Jews were ordered to identify themselves – first the foreigners and then the French. But until September 1943 the

---

* Later well known as the distinguished politician Simone Veil.

Jacobs, like other Jews in Nice, had felt themselves safe under the liberal regime of the Italians.

Almost immediately after the arrival of the Gestapo, Simone's best friend from school was arrested with her parents (and later gassed on arrival at Auschwitz). The only answer for the Veil family was to split up and hide. They managed to acquire false identity cards and went to live with different people. The headmistress of Simone's school had told her that she would have to stay away from school as several girls had been arrested and she could not take the responsibility. Unhesitatingly, her French professor of literature took her into her family; here Simone was brought books to study and homework by fellow pupils.

But the *baccalauréat* was so important that it would have been worthless to her under a false name, so when the day of the exam came, she sat it as Simone Jacob rather than under the name on her new, false identity card. The day after completing it, en route with a companion to meet friends to celebrate, she was arrested and taken to the Gestapo headquarters at the Excelsior. There the fact that her papers were false was discovered when she was confronted with an identity card bearing her recognisable signature in the green ink she always used. The boy she was with went to warn her family, but the Gestapo followed him and they were caught. All were taken to Drancy; thence Simone, her mother and one sister were sent first to Auschwitz and then to Belsen (where her mother died of typhus shortly before the Liberation).

When Cocteau thought of reviving his play *Antigone* in 1944[*] he asked Chanel to work with him again. She had already created the clothes for a number of his productions, most recently *Les Chevaliers de la table ronde* (in 1937) as well as for Jean Renoir's 1939 film *La Règle du jeu* – reminiscent of her Westminster days with its plot centred on a large house party gathered for a hunt. She had also designed the costumes for that earlier, 1927 Cocteau *Antigone*,[†] for which Picasso had created the sets.

---

[*] In the event, it was put on by Jean Anouilh.
[†] First performed as a play in 1922.

Despite the fame of both men, it was Chanel who had stolen most of the headlines for the clothes made of Scottish wools and tweeds chosen by Cocteau ('Chanel becomes Greek', said *Vogue*). To persuade her, Cocteau had written her a long and carefully flattering letter. 'Your work is . . . "a kind of miracle", [you have] worked in fashion according to rules that seem to have value only for painters, musicians and poets. Pablo Picasso said that you are "the woman with the most sense in Europe". I completely agree . . .'

The chance of again working closely with Picasso may also have been a draw: Chanel had first met him through Misia Sert during the time of their early intimacy and had, as she later admitted, been enthralled by him. 'He was wicked. He was fascinating like a sparrow hawk, he made me a little afraid. I felt it when he arrived; something would shrivel within me. He is there! I wouldn't see him yet, but I would know he was in the room. And then I would discover him. He had a way of looking at me . . . I trembled.'

So close did they become when they worked together on *Train Bleu* that she kept a room ready for him at her then apartment on the rue St-Honoré where he could stay when he wanted to escape from domesticity but did not want to be alone. For Chanel this would have been welcome: a feeling of loneliness was at the core of her being. 'At the age of six I am already alone,' she told her friend and biographer Paul Morand. Lover after lover had 'left' her; some, like Boy Capel and Iribe, through death, others through social pressures. Nor had she any children although, according to some stories, she had longed to conceive during her affair with Bendor.

For Chanel, to be needed for her creative powers by Cocteau must have been a boon. Her work, which she had given up so abruptly, had been her life. Years later, she told Louise de Vilmorin, one of her biographers: 'A loveless childhood developed in me a violent need to be loved. This need . . . explains, I think, my whole life. I consider my success as proof of love, and I like to think that, when people love what I create, they are loving me as well, loving me through my creations. When I realised that my business had a life, my life, and a face, my face, a voice, my own, and when I realised that my work loved me, obeyed me, and responded to me, I gave myself over to it completely and I have had since then no greater love.'

CHAPTER 16

>─┤◆├─○─┤◆├─◁

The Resistance Grows Stronger, the Starving People Weaker

In the months before the Liberation, life on the Riviera became both more confused and crueller. The Resistance had grown in strength and daring, meaning that there were more frequent reprisals from the Germans against civilian hostages; betrayals too had increased, sometimes because of the larger sums now offered to informers, sometimes out of revenge, while the Vichy police and the Milice continued their round-ups. 'No one who has not lived in an occupied country can realise the humiliation and frustration of the natives,' wrote Elsie Gladman of that time. The hospital itself was frequently visited without warning by plain-clothes agents to seek out anyone who might be hiding there, and all patients had to be checked and signed for.

Pétain was now widely recognised to be no more than a willing puppet for the Germans. Gloomy and apathetic, he had more or less given up governing – it was Laval who was now in the driving seat. As the joke emanating from Vichy, recorded by Jean Galtier-Boissière, had it: 'The latest from Vichy. "You know the Marshal is dead?" "No! Since when?" "Three months ago, but his entourage have hidden it from him."'

Hunger and the apathy resulting from it had taken hold. 'If one lives on the Riviera it is very hard to believe in the Resurrection of France,' wrote Elizabeth Foster. 'Nice is still a corpse and a repulsive one at that. But even Nice will join in the procession and rejoice, although she won't strike one blow for her own liberation. Not a sound or a movement.'

Orders and counter-orders caused confusion. No one knew from minute to minute what they might or might not do – whether they might go out or had to stay in because of a sudden curfew, whether they must close the shutters or could leave them open.

In the first four months of 1944, more Jews were arrested in France than at any time in the previous year, partly because Vichy initiated a campaign against 'lazy Jews' as not enough of them had voluntarily joined labour camps.

One of them was a friend of Chanel's, the Jewish poet Max Jacob, an intimate of Picasso and Cocteau who had converted to Catholicism many years earlier, left Paris and settled in St-Benoît-sur-Loire in 1936, where he lived and worked quietly. On 2 February he wrote to Cocteau, asking if he could enlist Chanel to help his imprisoned sister. ('I'd like to write to her. Maybe you can go and see her. Together, you two can save my sister.') Chanel turned to Sert and Cocteau to Georges Prade, a publisher friend of his who was an acquaintance of the all-powerful Otto Abetz. Three weeks later, Jacob himself was arrested by the Gestapo and interned at Orléans prison, whence he wrote a heartrending letter to Misia Sert. 'In my anguish I call for help . . . my older sister has died of grief. My brother-in-law dead in a concentration camp. My brother taken off to prison. I've borne it all, resigned to the curse of my poor race. But now the crowning horror: my youngest sister, my favourite, the one I called "ma petite" has been arrested with no pretext, taken to the depot, then to Drancy. It's for her that I ask your intervention, before they drag her off to Germany to die in some dark cell.'

Misia turned at once to Sert, who immediately pulled every string he knew. But it was no good. Max himself was taken off to Drancy, and although Prade telephoned Cocteau on 28 February saying he thought they would succeed, as Sert had finally been able to obtain the order for his release, it was too late. Max died, supposedly of pneumonia, on 5 March, the day before he was to be transported on the next convoy to Auschwitz.

On 14 April a directive was issued that 'All persons who are considered Jewish according to the law must be arrested without consideration for nationality or other circumstances.' This meant snatching them not only from the streets but from prisons, camps, children's homes, hospitals and old people's shelters.

As the Allies advanced up Italy, those who could listen clandestinely to their radios felt that liberation could not be far off. Adding to this belief was the appearance and attitude of the conquerors. On the Riviera, the German soldiery consisted of either very young or much older men: the Russian front was mopping up the tougher and more experienced. To save on petrol, dogs that measured forty-five centimetres at the shoulder were now requisitioned to pull light carts.

Bombing raids – the Allies aimed for railway lines or stations – had cut off transport and therefore food, so shortages were worse than ever. Often the raids caused cuts in the electricity supply and, as candles were unobtainable, only those who had a stock of them had a little light. The Germans, playing on French bitterness over the Allied raids, stepped up their propaganda efforts. Their theme was that the raids were useless and that therefore French lives and property were being sacrificed in vain.

At last a local newspaper – there had been none since the disappearance of *L'Éclaireur* – was being distributed. The *Petit Niçois* was for many the only way to keep up with the orders from the Germans, with news of when and where the daily food distribution would take place. These changed constantly, with penalties for disobedience, sometimes so quickly that other methods had to be used. 'A loudspeaker proclaimed that we might go out from 1 a.m. till 2 p.m. but must remain indoors from 2 p.m. to 6 p.m.,' wrote Elizabeth Foster in late May. 'No one knows what this means but the market was opened and the cook managed to get us aubergines and pears.'

On 5 June Rome was liberated by the Allies. Elizabeth and a friend celebrated this with an 'unhoped-for dish of macaroni' and a bottle of champagne given to her six months earlier for that very purpose. More exciting still, on the morning of 6 June 1944, thereafter known as D-Day, Operation Overlord went into action. American, Canadian, British and Free French troops, more than 150,000 in all, began the Normandy landings that would lead to the Liberation of France. In Vichy, Pétain declared that 'the battle which is taking place on our soil does not concern us'.

'Well, it has come at last, the long-expected zero hour,' wrote Elizabeth. 'You can – no, I do not believe you can – imagine what it means to us prisoners. We have days, weeks, perhaps months of patience before us and every prospect of things being worse before they are better, but we can stick it out now that the moment of action has come. I have sat glued to the radio all day trying to piece each fragment of news into a coherent idea of how it all goes . . . it is evening and so ends what the Algiers Radio calls "An unforgettable Day of Joy and Hope".'

News of the D-Day landings spread through wireless sets hidden in cellars and was whispered in queues for the solitary slice of bread that was all that was usually available. More and more sanctions, on anything that could in any way aid a potential invasion by the Allies, were imposed by the Germans, who were now also increasingly threatened by the Resistance, emboldened as defeat of the Nazis looked probable, and spurred on by de Gaulle in England.

On 11 June Elizabeth recorded that 'it has been announced that a thousand doctors must go to Germany'. At the end of the month all cars, vans and motorbikes were forbidden, as well as telephones and telegrams. On 1 July a curfew was imposed from 8 p.m. to 6 a.m., all cinemas, cafés and bars were closed until 13 July, as punishment for the killing of Germans.

New anti-tank barricades and trenches were constantly being constructed, many of them with the help of local men, who received hot meals in return. This was often a two-way traffic: through the workers, lured by much-desired food (on 5 July the bread ration had been halved), trickled plenty of information to the Allies.

Then came an episode that sent a shock of revulsion through the Niçois, and left some small children traumatised. On 7 July 1944 two young *résistants*, Séraphin Tamia and Ange Grassi, were hanged by the Germans on the avenue Jean Médecin after being terribly tortured. They were captured because someone had betrayed them and the hanging was in retaliation for the killing of two German officers and two German soldiers. To drive the lesson home, all traffic was forced to divert into the avenue and pedestrians too were obliged by the Germans to walk past the swinging corpses.

'A shudder of horror went thro' Nice yesterday afternoon,' wrote Elizabeth the following day. 'It had been a perfect cloudless summer's day, no alert since the night before, only an occasional distant cannon shot or explosion, the afternoon was radiant and suddenly came the dreadful news. Two soldiers of the underground front, "franc tireurs", the German communiqué calls them, had been caught, condemned to death by a military tribunal and the sentence immediately carried out by hanging on the avenue de la Victoire,* just opposite the Galeries Lafayette ... in the very centre of the business district, shops and banks, the Casino Municipal and the most crowded cafés ... there these poor bodies were left hanging.'

This grisly sight remained for three days. Several children† could not walk down that street again for the rest of their lives.

'After the gloomiest national holiday ever known in Nice, not a flag to be seen, the streets deserted, all manifestations and meetings, public and private forbidden, it was moving and comforting to listen this morning to the radio and to hear the bells sounding in Normandy, the "Marseillaise" sung and to feel the pulse of rejoicing by the people,' wrote Elizabeth Foster on 15 July.

In the small inland towns and villages, the Germans continued their sweep for more manpower.‡ In Vence, a little way inland from Nice and Antibes, one of its inhabitants, André Mellira, then a schoolchild, remembered: 'On 17 July 1944, our town

---

* The avenue Victoire had been renamed the avenue Jean Médecin after the 1918 armistice, but some people still referred to it by its old name.

† Reported to me by their descendants.

‡ By the end of the war, 650,000 French civilian workers had been sent to work in German factories, 60,000 had been deported to German concentration camps and 30,000 French civilians shot as hostages or members of the Resistance.

crier with his loudspeaker proclaimed that all the men were ordered to attend in the square of the great park. Patrols were sent to beat the countryside to bring in those who were there. I recognised one of our more distant neighbours climbing the route to Cagnes escorted by Germans. At the *place*, barriers stopped women having access. Members of the German security service come from Nice sat at a table with an interpreter; the men went past the table one by one with their identity papers. Most passed but a number of young ones were taken to Nice, and some deported.

'As the summer continued, the situation of the inhabitants deteriorated. The buckets of oats for the horses were replaced with buckets of chopped-up potatoes. Alerts were more and more frequent. Sometimes our teacher would take us into the woods where we would construct shelters.

'The enemy had become nervous and regularly requisitioned young men to dig trenches round the town. The work went slowly and stopped altogether when the supervisors' backs were turned. The fields were filled with barbed wire and piles of stones, no doubt to stop planes landing.

'Food got more and more difficult. Luckily we had fruit and vegetables. My father didn't smoke so bartered his tobacco ration for sugar from the chemist and for potatoes from a peasant at St-Paul.' They also had that once-plentiful but now rare commodity, olive oil, with two fruitful olive trees that had produced enough olives to make forty-five litres of olive oil, 'which we brought back on foot from the mill at Cagnes'.

The food situation was worse in towns, with the bread ration halved again, and Nice the only town to have any; other places subsisted on a kind of biscuit. So crushing was this shortage that two bakers were murdered and their bakeries ransacked. 'Yesterday a miracle happened,' wrote Elizabeth Foster. 'I came into the sitting room to see a glass of milk on the table. I could not believe my eyes. It was the first milk I had seen in two years. It opened visions of a world where milk and butter exist in reality, not just in dreams.'

Clothes were often bartered for food. 'Another nurse and I put into a bag some of our clothes – woollen jumpers, old coats, etc.,' wrote Elsie Gladman. Sharing the hospital's only bicycle, they made their way up into the small villages in the hills behind, where they were able to exchange their used garments for home-cured ham and pork, hidden by the villagers from the Germans.

All day long the siren howled its constant alerts, sending those who could do so darting down to cellars as the noise of explosions filled the air. Waves of Flying Fortresses passed overhead, so high that, as frightened birds flew about, they seemed larger than the huge bombers above. 'As I looked up, I knew that the hour of our deliverance was nigh,' wrote Elizabeth. 'Our alerts are so continuous that one wonders why they trouble to sound the all-clear. Will the end come today or tomorrow?'

The Resistance was stepping up its efforts. One of its members, Le Bas, whose vehicle assembly and repair workshop had been requisitioned by the Nazis, got on terms with the German officer who took over its running. Thanks to this rapport he learnt of the imminence of a punitive expedition against the village of Allos, where a German soldier had been killed, and was able to warn the local *maquis*, who prepared an ambush. The vehicle at the head of the German column was stopped at a horseshoe bend by a shot from a bazooka and its occupants, including the head of the expedition, were killed, which made the others decide to turn round. Another of Le Bas's exploits was his exploration of the coastline at Nice, now a forbidden zone. He did this on the pretext of testing the German vehicles entrusted to his workshop. His reports on the defences (blockhouses, carpets of nails, various traps) were of much more use to the Allies than a photograph.

Robert Streitz, through various contacts, was also able to channel information through the Resistance network to the Allies. He had come across a man he used to know well, a Russian engineer named Toumayef, with whom a friendship had developed when the two of them had gone on some memorable skiing trips together before the war. Toumayef was working for the Todt Organisation, the large German civil and military engineering group founded by the senior Nazi Fritz Todt, responsible for a huge range of engineering projects, not only in Germany but in occupied countries. Todt was notorious for using forced labour and Toumayef, an unwilling conscript, furnished Streitz with the plans of a submarine base being constructed in the bay of Passable and also those of the fortification of the Château in Nice. Even better, he told Streitz that the bunkers of artillery of that sector were unusable because of faulty ventilators.

A second good source for Streitz came via his Austrian wife, who knew an Austrian major who was – of course secretly – anti-Nazi. From time to time, he was able to pass on to his countrywomen information on the garrison and on the movement of troops. 'We learnt the essential points of the order of defence by the infantry division that occupied the terrain between Cannes and Menton,' wrote Colonel Galizzia, head of the Nice Resistance network, in his post-war history. 'That is to say, how long their resistance on the beaches would last (one hour), their fallback position and their chief way of getting there – the Route Napoléon. My own excursions on a bicycle had shown me that the area round Nice was emptying.' It was Streitz, he wrote, who added the final touch. He had persuaded his friend Toumayef to smear sand over the workings of the jackhammers that were being used to dig holes for mines on the wharves and jetties of Port Nice, so that their constant breakdowns hindered the work.

Everyone knew that invasion was only days away – but not where it would come. The landing area chosen was almost fifty kilometres (measured straight across), but the coastline, with its many deeply indented bays, added up to much more. Earlier, paratroopers had been dropped inland, each man equipped with everything from arms, ammunition and three days' rations to francs, cigarettes and morphine. Round their necks they wore silk scarves printed with maps in green, brown and blue of the main road network in Provence.

'AT LAST!' wrote Elizabeth Foster on 15 August. 'All night long aeroplanes roared overhead. I slept in brief snatches and each time I woke that never-ceasing roar continued. At four in the morning there was a deafening crash. At five things seemed quiet except for the distant fire of naval guns. I went to bed to doze until the morning radio at 6.30. At 7.30 the *femme de ménage* came in with news of a landing somewhere in southern France. Then a loudspeaker giving the order of the German commander that everyone must remain indoors. At 3 p.m. the radio gave the news that the Allies had landed at various ports from near Cannes to Fréjus, with very little opposition.' The landing was watched by Britain's Prime Minister, Winston Churchill, from the deck of the destroyer HMS *Kimberley*.

That day, the 15th, was Napoleon's birthday, and the Resistance in the Var used Napoleon as its codeword. At early dawn mist and fog obscured the shoreline, so that the air attack did not begin until 5.30 and shelling one hour later.

In Cannes, the Germans had blown up the *quais*. They had already put barrels of explosives through manhole covers into the sewage system; these were now detonated, destroying buildings facing the pier.

At Elsie Gladman's hospital nearby, as the Allied bombers thundered overhead, their target the gun emplacements on the hills above, the nurses spread a huge Red Cross flag over their courtyard, which they hoped would protect them. Two doors away, the Germans had an arms depot and a gun, which they also covered with a Red Cross flag.

For Elsie Gladman there was personal sadness. On the night before the Allies moved in, while Elsie listened to the firing all around them, the Germans murdered twenty of their captives, already weak from hunger and repeated torture. Among them was her Greek friend Hélène Vagliano, who had worked for the Allies by transmitting messages to the various French *résistant* groups, through her own portable broadcasting set carried in a shopping basket on her bicycle, while knowing that it was certain death if she was caught.

Hélène had been betrayed to the Gestapo by another woman and arrested on 29 July. She had been taken to Gestapo headquarters, tortured and mutilated, but she remained silent. As the Allies approached, the Germans, knowing the fate that would await them if this cruelty became known, loaded the prisoners into a truck and drove them to the bank of the River Paillon, where they were lined up facing the water and then machine-gunned by a squad of secret police. One of them was Hélène; her death was the macabre fulfilment of the prophecy made to her in 1940 by the clairvoyante whom she and Vera Boissevain had visited together.

Even on 15 August, when the Allies landed only a few kilometres from Cannes, the town was kept in a state of siege, with its people only allowed on the streets from 7.30 a.m. to 8.00 a.m. This close control lasted for nine days, until finally the German soldiers went, some on foot, some on bicycles, leaving machine-gun bullets strewn over pavements, blowing up miles of railway track and bridges as they retreated and shooting many whom they suspected of being Resistance workers in a last burst of horror before they left.

One of the first into Cannes was Marcel Block's son Peter, still unaware that his father had been sent to Auschwitz,* dropped as a paratrooper sixteen kilometres inland behind St-Raphael. 'There was practically no resistance from the Germans,' he said. 'At that stage of the war, a lot of their troops were non-German. We were pathfinders, mainly American, but Churchill had insisted there must be a British component. We got a great welcome – we drank champagne all afternoon.'

The scent of freedom took longer to reach Paris, where the Germans remained in charge, continuing with round-ups and arrests until the last minute. As the Allies fought their way through France, Chanel gave shelter to a friend who seemed to be wanted by both sides. Serge Lifar had been to the German Embassy on the morning of 11 August where his friend the Swedish Consul Raoul Nordling was trying to negotiate with the Germans to secure the release of hostages and the cancellation of convoys to Auschwitz. Walking back to his hotel in the twilight, Lifar saw four German officers sitting silently in a car outside.

From the hotel's shadowed interior, the manageress gestured to him to keep on walking. Lifar, fit and active from his years of

---

* See Chapter 13.

dancing, ran in the growing darkness to the rue Cambon, where he slipped into no. 31. Here he stayed, with Chanel looking after him. 'It was the only house in Paris that received me and maybe saved my life,' he said, 'for I was an undesirable everywhere. A sort of living corpse.' (Later, Chanel confided to a friend: 'I couldn't walk around the apartment even half undressed because Serge might be hiding in a closet.')

An orderly retreat of top German officials began the next day. Otto Abetz and his wife left by car in the evening. Von Dincklage had already gone, begging Chanel to accompany him, but she refused. Another who left was Gerhard Heller, but not before saying goodbye to Florence Gould.

On 13 August Galtier-Boissière noted the number of people enjoying themselves in the sunshine, as if all were well with the world, although the first signs that the Resistance was gathering its forces had appeared. 'The sunny banks of the Seine are black with people. Thousands of Parisians are bathing while the battle rages sixty kilometres away. For the first time there are posters of the Resistance on the walls and others detailing German atrocities. People gather to read them.'

Simone de Beauvoir wrote feelingly of the contrast between sunlit pleasure and sudden death. 'The morning seemed calm; on the banks of the Seine, you could see fishermen throwing out lines and some young men sunbathing in their swimsuits, but the FFI [the underground French Resistance] were hiding behind the balustrades of the embankments. A German truck passed beneath the window; two young soldiers, both very blond, stood upright, holding sub-machine guns; twenty metres away, death lay in wait for them. One felt like shouting, "Beware!" There was a burst of gunfire and they fell.'

On 15 August news of the Allied landing on the Riviera and subsequent Allied advance reached the French capital, a signal for fighting and tumult to begin. In a last fling, Brunner managed to send a final convoy to the death camps, 1,654 men (among them 168 captured Allied airmen) to Buchenwald and 546 women, all political prisoners, to Ravensbrück.

As the Germans began their evacuation, the Paris police, postal workers and metro workers went on strike, followed soon by every other worker. Paris was now a city in revolt, its citizens, led by the FFI, on the attack. There was gunfire everywhere – some of it from the shooting of some young FFI members in the Bois de Boulogne.

On 17 August Galtier-Boissière was writing gleefully: 'The great flight of the Fritzes. On every street, hundreds of lorries, hundreds of packed cars, ambulances carrying the wounded. The Paris police are on strike. Coming from sumptuous hotels, sparkling torpedoes of monocled generals, accompanied by blonde women elegantly dressed who seem ready to go to some stylish *plage*.' The same day, Pétain and Laval were driven under armed guard to Sigmaringen, a castle on the Danube near Stuttgart.

As fighting continued where the Germans had dug themselves in, the FFI took over the ministries. From then until the German garrison surrendered on 25 August there was bitter street fighting. The FFI built 600 makeshift barriers against German panzers from plane trees they and fellow citizens felled, building them up with sandbags they dragged along the pavements. People stitched *tricolores* and hung them out of windows as air battles raged overhead and came out of apartment buildings to bring the fighters food and ersatz coffee. Despite the pockets of German snipers and the FFI deaths, victory was in the air. 'Freedom is returning,' wrote Jean Guéhenno. 'We don't know where it is, but it is all around us in the night. It is approaching with the armies.'

At 3.30 that afternoon Major-General von Choltitz, Hitler's commanding officer in Paris, surrendered. He had been Paris's military governor for just over a fortnight, with instructions to be prepared to leave no Parisian religious building or historical monument standing. 'The city must not fall into the enemy's hand except lying in complete rubble,' read Hitler's cable, orders he ignored.

With uncertainty as to the moment of deliverance, the battles continued. Guéhenno himself returned home at about 10 p.m., to be rung by friends 'saying they can see huge fireworks over the Hôtel de Ville, with red and blue rockets answering them in the south and west. It was the signal. The first tanks of General

Leclerc's [Free French] army had just rolled up to Notre-Dame. And then all the bells of all the churches rang in the night, drowning out the rumbling of the big guns . . . Freedom – France is beginning again,' rejoiced Guehénno.

Wine flowed, the starving French* wept, laughed, embraced and sang the 'Marseillaise' in an exuberance of both joy and the disappearance of fear – gone was the terror of being pounced on as a hostage by the Gestapo and shot in retaliation for some successful action of the Resistance. Soldiers, their faces covered in lipstick, accepted flowers and kisses. It was, wrote Colette, an evening 'when night rose like a dawn'.

That night at the Hôtel de Ville, General de Gaulle declared: 'Paris! An outraged Paris! A broken Paris! A martyred Paris! But . . . a liberated Paris! Liberated by itself, liberated by its people with the help of the armies of France, fighting France, of the only France, the real France, the eternal France!' It was stirring stuff, even if a touch fanciful: many of the first company of French to enter Paris were Spanish Republicans,† and de Gaulle himself was only there through the aid of the Allies.

The next day, ignoring German sniper fire, de Gaulle led a victory parade of French forces down the Champs-Élysées, where for the past four years jackbooted German troops had marched daily, to the Arc de Triomphe. It was watched by everyone who could get near it, either standing in the crowds or hanging out of windows.

Chanel viewed the victory parade from José-Maria Sert's balcony, hung with some of his antique velvet for the occasion, which overlooked the place de la Concorde. Among the party of fifty, gazing at the spectacle with excitement, joy or apprehension, were Serge Lifar and Colette and Maurice Goudeket, whom Sert had sent his chauffeur and limousine to pick up. (The day

---

* It was four years since an adult had been allowed a fat ration, and since the Normandy landings and bombing of railways food had become even scarcer.
† Eighty per cent of the company led by Captain Raymond Dronne were Spanish Republicans, banished to Morocco by Franco, where they were recruited by General Leclerc.

before, Colette had said she would not believe in the Liberation until she had seen a Scottish officer, complete with kilt, in front of her. The devoted Maurice ran out and found one, whom he invited to lunch, a tin of black-market bully beef.)

Afterwards there was a feast. Laid out on Sert's magnificent tortoiseshell dining table were his heavy gold platters heaped with good things from Spain: ham, sausages, piles of fresh fruit, limitless champagne. As the guests ate, the windows suddenly shattered. It was gunfire – no comfort that it was from the exuberant liberating troops. Everyone fell on the floor or hid under tables as bullets spattered Sert's wonderful tapestries, only turning to the food again when the *feu de joie* was over. (On the Riviera the great excitement was the promise of a Victory Bun, for which, remembered Elsie Gladman, everyone had to register at the baker.)

De Gaulle's triumphal march ended at Notre-Dame for a Te Deum of thanksgiving. In the cathedral, a shot fired accidentally rang out. Malcolm Muggeridge, then a member of MI6, based in Paris, recorded: 'The huge congregation who had all been standing suddenly fell flat on their faces. There was a single exception: one solitary figure, like a lonely giant. It was, of course, de Gaulle. Thenceforth, that was how I always saw him – towering and alone; the rest, prostrate.'

Anaïs Nin, famous for pouring out every last thought into her journals, perhaps summed up best the feelings on that day. She wrote simply: 'JOY. JOY. JOY. JOY. JOY. JOY. JOY. JOY. JOY.'

CHAPTER 17

>─◆>─○─<◆─|─<

Last Days

Early in September 1944, two young men in sports shirts and sandals knocked on the door of Chanel's room at the Ritz and told her to come with them. 'On whose orders?' she asked. 'On those of Le Comité d'épuration,' she was told. These words were enough to strike terror into anyone.

Immediately after the Liberation came a period that most Frenchmen would prefer to forget. It was known as the *épuration sauvage* – the savage purification. *Résistants* turned on those they had marked down as collaborators, neighbour denounced neighbour, the prisons were stuffed with people who had committed real or imagined crimes. The épuration sauvage swept across the country. 'It is like some terrible epidemic,' wrote Cocteau of that time.

Women accused of *collaboration horizontale*, or sometimes merely suspected of it, had their heads shaved. The *tondues* – the shorn women – were often paraded through the streets on the back of a lorry; some were daubed with tar, some stripped half naked, some marked with swastikas in paint or lipstick. Some were young mothers whose husbands were prisoners of war and who, with no means of support, had gone to bed with Germans for food or other favours for their families; others were prostitutes, plying their trade irrespective of the nationality of the customer ('All men look the same with their clothes off,' said one). Several were merely cleaners who had cleaned German offices. Often, it was simple jealousy of those who through youth and prettiness had managed to eat well through a German 'friend'.

Milice members, more hated even than the police (who were prudently lying low) were often shot out of hand, either murdered by vengeful civilians and *résistants*, or after a speedy court martial. Those who could do so fled to Germany, where most were impressed into the Charlemagne Division of the Waffen-SS.

As for civilians, the first to be pounced on were those writers who had written openly pro-German articles, if only because there was evidence of collaboration in print for all to see. 'It sometimes seemed as if everyone was informing on everyone else,' said Malcolm Muggeridge. 'The truth is that under the German occupation everyone who did not go underground or abroad was in some degree a collaborator and could be plausibly accused as such.'

Deciding what was collaboration and what was not was a difficult question. Denouncing others or actively helping the Germans clearly was, but what about events in the daily grind of life or the battle for survival? Almost every artist, actor and writer had worked during the occupation. As only German-approved paintings, plays, books and newspapers could see the light of day, was this collaboration if it was the only way of earning enough to feed your family? Was it collaboration to attend the salons of those friends whom you knew entertained the enemy? Was continuing to work under Vichy collaboration? If you were an officer of that state, was upholding its laws, even those you knew to be inhuman, collaboration?

In the period between 1944 and 1951, 6,762 people were sentenced to death by the official French courts. Of those, 3,910 were tried in absentia. However, only 791 collaborators were actually executed; more were subjected to the *dégradation nationale* punishment, which included the loss of their political, civil and professional rights.*

Chanel's crime, of course, was having a German lover

---

* As a comparison, the Axis occupation forces and their allies in the French Milice killed 30,000 French people, while of the 76,000 French Jews who were deported by the Vichy government, only 3 per cent survived.

– something she had never bothered to conceal. When the two young *résistants* came for her that September day she drew on her gloves, picked up her handbag and walked out of the room in front of them, leaving her maid in tears and Serge Lifar, a prime target of theirs, still sharing her tiny Ritz apartment, hiding in a cupboard. (Soon afterwards, Lifar gave himself up, to the Comité d'épuration of the Opéra.) Later he said of her: 'Coco behaved like a queen, like Marie Antoinette being led to the scaffold. She left with the two Frenchmen who came to arrest her with her head held high.'

When shown a photograph of von Dincklage and asked if she knew him, she answered: 'Of course. I've known him for twenty years.'* When asked, 'Where is he?' she replied: 'He's a German so I suppose he's in Germany.' A few hours later she was released. No one really knows how or why, although there was much speculation that it was her friendship with Winston Churchill that had kept her out of trouble; the wife of the manager of the Ritz, a woman usually well informed about its inhabitants' doings, believed she had shown them letters from Churchill assuring her of his friendship and support. Another factor might have been that while the other couture houses had sold freely to German wives and mistresses, she had closed hers at the beginning of the war, thus refusing to deal with the enemy.

Perhaps the clincher was that the moment the Americans had entered Paris, she had said that every GI could have a free bottle of Chanel No. 5 for wife or sweetheart. Those who could not speak French simply held up five fingers to show they wanted a bottle of the most famous scent in the world. With a queue stretching round the block, it is likely that a large number of American soldiers would not have taken kindly to anything happening to Mademoiselle Chanel. Or, as Malcolm Muggeridge put it: 'By one of those majestically simple strokes which made Napoleon so successful a general, she just put an announcement in the window of her emporium that scent was free for GIs,

* Spatz had first entered France in 1928. During the playboy life he led thereafter, Chanel might easily have come across him, if not made a less fleeting acquaintanceship.

who thereupon queued up to get the bottles of Chanel No. 5 and would have been outraged if the French police had touched a hair of her head. Having thus gained a breathing space, she proceeded to look for help à gauche et à droite, and not in vain thereby managing to avoid making even a token appearance among the gilded company – Maurice Chevalier, Jean Cocteau, Sacha Guitry and other worthies – on a collaborationist charge.'

On the Riviera, final liberation was proceeding slowly. 'The Germans are still here, though they are said to have been withdrawn to Cimiez to await orders,' wrote Elizabeth Foster on 18 August. 'The German commander has just issued an order saying we are forbidden to leave our houses except from 2 p.m. to 6 p.m. I don't know how we shall be fed for the markets are open only in the morning. They have been practically empty for the past three days. No bread today but we were given a little macaroni and our August sugar ration. No fruit, no vegetables and of course no meat.' The present of six potatoes (to be shared among three) was a boon.

Cannes was the first city to gain its freedom as the Resistance, no longer scattered but well organised, rose against the remaining members of the Wehrmacht. A number, mostly Poles, Czechs and Romanians, gave themselves up. As in many towns, the first to feel the vengeance of the liberators were the women and girls who had had relationships with Germans. Rounded up by their fellow French, they were put in the Hôtel Montfleuri and their heads shaved before they were paraded through the streets. One American soldier, asked what he most remembered about the Liberation on the Riviera, said: 'The streets full of hair' – the shearers had got to work at once and the discarded tresses lay on pavements or in gutters.

Antibes too was liberated, on 24 August, by the local Resistance, joined by its inhabitants. They began by commandeering the main post office, railway station, docks and electricity depot, and countering German resistance until the first American troops arrived. The advance of Allied forces had been slow, as the Germans had mined the coastline. They were helped by information from the *résistants*, some of whom had cycled along the coastline through lesser-known roads, checking German movements.

The constant bombing of railways and major roads to stop the Germans regrouping inland, the blowing-up of bridges and miles of railway line by the Germans as they retreated eliminated most forms of transport and meant that nothing could be brought into the markets. Most shops now barricaded their windows because they feared riots and break-ins from the starving population.

'Everyone seems to have forgotten Nice, the fifth-largest city in France,' wrote Elizabeth on 24 August. By now, the time and distribution points of daily rations, such as they were ('No bread today, for the second day running'), were announced by loudspeaker, with everyone asked to tell their neighbour. Days were punctuated by sporadic bombing and cannon fire and, now, the noise of German lorries thundering past.

On the afternoon of 28 August, the German withdrawal began. It was an army far different from the fearsome grey-uniformed force that had entered almost a year earlier, full of the elderly and teenagers, and their vehicles were anything they could lay their hands on: lorries, tanks, requisitioned cars, even bicycles. As they headed for Italy they camouflaged themselves with branches in an attempt to avoid the relentless onslaught from above. When night fell, those in the hills above came down to join the retreat, firing as they went.

Finally, on 29 August, Nice was in the hands of its own people and the *résistants* rather than the Germans. Slowly, flags and *tricolore* streamers began to appear; and by the afternoon, the rioting and revenge had begun, much of the brunt of it borne by those of Italian descent. Before any form of legal trial had been put in place, there were beatings, pillage and killings. Men – and often women – were shot with either a bullet to the back of the neck or by a burst of machine-gun fire.

The Bishop of Nice managed to save a convent of Italian nuns from having their heads publicly shaved and their habits torn off. The first collaborators were arrested, posters of Marshal Pétain torn down, and swastikas painted over. By 31 August there had been more than a hundred summary executions and a number of unexplained disappearances.

The two main black-market stores were broken into and their stocks seized by the authorities for distribution. On 2 September Elizabeth Foster was writing: 'I have just had my first piece of white bread for four and a half years! I had forgotten how white real bread is and how good it is even butterless.' But not until mid-September did bread, though nothing else, appear regularly.

By the end of the month the morning paper, now permitted again, was full of outbursts from the Nice officials over the 'tragic, catastrophic' food situation, with appeals to the peasants in the surrounding provinces and North Africa for food. As Elizabeth wrote: 'The promised ships full of meat and oil do not arrive,* we have no potatoes, sugar, wine or farm produce. Of course no cheese or milk, except a little for babies.' Four ships had been sunk in the harbour by the departing Germans and food could not come by sea until the mines and this wreckage had been cleared. German prisoners were now removing obstructions and fortifications from the Promenade des Anglais. Much of Nice was mined – the gardens, the Promenade des Anglais and the boulevard Gambetta.

As the cold weather, early for once, began, hardship worsened. On 14 November Elizabeth commented: 'Coal is non-existent and wood very hard to obtain. Except for the American bread we are again worse off for food than before the Liberation. Sugar, fat substances, meat and macaroni have all vanished. We are getting thinner and thinner. I thought it wasn't possible but it is. But we are free at last from a five-year nightmare.'

For Chanel, the gradual ending of the war meant a period of what must have felt like limbo. She had no work, her lover had gone and many of her friends had either disappeared, were suffering punishment for collaboration or lying low. Nor could she have known if she herself was free of suspicion. Always the pragmatist, the following year she moved to Switzerland. Through a friend of the photographer Horst, she managed to send $10,000

---

* One was struck by a mine and sunk.

to von Dincklage, which enabled him to join her there.

Finally, it must have seemed safe for her to spend time in France again. The place that drew her back, to which most of her visits were made, was, almost inevitably, the one house that she would have called her real home – La Pausa.

EPILOGUE

>-◆-○-◆-<

The Riviera itself recovered comparatively quickly. German prisoners were used to remove the thousands of mines their own troops had laid anywhere they thought the Allies might land. The first Cannes Film Festival was held in September 1946, marking the return of French cinema to the world's screens; the Blue Train returned in 1949, the age of mass air travel arrived shortly thereafter. As early as 1947 the number of visitors to the coast equalled the pre-war record. But the majority were of a different type, with much more modest finances; to cater for the steadily increasing numbers of tourists, the building of establishments far more modest than the great pre-war luxury hotels ran rife.

Chanel's close relationship, so often antagonistic, with Misia had continued. José-Maria Sert died suddenly in November 1945. Seriously ill with jaundice, he had ignored his doctor's warnings and continued to travel, enjoy cocaine and morphine and eating what he wanted, with the inevitable result. He was buried in Vic Cathedral, in Catalonia, which he had spent a lifetime decorating. 'With him', wrote Misia, 'disappeared all my reasons to exist.'

To the seventy-three-year-old Misia, who still looked extraordinarily young, he left his apartment in the rue de Rivoli, with its immensely valuable furniture, library, paintings and objets d'art. Here she lived, in this shadowy Ali Baba's cave, occasionally selling one of the magnificent commodes or bibelots when she needed money. Now almost blind, Misia had become heavily, and openly, dependent on drugs. Even chatting at parties or walking down the street, she would pause to jab a needle through her skirt. In Monte Carlo she walked into a pharmacy and asked for morphine while a terrified Chanel pleaded with her to be more careful; one day she was arrested and spent twenty-four hours in a filthy cell before friends were able to obtain her release. After this, she rapidly went downhill. In September 1950, aged seventy-eight, she died in Paris with Chanel at her bedside.

The next morning Chanel sent everyone out of the room and had Misia's body moved to Sert's canopied bed. Then, alone, she dressed and made up her friend. When, after an hour, she threw open the door, everyone who entered gasped. There lay Misia, dressed in white, lying on a bank of white flowers, beautiful as ever, with hair deftly arranged, her cheeks a pale blush-pink, a pale-pink satin ribbon across her breast and on it a single pale-pink rose. It was Chanel's last gift to the woman to whom she had been closer than anyone on earth.

Serge Lifar, accused of entertaining Hitler and his troops (he had even boasted about his close links with Germans), was punished by a year's forced retirement from work – the longer after the cessation of hostilities, the less savage retribution tended to be. He quickly found work in Monte Carlo. In 1947 he was able to return to his old post as ballet master, although he complained that for ten years after the war Parisians still crossed the street to avoid him when they saw him coming.

Jean Cocteau, inexplicably, was left alone, but felt so guilty he developed a severe nervous rash.

In late April 1945, as the Allied armies approached Buchenwald, Léon Blum, the former Prime Minister imprisoned there by the Germans, was transferred to Dachau. In the last weeks of the war the Nazi regime gave orders that he was to be executed, but the local authorities decided not to obey them. He was rescued by Allied troops in May 1945. While in prison he wrote his best-known work, the essay *À l'échelle humaine*, 'On a human scale'.

Three months after the war ended, Pétain was tried for his collaboration with the Nazis and convicted. The eighty-nine-year-old Marshal was sentenced to death by firing squad, but de Gaulle, taking into account Pétain's age and his First World War record, commuted this to life imprisonment. He was sent to the Île d'Yeu, on the Atlantic coast of France, where he died in 1951, aged ninety-five.

Laval was executed by firing squad, telling the soldiers: 'I don't hold this against you. Aim for the heart. Vive la France!'

Vera Lombardi, by dint of using her aristocratic contacts in England, which included an appeal to Churchill, was finally allowed to leave Madrid for Italy in January 1945.

Somerset Maugham returned to the Villa Mauresque in 1946. He spent the rest of his life living and working there, interrupted only by long spells of travelling. After Gerald Haxton's death he began a relationship with Alan Searle, a young man from the London slum area of Bermondsey.

Pablo Picasso returned to the Riviera first to visit for months at a time, then, as a global celebrity, to live there with various wives and mistresses.

Soon after her escape from the Riviera Enid Furness, down on her luck – a legal battle was tying up her inheritance from Lord Furness – met one of her former lovers, Lord Castlerosse, now Lord Kenmare. They soon married and Castlerosse's doctor warned Enid that her new husband had a weak heart and was to abstain from sex as it would surely kill him. Less than a year after they were married he died of a heart attack, but as Enid pointed out, 'It was one of the only pleasures left to him in life. How could I ration him?'

Winston Churchill often returned to the Riviera. On one of his first visits he went to the Monte Carlo Casino to pay the debt he left owing in 1939. The Casino never cashed his cheque but had it framed.

The Duke of Windsor, with the Duchess, having spent most of the war years as Governor of the Bahamas, returned to Europe in 1945, spending time in Paris and at the Villa La Croë before accepting an offer from the French government of the lease of a handsome three-storey house, 4 route du Champ d'Entraînement in the Bois de Boulogne, offered to them at a peppercorn rent for a lease of fifty years. There they led a gilded but essentially pointless existence.

After the war, Florence Gould's salons continued; she simply added names from the new regime to replace those who had returned to Germany. To Gerhard Heller she sent a card, saying: 'Come back soon, our Thursdays await you,' before moving back to the Riviera, where she continued entertaining and became a noted philanthropist. In 1984 her famous jewellery was sold at Christie's in New York for $8 million, an auction record for a jewellery collection.

Aldous Huxley, who had settled in Los Angeles, spent most of the rest of his life there. As well as fifty books, he wrote film scripts. He died in 1963, on the same day that President Kennedy was assassinated.

Gaby Fisher was able to rejoin her family, all of whom survived. She finished her studies in Israel, where she became a teacher.

Simone Veil, whose mother died just before the war ended in 1945, survived Auschwitz. She became a lawyer, and had a brilliantly distinguished career as a politician and Minister of Health under Giscard d'Estaing. She was made an honorary dame, and became the sixth woman to enter the Académie française.

Elsie Gladman went home to see her family, 'who were shocked by my emaciated appearance'. When no longer skin and bones, she returned to nursing on the Riviera, this time in Nice, at the Queen Victoria Memorial Hospital (later the British-American Hospital), where she worked as matron for seventeen years.

Miriam Selz stayed at the convent deep in the countryside until December 1944. Her mother wanted her to give up Catholicism but she refused. 'I am a Catholic and I want to stay a Catholic. If I return to Judaism I won't know who I am. I want to stay what I have lived for the past three or four years.'

Serge Klarsfeld grew up to become a lawyer, historian and Nazi hunter. He and his wife Beata were instrumental in the arrest and eventual condemnation of Klaus Barbie (the German SS officer who was also known as the Butcher of Lyons).

Françoise Frenkel wrote an account of her adventures in 1945, but few copies were published and the book was quickly forgotten. She died in Nice in 1975; thirty-five years later her book, *No Place to Lay One's Head*, was rediscovered in a car-boot sale and republished in France.

All the girls Mère Irène hid kept in touch with her, telling her of every major life event. Occasionally she met them again in Paris. At the Liberation, she received un *Hommage de gratitude* from the Comité Niçois de défense des Juifs.

After the Liberation, Joseph Sungolowsky's father Aron, who had become rabbi of the Ashkenazi community in Nice, thanked Monsignor Paul Rémond officially on behalf of everyone for his clandestine help.

In 1951 Étienne Balsan died in a car crash, and Schellenberg, after six years' imprisonment, went to Switzerland and made contact with Chanel. His wife declared that Chanel financed the purchase of a house in the Italian lakes for them – perhaps to buy his silence.

After a few collections featuring 'trench-brown' and camouflage-print taffeta, Elsa Schiaparelli spent most of the war years in America. She returned to Paris afterwards, but her fashion house struggled in the changed fashion climate and she finally closed it down in 1954 – the same year that her rival Chanel returned.

The year 1953 brought many changes. Bendor, Duke of Westminster, died and Chanel sold La Pausa, her last link with her former lover. *Vogue* called it her 'labour of love'. After her long struggle with the Wertheimers, she and Pierre Wertheimer had made it up and come to terms: he had given her a larger share of profits and agreed to relaunch her. She reopened her couture salon, an extraordinary and brave step for a woman of seventy who had been out of the worlds of fashion and society for almost fourteen years. When asked by Marlene Dietrich why she was doing this, she replied: 'Because I was dying of boredom.' It was the truth. As she once said: 'Work has consumed my life. I have sacrificed everything to it, even love.'

Once more she began to work six days a week. The first collection was a flop ('a fiasco', said the *Daily Mail*, although French *Vogue* was more positive). But within a year she was back, famous again, with the little tweed suits that shout 'Chanel' – in 1964 Orbach's sold 200 copies of these suits in one afternoon – and the introduction of the iconic quilted handbag,* with lipstick slot and a secret compartment that she said was for love letters.

Her final collection was for spring/summer 1971. A few weeks before her death on 10 January 1971 at the age of eighty-eight, the second-most important Chanel scent, No. 19, was launched. 'Work has always been a kind of drug for me,' she once said, 'even if I sometimes wonder what Chanel would have been without the men in my life.'

One of them was to pay her perhaps the most touching tribute she ever received. Before he died Pierre Reverdy wrote a poem to the woman he had loved for the past forty years:

Dear Coco, here it is
The best of my hand
And the best of me
I offer it thus to you
With my heart
With my hand
Before heading toward
The dark road's end
If condemned
If pardoned
Know you are loved

---

* The 2.55, with plaited leather and gilt chain shoulder straps.

ACKNOWLEDGEMENTS

There are many people I would like to thank for their help in the making of this book but first, my gratitude to Jacqueline Hastings, and to her husband Bruce, is enormous, both for their superb detective work and their help in smoothing my path with introductions. My grateful thanks go to Mike Fiddler for allowing me to quote from his article in *Riviera Buzz*, his helpful suggestions, and for letting me see his grandfather's diary. Others to whom I owe a debt are Raymond Ardisson – tireless in sending me much useful material – and Corinne Attwood for her excellent German translations. Barbara P. Barnett sent me much useful material, and Peter Block let me see all he had gathered about his father. I am indebted to Lady Butter, Charles de Croisset and Veracha Evans-Lombe for her recollections of her parents Laurens and Vera Boissevain; and to Federico Finotti for the transcription of his father's wartime diary, Gaby Glassman for her story of her father, Ann Wochiler for stories of her parents and others (including papers that will eventually go to the Mémorial de la Shoah in Paris or the Wiener Library in London) and to Dennis Youdale for stories of his childhood on the Riviera. Mme Patricia Marinovich, owner of the Restaurant Roquebrune, was extremely kind in giving me her mother's and grandmother's recollections of Chanel, and I owe a debt of gratitude to Ghislain Poulain, Pierre Oporto, Marsou Viano and the local historian Jean-Claude Volpi for all they told me about life on the coast during the years in which I was interested. I owe a huge debt of gratitude to my friends Angela Levin and Bob Low for having me to stay in Jerusalem while I was researching, to Reut Golani of Yad Vashem Holocaust Resources for her efficiency and helpfulness and to the always amazing staff at the London Library. Last but not least, I would like to thank my wonderful editors Holly Harley, Linden Lawson and Alan Samson.

Much of the information in this book has been gleaned from interviews with the above as well as published writings (see Bibliography), but other sources are as follows:

A.S. Dean's diary can be found in Documents 20321, Imperial War Museum, London

Constance Edser's remembrances are in Oral History, Catalogue no. 331556, Imperial War Museum

Gaby Fisher's remembrances are in 0.3 File no. 10652, Yad Vashem, Jerusalem

Elizabeth Foster's diary is MS Am 1612, Houghton Library, Harvard University, Cambridge, MA

There is an interview with Enid Furness in *Australian Woman's Weekly*, 4 July 1942

Colette Halber's story is in 0.3 File no. 11603, Yad Vashem

Elizabeth Blair Hales kept a diary of her escape from wartime Paris; it can be found under *Fleeing Hitler*, a project by Dr Hanna Diamond

A.E. Hotchner describes Göring in Paris in *Vanity Fair*, 21 June 2012

The story of Mère Irene is in Record Group O.33, File no. 5063 in the archives of Yad Vashem

Captain William Geoffrey Jameson's memoir, by Hugh Shuttleworth, was published in *Shipping, Today and Yesterday*

Henri Korb's story is in Record Group 0.33, File no. 5592, Yad Vashem

Miriam Selz's story can be found in File no. 11040, Record Group 03

The story of Paula Tattmar is in Oral History/Accession no. 1990.339.76/RG no. RG-50.161.0076, United States Holocaust Museum, Washington

Gaby Schor's recollections are in file no. 0.3 10652, Yad Vashem

The story of Robert Streitz's work for the Resistance can be found in 'Histoire abrégée du poste S.R. de Marseille et de Nice' by Colonel Gallizia, in *Amicale des Anciens des Services Spéciaux de la Défense Nationale*, 132 (1986)

Joseph Sungolowsky's story is in File no. 03/10661, Yad Vashem.

BIBLIOGRAPHY

Adam, Peter, *Eileen Gray: Architect/Designer: A Biography* (Thames & Hudson 1987)

Ballard, Bettina, *In My Fashion* (Secker & Warburg 1960)

Bedford, Sybille, *Quicksands: A Memoir* (Hamish Hamilton 2005)

Blume, Mary, *Cote d'Azur: Inventing the French Riviera* (Thames & Hudson 1992)

Ed Bryer, Jackson R. and Barks, Cathy W., *Dear Scott, Dearest Zelda: The Love Letters of F. Scott and Zelda Fitzgerald* (Bloomsbury 2002)

Cameron, Roderick, *The Golden Riviera* (Weidenfeld & Nicolson 1975)

Castle, Charles, *La Belle Otero* (Michael Joseph 1981)

Cavendish O'Neill, Pat, *A Lion in the Bedroom* (Park Street Press 2005)

Chaney, Lisa, *Chanel: An Intimate Life* (Fig Tree 2011)

Cocteau, Jean, *Opium: The Diary of His Cure* (Peter Owen 1957)

Collas, Philippe and Villedary, Eric, *Edith Wharton's French Riviera* (Flammarion 2002)

Connolly, Cyril, *The Unquiet Grave* (Hamish Hamilton 1931)

Coward, Noel., *An Autobiography* (Methuen 1986)

De la Haye, Amy, *Chanel: Couture and Industry* (V&A Publishing 2011)

Diamond, Hanna, *Fleeing Hitler: France 1940* (Oxford University Press 2007)

Donaldson, Frances, *Edward VIII* (Weidenfeld & Nicolson 1974)

Downing, Rupert, *If I Laugh* (Harrap & Co 1940)

Feuchtwanger, Lion, *The Devil in France* (Hutchinson 1942)

Field, Leslie, *Bendor: The Golden Duke of Westminster* (Weidenfeld & Nicolson 1983)

Forbes-Robertson, Diana, *Maxine* (Hamish Hamilton 1964)

Frenkel, Françoise, *No Place to Lay One's Head* (Pushkin Press 2018)

Galante, Pierre, *Mademoiselle Chanel* (Henry Regnery Company 1973)

Galtier-Boissière, Jean, *Mon Journal pendant l'Occupation* (La Jeune Parque 1944)

Gladman, Elsie, *Uncertain Tomorrows: A Nurse's Life on the Riviera – in Peace and War* (Librario Publishing 2000)

Gold, Arthur and Fizdale, Robert, *Misia: The Life of Misia Sert* (Macmillan 1980)

Graves, Charles, *None but the Rich* (Cassell 1963)

Guéhenno, Jean, *Diary of the Dark Years, 1940–1944* (Oxford University Press 2014)

Hastings, Selina, *The Secret Lives of Somerset Maugham* (John Murray 2009)

Heller, Gerhard, *Un Allemand à Paris, 1940–1944 (Éditions du Seuil 1981)*

Herbert, David, *Second Son* (Peter Owen 1972)

Jones, Ted, *The French Riviera: A Literary Guide for Travellers* (I.B. Tauris 2004)

Kanigel, Robert, *High Season in Nice* (Abacus 2003)

Kennett, Frances, *Coco: The Life and Loves of Gabrielle Chanel* (Victor Gollancz 1989)

Koestler, Arthur, *Scum of the Earth* (Jonathan Cape 1941)

Lambert, Raymond-Raoul, *Diary of a Witness, 1940–1943* (Librairie Arthème Fayard 1985)

Lancaster, Marie-Jacqueline, *Brian Howard, Portrait of a Failure* (Anthony Blond 1968)

Lottman, Herbert, *Colette* (Secker & Warburg 1991)

Lovell, Mary S., *The Riviera Set* (Little, Brown 2016)

Luce, Clare Boothe, *European Spring* (Hamish Hamilton 1941)

Lynn, Andrea, *Shadow Lovers: The Last Affairs of H.G. Wells* (The Perseus Press 2001)

Madelson, Axel, *Chanel: A Woman of Her Own* (Holt Paperbacks 1990)

Marsh-Feiley, Reginald, *A Poor Lookout* (self-published, lulu.com 2010)

Maugham, Robin, *Recollections of W. Somerset Maugham* (W.H. Allen 1978)

Maugham, W. Somerset, *Strictly Personal* (William Heinemann 1942)

Mauthner, Martin, *German Writers in French Exile, 1933–40* (Vallentine Mitchell 2007)

Maxwell, Elsa, *R.S.V.P.* (Little, Brown 1954)

Mosley, Leonard, *Castlerosse* (Arthur Barker 1956)

Muggeridge, Malcolm, *Chronicles of Wasted Time*, vol. 2 *The Infernal Grove* (William Collins 1973)

Nicolson, Harold, *Diaries and Letters, 1930–39*, ed. Nigel Nicolson (Collins 1966)

Oppenheim, E. Phillips, *The Pool of Memory* (Hodder & Stoughton 1941)

Picardie, Justine, *Coco Chanel: The Legend and the Life* (HarperCollins 2010)

Pryce-Jones, David, *Fault Lines* (Criterion Books 2015)

Pryce-Jones, David, *Paris in the Third Reich: A History of the German Occupation, 1940–44* (Collins 1981)

Richardson, Joanna, *Colette* (Methuen 1983)

Riding, Alan, *And the Show Went On* (Duckworth 2011)

Ronald, Susan, *A Dangerous Woman* (St Martin's Press 2018)

Rose, F., *Saying Life* (Cassell 1961)

Say, Rosemary and Holland, Noel, *Rosie's War* (Michael O'Mara Books 2011)

Sert, Misia, *Two or Three Muses* (Museum Press 1953)

Servadio, Gaia, *Luchino Visconti: A Biography* (Weidenfeld & Nicolson 1981)

Sheean, Vincent, *Between the Thunder and the Sun* (Macmillan 1943)

Sica, Emanuele, *Mussolini's Army in the French Riviera* (University of Illinois 2016)

Simon, Linda, *Coco Chanel* (Reaktion Books 2011)

Snow, C.P., *A Variety of Men* (Macmillan 1968)

Soames, Mary, *Speaking for Themselves: The Personal Letters of Winston and Clementine Churchill* (Doubleday 1998)

Spotts, Frederic, *The Shameful Peace* (Yale University Press 2008)

Standish, Robert, *The Prince of Storytellers* (Peter Davies 1957)

Steegmuller, Francis, *Cocteau: A Biography* (Macmillan 1970)

Swanson, Gloria, *Swanson on Swanson* (Michael Joseph 1981)

Veil, Simone, *A Life* (Haus Publishing 2009)

Vinen, Richard, *The Unfree French: Life under the Occupation* (Allen Lane 2006)

Vreeland, Diana, *D.V.* (Alfred A. Knopf 1984)

Waterfield, Giles, *The Long Afternoon* (Review 2000)

Wells, G.P., ed., *H.G. Wells in Love* (Faber and Faber 1984)

Westminster, Loelia, Duchess of, *Grace and Favour* (Weidenfeld & Nicholson 1961)

Windsor, The Duchess of, *The Heart has its Reasons* (Michael Joseph 1956)

Zuccotti, Susan, *The Holocaust, the French, and the Jews* (Basic Books 1993)

Articles and Magazines

The Field, 19 February 2015

'Destry Rides Again', *Vanity Fair*, 13 February 2009

Jewish Telegraphic Agency, 6 October 1940

'The Magnificent Jewels of Florence J. Gould', Christie's New York catalogue, 11 April 1984

INDEX

>-+•>-•0-•<+•-<

Anne de Courcy

ANNE DE COURCY is the author of several widely acclaimed works of social history and biography, including *The Husband Hunters, Margot at War, The Fishing Fleet, The Viceroy's Daughters,* and *Debs at War*. She lives in London and Gloucestershire.